Korea & Taiwan

a travel survival kit

Korea & Taiwan – a travel survival kit
2nd edition

Published by
Lonely Planet Publications
PO Box 88, South Yarra, Victoria 3141, Australia
PO Box 2001A, Berkeley, California, USA 94702

Printed by
Colorcraft, Hong Kong

This edition
August 1985

National Library of Australia
Cataloguing in Publication Data

Crowther, Geoff, 1944-
Korea & Taiwan

2nd edition.
ISBN 0 908086 71 7

1.Korea (Republic) – Description and Travel – guide-books. 2. Taiwan – Description and travel – 1975– – Guide-books. I. Title.

915.19'50443

ACKNOWLEDGEMENTS

The first edition of this book came together during 1982 and 1983 following two trips to Korea by the author. Initially, the only grass-roots information I had to go on was what I could glean from the out-of-print Peace Corps guide to Korea kindly supplied to me by Patrick Linden of the USA and the many glossy, though very informative, leaflets and booklets put out by the Korean Tourist Office. These sources of help, however, quickly became of secondary importance after I met Choe Hyung Pun of Taejon. She travelled round Korea with me on both occasions and without her enthusiastic support, suggestions and her ability to translate on numerous occasions what followed might have been a hopeless muddle. I also must thank Mr Kwon Young Joung of Kyongju for his matchless hospitality on both occasions that I visited that city and for his energy in taking me to sites and places I would otherwise never have heard of. Another important contribution was that by David Yu of Melbourne, Australia, who did the Chinese script in the Taiwan section.

This second edition was much more of a team effort by Choe Hyung Pun (who visited Korea once again for three months) and myself together with much appreciated and valuable contributions by Hyung Pun's family members, Mr Kwon Young Joung and travellers out there on the road who include Kevin Dwyer (USA), Fred Dong (USA), Dina and David Gidron (Israel), Keith of the Taipei Hostel (Taiwan), Bill Moses (Canada), Bjorn Ohlsson (Sweden), F Planzer (Taiwan), Paul Ratterman (USA), Sen & Jos Sewell (Japan), Mark Shen (Taiwan), Steve Smith (USA), Todd Stradford (Japan), Sunny (Australia), John & Evelyn Williames, Cecilia Zilka (Japan), Jackie Feldman (Isreal).

My sincere thanks must also go to Margaret Moult and Pru of Burringbar, Australia, without whose commitment, good humour, lack of regard for comfort, and typing skills this book would have been considerably delayed. And last, but not least, many, many thanks to the Lonely Planet team.

For the last edition I did all the Korean script for the book but for this edition Choe Hyung Pun has done both the Korean and the Chinese script.

To the technical and/or ecologically minded this is the first Lonely Planet book written on a solar-powered, Kaypro 4 micro-computer using a four-panel Solarex X100GT rig together with a bank of six ex-Telecom 2 volt batteries and a Santech AC inverter without generator back-up. It's been an interesting experience but I keep coming across accounts of RSI (tenosynovitis) though I doubt I'll ever make the grade being a two-finger 'journo'.

A WARNING & A REQUEST

Things change – prices go up, good places sometimes go downhill, bad places go bankrupt and nothing stays the same. So, if you find things better, worse, cheaper, more expensive, recently opened or long ago closed please tell us. Your letters are very important both for cross-reference and for expanding the scope of the guide. It's very encouraging to hear from travellers who use the guide (whether their comments be positive or negative). Your contributions help to improve the quality of the guide and are much appreciated especially by travellers who will follow you. Naturally, if you write us an informative letter we'll send you free a copy of the next edition of the book or any other of the Lonely Planet series which you request. Happy travelling!

Contents

Introduction

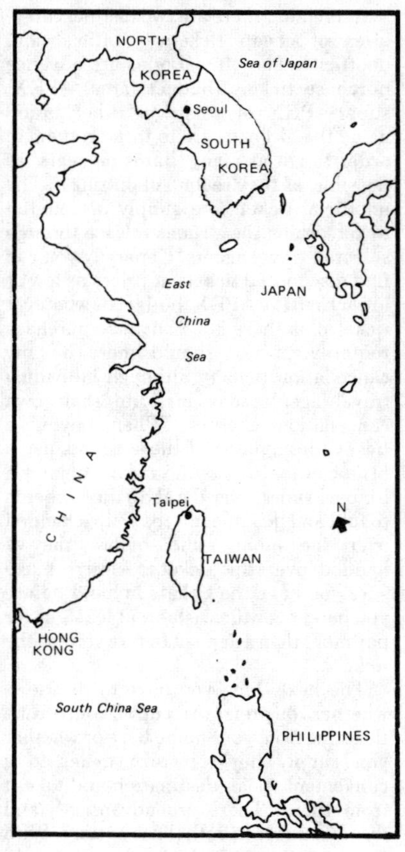

Most people intent on visiting North-East Asia think first of Japan and China. This is inevitable if only because of their size, influence and press coverage. Yet they share this area of the world with two smaller countries which are not only unique but equally as fascinating. Both Korea and Taiwan are beautiful mountainous countries intensely proud of their respective cultural heritages and intent on preserving them. Not only that but the people of Korea have a refreshingly spontaneous nature about them which contrasts markedly with the ritualised formality of the Japanese. Both countries are undergoing a remarkable industrial transformation yet this process still has a long way to go before it will encroach on the natural beauty of the mountains, forest, beaches and ancient monuments. If you're looking for somewhere where you can explore incomparably beautiful ancient temple complexes high up in misty, forested mountains, island-hop all the way round the coast and also have the choice of the usual facilities and services of modern cities then don't miss these countries.

Getting There

Most travellers heading for South Korea and Taiwan also plan to visit Japan, Hong Kong and one or more countries in South-East Asia. To do this with the minimum expense requires some forethought as there are a bewildering number of possibilities and airline ticket deals available. Unfortunately there is no magic key which will instantly unlock the mysteries of this market. A great deal depends on such factors as which country you live; what travel agencies you have access to; whether you can buy your ticket in advance; how flexible you can be about your travelling arrangements; how old you are (you're at a considerable advantage if you're 26 years old or under), and whether you have an International Student Card. Nevertheless, there are certain ways to go about getting the best of current deals – bearing in mind the old adage that no matter how little you paid for your ticket you will inevitably meet someone, somewhere who paid less.

The first thing to do is equip yourself with as much information as possible and to be familiar with ticketing jargon. One of the best sources of information is the monthly magazine *Business Traveller*, available from newstands in most developed countries or direct from 60/61 Fleet St, London EC4Y 1LA, England, and from 13th floor, 200 Lockhard Rd, Hong Kong. Another is the magazine *Trailfinder* from Trailfinders Travel Centre, 48 Earls Court Rd, London W8 6EJ, England. If you live in the UK (or Europe for that matter) then the weekly publication *Time Out* from newstands in London or from Tower House, Southampton St, London WC2E 7HD, contains what must be one of the world's best collection of bucket shop (ie discount airline ticket shops) ads. Similar publications exist in other parts of the world. A little research will uncover them.

Remember there are two distinct categories of cheap tickets – official and unofficial. The official ones are advance purchase tickets, budget fares, APEX, super-APEX or whatever other brand name the airlines care to tack on them in order to get as many 'bums on seats' as possible, as they're fond of putting it. The unofficial tickets are simply discounted tickets which the airlines release through selected travel agents. Generally you can find discounted tickets at prices as low or lower than the APEX, budget or whatever ticket plus there is no advance purchase requirement nor should there be any cancellation penalty although individual travel agents may institute their own cancellation charges. When buying a ticket through one of these agents use a little caution. It's by no means unknown for backstairs, over the shop travel agents to fold and disappear after you've handed over the money and before they've handed over the tickets. Always make sure you have the tickets in hand before you hand over the cash or, at least, never pay more than a deposit before you see the tickets.

The next thing you have to decide is whether you prefer to fix up all your airline ticketing from your home base or whether you simply buy a return ticket to a convenient Asian destination and take it from there. There are advantages and disadvantages in both these options. With few exceptions it is always cheaper to add on nearby destinations to a long-haul ticket rather than buy a straight A to B long-haul ticket and then start all over again arranging another ticket which will loop you round a cetain area. But this isn't always the case especially if you live in Australia where there is little if any 'unofficial' discounting by airlines. If you do opt to buy tickets in Asia then Hong Kong is the best place to buy by far.

Bangkok and Singapore, which used to be No 1 and No 2 places to buy tickets, respectively, have now definitely been superceded by Hong Kong. If you're coming from Europe then you're a winner here since air fares, especially from London to Hong Kong, are currently one of the best deals you'll come across anywhere in the world.

From Europe

The regular economy one-way fares London-Hong Kong are £500. The apex one-way fare is £250 and the return fare £500. 'Firecracker' (another name for standby) fares are £190 one-way and £280 to 380 return. Airlines serving the London-Hong Kong route are British Caledonian, British Airways and Cathay Pacific.

If your ultimate destination from Europe is Australia but you'd like to make a loop around north-east Asia before going there then London – Hong Kong – Sydney or Melbourne would be around £360 one-way while terminating in Perth would be about £380 one-way. Good agents to check with in London for these sort of tickets include Trailfinders and Student Travel Australia (latter on Old Brompton Rd). Or check the many bucket shop travel ads in *Time Out* or *Australasian Express*.

From the USA

The cheapest tickets from the USA are invariably obtained in San Francisco, which has become America's bucket shop capital for the Orient. These bucket shops are entirely in the hands of ethnic travel agents who offer 'unofficially discounted' tickets on most major airlines. The reason for all this is that the transpacific is second only to the transatlantic as an area of massive seat over-capacity.

The cheapest fares through these agents are on Korean Air (KAL), the Taiwanese China Airlines (CAL) and Philippine Air (PAL), which cut up to 30 % on published APEX fares and 60% on full Economy fares. One-way trips usually

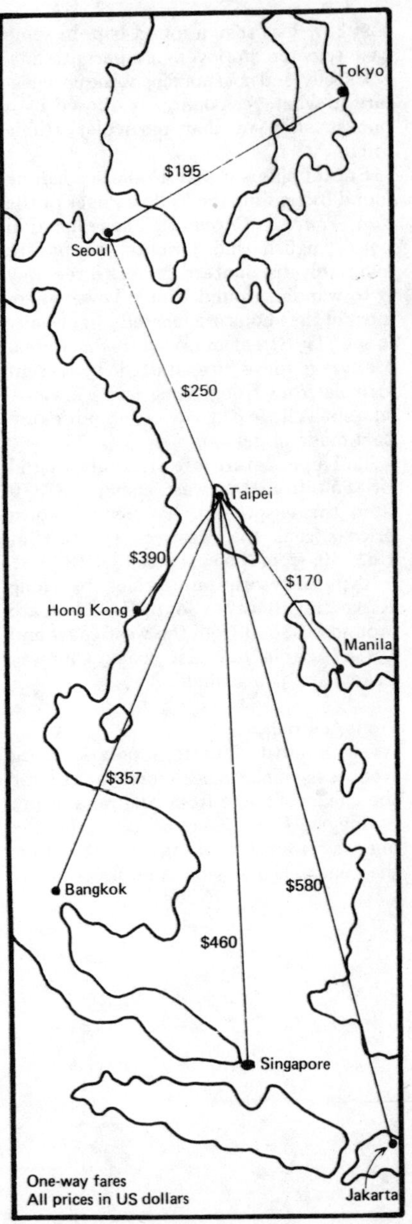

cost 35% less than a round-trip. In some case selected stopovers are permitted.

Usually, and not suprisingly, the cheapest fare to whatever country is offered by a bucket shop of that particular ethnic origin.

Bucket shops in San Francisco can be found by reading the Yellow Pages or the *San Francisco Chronicle*. Those listed in both English and Oriental script are invariably discounters. A more direct way is to wander around China Town where most of the shops are located – especially in the Clay Street and Waverly Place area. Many of these are staffed by recent arrivals from Hong Kong and Taiwan – who speak little English – so enquiries are best made in person.

To Taipei, return fare prices are around US$650 from the west coast, US$870 from the east coast. To Seoul, return prices from the west coast start at US$740, from the east coast US$940.

Typical return fare prices to Hong Kong, the gateway to South-East Asia, are around US$500 from the west coast and US$870 from the east coast. One-way tickets are also available.

From Australia

As with most departure points, Hong Kong is the place to head for if you're after the cheapest route from Australia. From Sydney to Hong Kong is A$591 for the one-way Apex low season fare, A$714 for the same in high season. A return economy excursion fare is A$1283. Direct flights to Seoul, return only, are economy A$2384, excursion A$1690

Around Asia

If you're footloose and free, haven't managed to find a travel agent who is willing to sell you a ticket to the Orient for a song, or simply like to play it by ear, then the accompanying map will give you a rough idea of what the 'best buys' are on the north-east Asian air ticket market at present. But remember to allow for inflation.

Round-the-World Tickets

Recently a number of airlines have been getting together to produce round-the-world tickets by combining their routes. These operate much like a normal mileage ticket where you can make as many stops as you wish so long as you continue in the same direction, with the important difference that you can only use services of the issuing airlines. Naturally they are a lot cheaper than a regular round-the-world mileage ticket.

Quite a few of these combination tickets will take you through Hong Kong or east Asia on your way round. Pan Am, one of the few airlines to have a round-the-world routing in their own right were the first in at this game but many other airlines have combined to offer similar round-the-world tickets.

Korea

Korea – Introduction

Despite the remarkable efforts of the national tourist organisation which produces an excellent range of well-illustrated and detailed brochures and maps, Korea still remains very much off the beaten track. Quite a few travellers get to the capital, Seoul, usually en route to somewhere else, and a few intrepid individuals make it to Cheju Island and Kyongju but hardly anyone seems to take time off here to explore Korea's numerous other attractions. Undoubtedly the magnets of Japan and China serve to distract most people's attention from this little-known country. Yet Korea is one of the most fascinating enigmas of the Far East and its history one of the world's most turbulent sagas of a small nation's struggle for survival against what would appear to be impossible odds. Sandwiched between vastly more powerful neighbours who, for at least two millenia, have frequently attempted to absorb it, it has nevertheless preserved its own uniquely different character and cultural identity.

You might be forgiven for thinking that the most coveted gems of Oriental culture are to be found either in Japan or China and that Korea merely offers a pale reflection of these. You would be wrong. Here you have some of the world's most enchanting countryside – beautiful, forested mountains offering endless trekking possibilities which, while seen at their most colourful either in the spring or autumn, are misty and romantic even during the wet season. And in them you will find sublimely crafted temple complexes whose origins stretch back 1500 years which you'll be hard-pressed to find the equal of anywhere. A visit to any one of these hauntingly beautiful places will leave an indelible impression. Many of them are still functioning monasteries and anyone expressing an interest in delving beneath the surface will find the monks not only very friendly but also hospitable. Then there are Korea's innumerable islands scattered like confetti off its southern and eastern shores, many of them with intriguing variations of the mainland culture. Very few of them have ever seen a visitor from abroad let alone had their paths tramped bare with tourist hordes.

And what of the people? Koreans are a proud, romantic, spontaneous and friendly people quite unlike their neighbours the Chinese and Japanese. You will not encounter here that feeling of disinterest which westerners often experience in those places. Even in cosmopolitan Seoul you'll be regarded with curiosity. Wherever you go, but especially in the smaller places, you'll be constantly approached by people wishing to strike up a conversation with you or take you to a place you might not have heard of, whether they be soldiers, hotel proprietors, students, businessmen or whatever. There people will try really hard regardless of language or cultural differences to establish some rapport with you yet always with humour and never in an overbearing manner. If you respond with friendship and a little imagination you will often find yourself the recipient of the most unexpected and often disarming hospitality. It's not that Koreans don't have fairly rigidly defined rules of social conduct and public behaviour in common with other Oriental people because they do and you will often be aware of this but as a foreigner they'll bend the rules double to spare you involvement and make you feel at home. Yet they don't do this as some sort of elaborate ploy to maintain any kind of supposed superiority. It's genuine and, when you renew a friendship established at some point in the past, you sure as hell know it.

Not surprisingly, history lies heavily on

these people. The cost of their survival as a nation has, at times, been devastating. The most recent example of this was, of course, the Korean War in the early '50s. Forced by circumstances to be always on the alert and prepared for the inevitable invasion, the armed forces have always been an important element of Korean society. This is no less true today than it has ever been. It would be fatuous to ignore the ubiquitous presence of the army (and its American allies) in South Korea – conscription is a three-year stint – or the fact that politically it remains a military dictatorship but it would also be a grave mistake to allow these realities to prejudice your view of this country and its people. These people are right on the front line. In the beginning it was China; then China and Japan; then Russia, China and Japan followed by Russia and America and now the two halves of Korea are pitted against each other. These people have felt the cold wind of super-power rivalry for centuries. They know it could all end tomorrow. Perhaps that's why they're so keen to establish friendships and exchange views with visitors from abroad; but then again perhaps it's just their natural disposition. But whatever the reasons, the line drawn here between guest and lifelong friend is very much a question of your own attitude.

There's one last plus which ought to put Korea firmly on the traveller's route and that is its relative cheapness compared to such places as Japan and China. Even in central Seoul you can find places to stay for less than US$4 (sharing) or US$7 for a single and out in the countryside it's often cheaper. Transport is well-organised – both buses and trains – all but the most rural of roads are paved. Korea is one of the unexplored gems of Asia and once you've been here you'll want to come back. It once acquired the nickname of 'The Hermit Kingdom', after it closed its borders to all foreigners for a time in the late 19th century as a result of what seemed like insuperable pressures from the outside, but after you've wandered round this country for a little while you'll realise what an inappropriate name it is for this exceptionally friendly and fascinating country.

Facts about Korea

HISTORY

Korean folk legends fix the date of the nation's birth by a semi-deity named Tangun around 2333 BC but, according to the latest research, its origins go back even further into the mists of time to 30,000 BC when migrating tribes from Central and Northern Asia first arrived in the peninsula. They brought with them their own folk myths and animistic religion as well as their own language, the latter a branch of the Ural-Altaic group which also includes Finnish, Hungarian and Turkish. This distinct language, though it borrowed Chinese script (until *hangul* was invented in the 15th century) and some of its vocabulary, has been of the utmost importance in maintaining Korean cultural identity down through the centuries.

The earliest influences assimilated by these nomadic tribes came from the Chinese who had established an outpost near present-day Pyongyang during the Han Dynasty. Constant wars with the Chinese dictated the necessity for an early alliance between the tribes of the north which eventually led to the formation of the first Korean kingdom, Koguryo, around the 1st century AD and the uniting of the northern half of the peninsula four centuries later following the demise of Han. Not being subject to the same immediate pressures, the related tribes of the south were slower to coalesce but by the 3rd century AD two powerful kingdoms – Silla and Paekje – had emerged to dominate the southern half of the peninsula.

The next four centuries – known as the Three Kingdoms Period – witnessed a remarkable flowering of the arts, architecture, literature and statescraft as Chinese influences continued to be absorbed, re-interpreted and alloyed with traditional Korean ideas and practices. Probably the single most formative influence was Buddhism which, in time, became the state religion of all three kingdoms. Buddhism has immeasurably enriched Korean culture and even though it was suppressed in favour of Confucianism when the Koryo dynasty was overthrown at the end of the 14th century it remains an integral part of modern Korea and has left an indelible mark on the language, manners, customs, art and folklore of the people. Even today, although it is no longer a dominant force in the spiritual life of the Korean people, Buddha's birthday still draws the multitudes to numerous temples throughout the country.

The Three Kingdoms Period was also the time when the developments which were taking place in Korea began to be exported to Japan. Architects and builders from Paekje, for instance, were primarily responsible for the great burst of temple construction which occurred in Japan during the 6th century. This transmission of cultural developments naturally accelerated during periods of conflict and there were times in Japan's early history when there were more Koreans involved in influential secular and religious positions than Japanese.

There was, of course, much rivalry between the three kingdoms and wars were fought constantly in attempts to gain supremacy but it was not until the 7th century that a major shift of power occurred. The rise of the T'ang Dynasty in China about this time provided Silla with the opportunity to expand its dominion over the whole peninsula. An alliance of the two was formed and the combined armies first attacked Paekje which fell shortly afterwards followed by Koguryo in 668 AD. The alliance, however, was short-lived since for the T'ang Dynasty it was a convenient ruse by which to establish hegemony over Korea. The Silla aristocracy had no intention of subscribing to such a plan and so, in order to thwart T'ang designs, switched allegience to the Koguryo resistance fighters. Together, the two Korean forces were able eventually to drive out the Chinese. Silla thus united the peninsula for the first time and this unification was to last through various changes of regime right up until partition after WW II. Yet Silla was to learn, as all other Korean dynasties have had to, that the price of this often precarious independence depended on the recognition of the vastly superior forces of China and its acknowledgement in the form of tribute. This traditional tributory relationship with China has more than once thrown Korea, through no action of its own, into the lion's den between contending armies from China at times of dynastic change and left it vulnerable to Japanese military adventures on its own territory and that of China's.

Unified, Silla presided over one of Korea's greatest eras of cultural development and nowhere is this more apparent than in the countless tombs, temples, pagodas, palaces, pleasure gardens and other relics which dot the countryside in and around Kyongju, the Silla capital. Buddhism in particular flourished with state funds being lavished on the construction of temples and images and monks despatched to China and India for study. The cohesiveness of Silla society was based on the twin pillars of *kolpum* – a rigid hierarchy of rank based on ancestry – and the *hwarang* – a kind of para-military youth organisation for the training and educating of the sons of the Silla elite. Yet it was the rigidity of this system which also brought about its eventual downfall. By the beginning of the 9th century, discontent among those who were excluded from power had reached such a pitch that the kingdom began to fall apart. Threatened by rival warlords to the north and west, the end came surprisingly bloodlessly when the last king of Silla, unwilling to contemplate further destruction, offered his kingdom to the ruler of Later Koguryo which had been set up in the northern half of the peninsula. As a result, the capital was moved to Kaesong, north of Seoul, the peninsula re-united and the last king of Silla was allowed to live out the rest of his days as an honoured guest in his rival's capital. Kyongju sank into obscurity and remained that way until 'rediscovered' in the 20th century – in many ways a fortunate event since had there been a major conflict at the time many of the priceless archaeological finds visible today in the National Museum at Kyongju would have been looted and lost forever.

The new dynasty, which took the name of Koryo, abolished *kolpum* and restructured the government placing emphasis on a Confucian examination system for state officials similar to that which prevailed in China except that eligibility for the examination was limited to the sons of the ruling oligarchy. With stability restored, the new dynasty prospered and it was during this time that Buddhism, through royal patronage, reached the height of its development and acquired considerable secular power through the acquisition of land and accumulation of wealth. In time, however, the Koryo government became as despotic and arrogant as that of Silla except that in this case it was the literati who monopolised the top positions rather than warrior-aristocrats. Disaffected military officers eventually reduced the power of these bureaucrats by assassinating one of the Koryo kings and installing his son as a puppet ruler. Yet, at the same time, events were taking place on Korea's northern borders which would radically affect the nation's survival as an independent kingdom.

Throughout the later years of the Koryo Dynasty marauding Khitan tribes began making life difficult for the kingdom and they were only kept in check by an alliance with the Mongols of China. The alliance was a reluctant one on the part of Koryo since it involved the payment of considerable annual tribute and it was eventually broken off. The reckoning didn't come until 1231 since the Mongols were preoccupied by their own internal problems but when it did the decision to rescind the treaty proved to have been a disastrous one. The Mongols invaded with vastly superior forces, quickly took Kaesong and forced the king to take refuge on Kanghwa Island where he remained relatively safe but totally powerless while the Mongols laid waste to the peninsula for the next 25 years. A truce was finally arranged, despite a die-hard Koryo faction, in 1259 when the Koryo monarch was restored to his kingdom (minus Cheju Island which the Mongols used for rearing horses) on condition that Koryo crown princes would be held hostage at Peking until the death of their fathers, that they would be forced to marry Mongol princesses and the tribute would be restored.

The tribute demanded by the settlement was, naturally, extortionate and included gold, silver, horses, ginseng, hawks, artisans, women and eunuchs but it wasn't the only thing which Koryo was compelled to provide. There were also demands to provide soldiers and ships for the ill-fated Mongol attempt to invade Japan between 1274 and 1281. These various exactions plus the powerful influence which the Mongol princesses wielded at the Koryo court led to intolerable strains being placed on the fabric of Korean society and were the root cause of the eventual downfall of Koryo. Still, Koryo survived for a little while longer and re-asserted its independence when rebellions in China led to the ousting of the Mongols and their replacement by the Ming Dynasty. There were reforms and wholesale purges of pro-Mongol aristocrats but the rot had spread too far and rebellions broke out which climaxed in the overthrow of the Koryo monarch and the foundation of a new dynasty by one of the king's former generals, Yi Song-gye.

The new regime staked its future on the ideals and practices of Neo-Confucianism which combined the sage's original ethical and political ideas with a quasi-religious practice of ancestor worship and the projection of the male head of the family as priest. At the same time, Buddhism, regarded as an enemy and rival, was suppressed, the monasteries' estates confiscated and their wealth sequestered. The religion has never recovered its former influence as a result of these events and even today, though few Koreans would acknowledge their religious affiliation as 'Confucianism', it remains the moral foundation of the nation with a powerful influence on family life.

The next 150 years were a time of relative peace and prosperity during which great strides were made under a succession of enlightened kings, the greatest of whom was probably Sejong (1418-1450). It was he who presided over the invention of a phonetic script – *hangul* – for the Korean language. The new script was an outstanding achievement and, since it was infinitely simpler than Chinese, led to a vast increase in literacy yet it was not introduced without considerable opposition among the intelligentsia many of whom regarded it as subversive and were worried about the reaction of the Ming court.

The period of peace came to a dramatic end in 1592 when the country was invaded by a newly-united Japan under Toyotomi Hideyoshi following Korea's refusal to join with them in an invasion of China. Exploiting to the full their superior weaponry – muskets supplied by the Portuguese – the Japanese over-ran the peninsula in just one month but at sea they were soundly defeated by Korea's most famous admiral, Yi Sun-sin, the inventor of the world's first iron-clad ships (known as turtle ships or Geobugseon, today 'immortalised' on every packet of cigarettes bearing that brand name). In their naval encounters with Admiral Yi Sun-sin, the Japanese lost more than 500 ships in less than six months. Unfortunately the admiral fell foul of the Yi court and was dismissed only to be recalled at a later date when his successor failed to match up. The war dragged on for four years until Korean guerrilla resistance and Chinese intervention forced it to a conclusion. Nevertheless, the Japanese invaded again the following year though this time the war was confined to the southern provinces and came to a speedier end when Hideyoshi died and the invaders withdrew.

The wars with the Japanese had been a considerable drain on Korean resources. Many craftsmen and intellectuals were taken prisoner and transported to Japan and almost all Korea's temples and palaces were burnt to the ground during this period. Yet there was to be no early respite. The early 17th century was a time of conflict in China. The Manchus there were in the process of overthrowing the Ming court with whom the Koreans had treaty obligations. Though unsure as to which side to declare for, the Korean court decided to side with the Ming thus incurring the wrath of the Manchus who, as soon as they had consolidated their hold over China, turned to invade Korea. The Korean forces were disastrously defeated and severe restrictions placed on their sovereignty.

Profoundly shocked and exhausted by this series of events Korea folded its wings and withdrew into itself over the next century while the pace of change all around it continued to accelerate – largely due to the spread of western ideas and contacts. Nowhere was this more apparent than in the number of converts to Catholicism and, later, to various sects of Protestantism. Frightened by the growing influence of these groups, the Yi court panicked and in the repression which followed hundreds of people were executed. But the major event which shook their confidence was the occupation of Peking by the French and British in 1860. In a vain attempt to shut off these dawning realities, the country was closed to all foreigners including the Japanese and it is as a result of this period that Korea acquired the name of the 'Hermit Kingdom'.

Naturally, an attitude such as this in the late 19th century couldn't be expected to survive very long and some 25 years later, as a result of independent occupations of Kanghwa Island by the French and Americans and a naval skirmish engineered by the Japanese which led to a treaty of 'friendship' (in the parlance of those days) and the opening up of Korean ports to Japanese traders, the policy of excluding foreigners was abandoned. Korea suddenly found herself blown like a leaf in the winds of imperial rivalry. Though she made a valiant effort to modernise and meet the challenge it was too late. The Tonghak uprising in 1894, by followers of a new religious sect founded in 1860 by Choe Che-U which combined elements of Confucianism, Buddhism, Taoism and Shamanism, set off a chain of events which led to the Sino-Japanese War, the defeat of China and the installation of a Japanese-controlled government in Seoul. But with China eliminated, Russia quickly jumped into the political arena and the Koreans became pawns in yet another struggle between giants. During this time pro-Japanese and pro-Russian governments followed each other in rapid succession, Queen Min – the real power behind the Yi throne – was assassinated by Japanese agents, and, for a year and a half, King Kojong took refuge inside the Russian legation. In the end the struggle for supremacy was settled by the Russo-Japanese War of 1904 and Korea occupied by the Japanese. Shortly after in 1910, following public riots and serious guerrilla activity by elements of the disbanded Korean army, the Japanese annexed the country, abolished the monarchy and began to mould the country's economy along lines which would best exploit their resources and maximise returns for their colonial masters.

Yet the Koreans, true to their origins as a defiant border people, were not so easily subdued. After the failure of a Korean delegation to gain recognition for their rights of self-determination at the

Versailles Conference following WW I, an independent movement was formed by a group of patriots. They leafleted Seoul and provoked public demonstrations against the Japanese occupation which quickly spread to the rest of the country. The Japanese troops and police panicked and in the brutal repression which followed over 7000 Koreans were shot and many thousands more seriously injured. Cosmetic reforms were brought in to try and contain the uprising but at the same time the ranks of the secret police were rapidly expanded and censorship tightened. As WW II drew near, Japan's grip over Korea was tightened even further. The Japanese language was made mandatory as the medium of instruction in schools, all public signs had to be in Japanese, the teaching of Korean history was banned and hundreds of thousands of Korean labourers were conscripted to assist the Japanese Army both in Korea and in China. It was a time which the Koreans quite rightly regard as one of attempted cultural genocide and the scars are a long way from being healed even today. Despite political shifts of power since WW II, Koreans still despise Japan for what it did in their country and regard it as the principal threat to their existence. It's more than likely you will come up against this lingering sore in conversations with Koreans.

If Koreans had imagined that the defeat of Japan in WW II would usher in a new era of peace then their hopes were quickly dashed. A deal had been struck between Russia, America and Britain over the fate of post-war Korea in which Russia was to occupy the peninsula north of the 38th parallel and America the country below this line. Though never intended as a permanent division it soon turned out that way once the occupying troops were in position and negotiations for a provisional government floundered when neither side was willing to make concessions which would result in its loss of influence over the new government. A UN commission was set up to try and resolve the problem and to oversee elections for a united government but it was denied entry to the north and was forced to confine its activities to the south. The new government which was elected in the south declared its independence and provoked the Communists in the north to do likewise. The stage was set for the Korean War.

By 1948 Russian and American troops had been withdrawn but while the Americans supplied only sufficient arms considered necessary for self-defence to the regime in the south the Russians provided the north with a vast array of weaponry with which to create a powerful army. On 25 June 1950 the North Korean army invaded. The Americans responded by sending in troops who were soon joined by contingents from 16 other countries following a UN resolution supporting the American action. The war went badly for the UN at first and its troops were soon pushed into a small pocket around Pusan but, following a daring landing at Incheon, its fortunes changed and within a month the North Korean army had been thrown back to the borders of Manchuria. But in November of the same year the Chinese entered the war and the UN troops were pushed back below the 38th parallel. The conflict continued for the next six months with both sides alternately advancing and retreating until a stalemate was reached just north of the 38th parallel. Negotiations for a truce were started but dragged on for two years eventually leading to the creation of the DMZ (De-Militarized Zone) and the truce village of Panmunjon where both sides have met periodically ever since to exchange rhetoric and denounce provocations.

At the end of the war Korea lay in ruins. Seoul had exchanged hands no less than four times and was flattened. Millions of people were left homeless. In the south, 47,000 Koreans had lost their lives and around 200,000 wounded: of the UN troops, 37,000 had been killed, most of them Americans, and 120,000 wounded. Combined military and civilian casualties in the north were estimated at 1½ to two million.

North Korea went on to become one of the most closed countries in the world ruled by the somewhat eccentric and ultra-nationalistic Kim Il-Sung whose position as head of state is maintained by a constant barrage of propaganda which gushes breathlessly about his boundless wisdom, doctrinal purity and unflagging efforts. If anyone deserves an accolade for having out-done Mao Zedong in the business of personality cults then it's Kim Il-sung.

In the south economic recovery was slow and the civilian government of President Rhee weak and corrupt. In 1961, following blatantly fraudulent elections, massive student demonstrations and the resignation of Rhee, a military dictatorship was established with General Park Chung-Hee emerging as its strongman. Pressures soon mounted for the return of a civilian government and so, in 1963, Park retired from the army, stood as a candidate for the Democratic Republican Party and, after its victory, was named as its leader. Park was re-elected as President in 1967 and again in 1971 though he only very narrowly missed defeat in 1971 by his rival, Kim Dae-Jung. On the positive side, Park created an efficient administration and was the architect of South Korea's economic 'miracle' but in October 1972, in an attempt to secure his position, he declared martial law, clamped down on political opponents and instituted an era of intensely personal rule. Like Kim Il-Sung, he created his own personality cult; his record on human rights became progressively worse and, finally, in October 1979, he was assassinated by his own chief of secret police.

After Park's death, there was a brief period of political freedom in which popular expectations of reform were aroused. They were short-lived. In May 1980, a group of army officers headed by General Chun Doo Hwan took control and arrested leading opposition politicians including Kim Dae-Jung. Student riots erupted in Kim's home town of Kwangju (Gwangju) which were brutally put down but feelings were running high and this action was followed by a local insurrection. A full-scale army assault was mounted and the insurrection savagely repressed. About 190 people lost their lives and hundreds were arrested. In the 'elections' which were held shortly after this, Chun secured his position as president but since more than 500 former politicians were banned from political activity during the campaign the result was a foregone conclusion. Kim Dae-Jung was tried for treason and sentenced to death but so transparent were the charges against him that Chun was reluctantly forced to commute his sentence following world-wide protests. Probably the single most important factor which saved Kim was Chun's need for a continued and substantial American base. US President Reagan had just come to power and was intent on keeping American forces there but Chun's insistence on going through with Kim's execution was placing in jeopardy Congressional approval for Reagan's wishes.
placing in jeopardy Congressional approval for Reagan's wishes.

Having consolidated his power base, Chun, on the other hand, lifted martial law, granted amnesty to quite a few detainees, and allowed the National Assembly to debate issues much more freely than was possible during Park's Presidency. It was rumoured, too, that passports were to be made much more freely available in the near future – something which is still by no means an automatic right at present. Press censorship, nevertheless, remains tight under a 'voluntary restraint' system and the authorities don't take kindly to any publications of a Communist nature – only recently a young publisher was sentenced to life imprisonment for publishing Korean-language editions of books by such people as Herbert Marcuse. Even more recently a corruption scandal involving millions of dollars was unearthed forcing the resignation of many high-ranking Government ministers and army officers. Chun can hardly be held responsible for this and seems determined to root out those involved as well as banning members of his family from holding important Government positions. The fairest thing which can be said is that it is a legacy of the Park regime, the last vestiges of which Chun is doing his best to sweep away.

Change is not going to happen overnight in South Korea and it's easy from the safety of distance to condemn the snail's pace at which it takes place but events there should be seen in the context of history, geography and the constant provocations by North Korea. Nevertheless, encouraging developments took place recently with the release from prison or from banning orders on political activity of opponents of the government. Even Kim Dae-Jung, who was released from prison in order to go to the United States for medical treatment (and who subsequently decided to stay when he was offered a lecturer's post at a prestigious American university), is talking about returning.

There was even a thaw in the normally ice-bound relations between North and South Korea in late 1984 following the devastating floods in the South. At that time North Korea offered the South substantial emergency aid such as food and cement and, although there was initially some suspicion of their motives, it was eventually delivered in convoys of trucks. The Chinese leadership, who excercise the major influence over the North Korean government, have also been pressuring Kim Il-Sung to make genuine moves in the direction of an accommodation with the South in keeping with their continued expansion of ties with the West and especially with the USA. The South, however, is likely to approach this with a considerable degree of caution – and with good reason. In late 1983, North Korean agents assassinated almost the entire South Korean cabinet in a bomb blast in Rangoon, Burma, where they were on an official visit. President Chun narrowly missed the same fate as a result of being held up in traffic. And then, of course, there was the shooting down of the Korean Airlines jumbo jet over the Kamchatka peninsula by the Russian air force in the same year but then neither the Pentagon nor the CIA is ever likely to come clean about their involvement in that affair.

GEOGRAPHY

The Korean peninsula borders on Manchuria and the USSR in the north, faces China in the west across the Yellow Sea and Japan to the east and south across the East Sea (Sea of Japan). Its overall length from north to south is approximately 1000 km while at its narrowest point it is 216 km wide. In terms of land area it is about the same size as the UK. The peninsula is divided roughly in half just north of the 38th parallel between the two countries, North and South Korea. The great bulk of the country is mountainous, the highest peaks being Mt Halla on Cheju Island in South Korea at 2000 metres and Mt Paektu at 2800 metres in North Korea.

In the south, agriculture is confined to the narrow, often terraced, valleys where the main crops are rice, barley, other cereal crops and tobacco. Horticulture is a rapidly expanding sector of primary industry. Cheju Island is the only part of the country where the climate is suitable for growing semi-tropical fruits – citrus and pineapples. Most of the mountains are forested and South Korea is one of the world's leading nations in reafforestation. The economy of South Korea, however, is dominated by manufacturing industries concentrated around Seoul, Taegu and Pusan. Despite the devastation of the Korean War which left the country in ruins by 1952, these industries have made great strides as a result of which Koreans now enjoy a standard of living rivalling that of the Taiwanese and Japanese. The main manufacturing products are iron and steel, chemicals, textiles and consumer products.

The population of South Korea stands at nearly 40 million.

LANGUAGE

Korea has its own alphabet known as *hangul* which was invented in the 15th century during the reign of King Sejong, a Chinese classics scholar and probably the greatest of all Korean kings. It certainly had to run the gauntlet of opposition in the early years from those at court who felt that the abandonment of Chinese and its substitution by something uniquely Korean would be considered subversive by Korea's nominal suzerain at the time – the Ming Empire of China – but its effectiveness in increasing literacy has ensured its survival. It's certainly a lot easier to learn than Chinese yet, even today, there's still a certain degree of social status attached to being able to read and write Chinese as opposed to Korean. This is the reason why you will often find maps, books and sometimes timetables published in Korea which are either partially or wholly in Chinese. Once you've got the hang of hangul – apologies for the awful pun – this can be a source of frustation but it doesn't compare with the confusion you're likely to experience initially with the two accepted systems of romanizing the Korean language. This is the main reason why you'll find a lot of hangul in this section of the book.

The two Romanization systems are the Ministry of Education system and the McCune-Reischauer, the latter being an internationally recognised scheme. To illustrate the differences between these two systems a few examples are necessary:

Pusan = Busan; Cheju-do = Jeju-do; Chongno = Jongro; Gyeongju = Kyong-ju; Halla = Hanra; Kangnung = Gangneung; Poshingak = Bosingag; Sorak-san = Seolag-san

The above should give you the basics of which letters are inter-changeable but beware of becoming the brunt of the standard joke among the expatriate/traveller community here. There are three cities here which, to the uninitiated, sound very similar – Gyeongju (Kyongju), Gongju (Kongju) and Gwangju (Kwangju). You wont be the first traveller who got on the wrong bus! The obvious thing to do in situations like this is to know the Korean characters of the places you're heading for. In most other guides about Korea you might come across the McCune-Reischauer system is used to render Korean into English (and the other European languages). In this guide we're giving you both but we're placing emphasis on the Ministry of Education system because this is a scheme which is adopted at transport terminals and on the official 'Tourist Guide Map' and other tourist leaflets. It may look a little more complicated but it's going to make it easier for you to get around.

Useful Korean Phrases

Numbers

1	*Il*
2	*Ee*
3	*Sam*
4	*Sa*
5	*O*
6	*Yuk*
7	*Chill*
8	*Pal*
9	*Ku*
10	*Sip*
11	*Sip-il*
20	*Ee-sip*
30	*Sam-ip*
40	*Sa-ip*
48	*Sa-sip-pal*
50	*O-sip*
100	*Paek*
200	*Ee-paek*
300	*Sam-paek*
846	*Pal-paek-sa-sip-yuk*
1000	*Chon*

2000 *Ee-chon*
5729 *O-chon-chil-paek-ee-sip-ku*
10,000 *Man*
20,000 *Ee-man*

Greetings

Good morning/Good afternoon/ Good evening
Annyong hasimnika 안녕하십니까

What is your name?
Irumi muosimnika?
이름이 무엇입니까.

My name is . . .
Na-ui irumun . . . imnida.
내 이름은 … 입니다

How are you?
Anahasiyo? 안녕 하세요

Hello
Yoboseyo 여보세요

Goodbye
Aniyong Ikeseyo.
안녕히 계십시요

Pleasantries, etc

Yes
ye 예

No
anio 아니오

Thank you
Kamsa hamnida 감사 합니다

Excuse me
Sille hamnida 실례 합니다

I am sorry
Mian hamnida 미안 합니다

Never mind
kokjong maseyo 걱정 마세요

This is good
Cho sumnida 좋습니다

This is bad
Nappumnida 나쁩니다

Can you speak English?
Yong-o hlasu issumnika?

Do you understand me?
Ihaehaseyo? 이해 하세요

Getting Around

Can you show me the way to . . .?
. . . un odiro gamnika?
… 어디로 가십니까?

Where is . . .?
. . . un odi issumnika?
… 어디에 있읍니까?

What is this place called?
Yogi-nun odimnika?
여기가 어디 입니까?

How many kilometres is it from here?
Yogi-esi myot kilomet im-nikka?
여기서 몇 킬로 미터 입니까?

How long does it take to get there?
Olmana kollimnika?
얼마나 걸립니까?

It takes (thirty minutes) (an hour)
(Samsip-pun) (han si-kan) kollimnida.
삼십분 한 시 간 걸립니다.

Stop here
Sewo jusipsiyo
세워 주세요

How much is the fare?
Olma imnika?
얼마 입니까.

Hassling

How much does it cost?
Olma imnikka? or Olmayo?
얼마 입니까? 얼마요?

It's too expensive
Nomu pisamnida
너무 비쌉니다

I'll buy this
I kos-ul sa kewsumnida.
이것을 사겠읍니다

Can I have the bill?
Kesanso-rul chu-seyo?
계산서를 주세요.

Korea – Facts for the Visitor

INFORMATION

The Korean National Tourism Corporation produces an extensive range of well-illustrated leaflets, booklets and maps with details of all the country's beauty spots, centres of interest and major cities. Many of these leaflets are available in Japanese, German and French as well as English. Almost all of them can be picked up at the two major points of entry:

Kimpo International Airport, Seoul
– 1st floor, Airport Terminal Building (tel 66 2182/3)

Kimhae International Airport, Pusan
(tel 98 1100)

Apart from the two international airports there are also Tourist Information Centres at the following places:

Seoul
31 1-ga, Taepyeongno, Jung-gu (tel 74 4034/72 5765), located at the rear of Seoul City Hall.

Pusan
Tourist Section, City Hall (tel 22 7289/23 1465)

Kyongju
Tourist Information Kiosk, Express Bus Terminal (tel 2 3843)

Outside the country the KNTC maintains offices in the following places:

Australia
Suite 2101, Tower Building, Australia Square, George St, Sydney 2000 (tel 02 27 4123/3)

France
Tour Maine Montparnasse Bldg, 4e Etage No 11, 33 Avenue du Maine, 75755 Paris Cedex 15 (tel 538 7123/7127)

Germany (West)
Wiessenhuetten Platz 26 6000, Frankfurt am Main (tel 0611 23 3226)

Hong Kong
Room 803B, Mohan's Bldg, 14-16 Hankow Rd, Kowloon (tel 3 66 2075/66 0946)

Japan
Room 120, Sanshing Bldg, 4-1 1-chome, Yuraku-cho, Chiyoda-ku, Tokyo (tel 03 580 3941/508 2384). There are branch offices in Kukuoda, Nagoya and Osaka

Sweden
Grev Turegatan 35, 4 TR, S-114 38, Stockholm (tel 08 61 8470/61 9460)

Switzerland
Postfach 7, 8126 Zumikon, Zurich (tel 01 918 0882)

Singapore
Suite 23068, 23rd floor, Raffles Place, Singapore 1 (tel 43 0441/2)

Taiwan
2nd floor, Jin Hsing Bldg, 195 Nanking Esat Rd, Section 3, Taipei (tel 741 1264/5)

UK
Vogue House, Hanover Sq, London W1 (tel 01 408 1591). You can also still get information from Park Travel, 31 Sackville St, London W1 (tel 01 434 3571)

USA
Suite 1500, 230 North Michigan Avenue, Chicago, Ill 60601 (tel 312 346 6660/1).
1501 Kapiolani Bldg, Honolulu, Hawaii 96814 (tel 808 946 9088).
5312A Bellaire Boulevard, Bellaire, Houston, Texas 77401 (tel 77401).
Suite 323, 510 Bldg, 510 West Sixth St, Los Angeles, CA 90014 (tel 213 623 1226/7).
Room 628, Korea Centre Bldg, 460 Park Avenue, New York, NY 10022 (tel 212 688 7543/4).

VISAS

Visas are not required by nationals of any of the west European nations except the Irish Republic. If you fall into this category you'll be given a 30-day, 60-day or 90-day stay permit on arrival depending on the passport you're carrying – for most of the above countries it is 60 days. All other nationals including Australia, Canada and New Zealand require visas. USA nationals also require visas, but they can get a transit visa on arrival by air, valid for 15 days, but is *not extendable*. Tourist visas are issued for a stay of 60 days.

Onward tickets and/or proof of 'adequate funds' are not required as a rule.

Visa extensions are becoming quite difficult to get and you may find that if you apply for one they demand that you have a sponsor or letter of recommendation from a Korean company or from your own embassy. Apply at the Seoul Immigration Office opposite Chong Dong Church at the back of Toksu Palace. The office is open Monday to Friday from 9 am to 6 pm and on Saturdays until 1 pm. Extensions cost W500 and no photographs are necessary.

Do not overstay your visa. The fine for doing this varies between W50,000 and W200,000.

Officially you're not allowed to work if you come in on either a stay permit or a tourist visa but many people do. There's plenty of work available teaching English – and other European languages – in Seoul. None of the schools or institutes which offer work to foreign language teachers will ask for a work permit but if you're thinking of doing this you should first ask around at the two main travellers' yogwans in Seoul to find out if any of the schools are currently exploiting this lack of legal status by paying low wages or, in one or two isolated cases, not paying at all.

Korean customs are pretty thorough and if you're bringing in expensive watches, cameras or casette players then the chances are that they'll be recorded in your passport which means you have to take them out with you or pay the import duty. All these things are much more expensive in Korea than they are in places like Singapore, Hong Kong and Japan. You're allowed to bring in 400 cigarettes and two bottles of spirits duty-free. The latter can be sold for about double the cost price without problem if you want to subsidise the cost of your stay.

CONSULATES & EMBASSIES

Some of the Korean embassies and consular offices abroad include:

Australia
: 113 Empire Circuit, Yarralumla, Canberra ACT 2600 (tel 73 3044). There is no Consulate in Sydney

Canada
: 151 Slater St, Suite 608, Ottawa, Ontario KIP 5H3 (tel 613 232 1715).
: There are also consulates at Toronto and Vancouver.

Hong Kong
: 3/F Korea Centre Bldg, 119-120 Connaught Rd, Central (tel 5 43 0224/7)

Japan
: 2-5 Minami-Azabu, 1-chome, Minato-ku, Tokyo (tel 452 7611).
: There are also consulates at Fukuoka, Kobe, Nagoya, Naha, Niigata, Osaka, Sapporo, Sendai, Shimonoseki and Yokohama.

New Zealand
: 12th floor, Williams Parking Centre Bldg, crn Boulecoutt St & Gilmer Terrace, Wellington (tel 739 073)

Philippines
: Room 201-208, Rufino Bldg, 123 Ayala Avenue, Makati, Metro Manila (tel 88 6423)

Thailand
: 6th floor, Pra-Parwit Bldg, 28/1 Surasak Rd, Bangkok (tel 234 0723/6)

Taiwan
: 345 Chung Hsiao East Rd, Section 4, Taipei (tel 761 9363)

UK
: 4 Palace Gate, London W8 5NF (tel 01 581 0247/9)

USA
: 2320 Massachusetts Avenue NW, Washington DC 20008 (tel 202 483 7383).

There are also consulates in Atlanta, Boston, Chicago, Honolulu, Los Angeles, Miami, New York, San Francisco and Seattle.

MONEY

A$1	=	W649
US$1	=	W832
£1	=	W915

The unit of currency is the won (W). There are coins of W1, W5, W10, W50, W100, and W500 though it's unlikely you'll see a one won coin anywhere except at a bank. Notes are in denominations of W500, W1000, W5000 and W10,000 though the W500 note is gradually being phased out. If you've ever visited Italy then bring the same wallet with you that you used there. Carrying Korean currency demands large pockets.

There is a street market for cash US dollars (and other hard currencies) which varies between 6% and 8% above the bank rate. Ask around in the travellers' yogwans or try some of the shops, particularly the electronic and camera shops, in the underground arcades around the GPO in Seoul. It's advisable to bring with you some cash US dollars if you're thinking of going on any of the tours organised by USO or using any of their facilities since you have to pay for these things in cash dollars though if it's just a drink or a meal you're buying they will reluctantly accept won. Outside banking hours money can be changed at most of the larger hotels though their exchange rates are somewhat lower than the banks. If you want cash dollars, the Exchange Bank of Korea will sell them to you at 2.2% commission provided you pay for them with hard currency travellers' cheques.

In some cities you may experience problems changing travellers cheques even though the banks display 'Authorised to change foreign money' signs. Kwanju is the worst place for this and there's only one bank in the whole city which will change cheques. In Sorak-dong you may well have to change at one of the large hotels.

You can reconvert up to the equivalent of US$500 into hard currency on leaving Korea if you have receipts to prove you changed the money in a bank in the first place. Inflation in Korea has been considerably reduced and, according to the government, now stands at around 5%.

Airport departure tax on international flights is W3500.

CLIMATE

Korea has four distinct seasons which are influenced predominantly by, on the one hand, winds from Siberia and the Gobi desert and, on the other, by the East Asian monsoons. Spring arrives in late March/early April with average temperatures around 10-12°C rising gradually through May and June to around 20°C. There is occasional light rain during these months. July and August are the hottest months with average temperatures hovering between 20° and 30°C. Humidity is high during these months – around 80% – as a result of the monsoons and there is occasional widespread flooding. Autumn, easily the most riotously colourful season to visit this country, comes in mid-October but is at its best in late-October and early November when temperatures average around 12°C. Very little rain falls at this time of year. Winter arrives with a vengeance in November and continues through to late March. During this time freezing winds from Siberia can push the temperature down to minus-15°C at night though, during the day, it generally hovers a few degrees on either side of freezing point. Winter is also characterised by a succession of three cold days followed by four milder days. Cheju-do's climate is naturally warmer all year than the mainland's and, even in winter, seldom drops below an average of 7°C.

The best times to visit Korea as far as temperature, rainfall and natural beauty go are April, May and June before the monsoons and September and October after the rains.

MAIL

Korea has a very well organised postal service and you shouldn't experience any problems either sending or receiving mail. Poste Restante 유치우편물교부 is available at all main city post offices but only in Seoul and Pusan will you find a distinct counter dealing exclusively with this. Elsewhere you may well have difficulty making yourself understood and may not even be able to locate a letter sent to you. The reason for this is that most postal clerks speak very little, if any, English and it's unlikely that a sorter would know what to do with a letter addressed (in English) to Poste Restante so if you do want mail sent to you at post offices other than Seoul and Pusan make sure they're addressed in Korean as far as the words Poste Restante go.

Most large post offices have a packing service available for parcels which relieves you of the bother of having to visit several different places to acquire boxes, polystyrene, tape and string. Their charges are very reasonable and they pack things very well. On the other hand, if you do get a parcel together yourself you don't have to leave it open for customs inspection before mailing.

ACCOMMODATION

Although there are many western-style hotels in all the main cities and tourist spots they're usually very expensive and won't leave you with much feeling for the country. As a budget traveller you'll find yourself staying in traditional Korean inns known as yogwans 여관 and yoinsooks 여인숙 which can be found everywhere. These are government classified according to the standard of accommodation which they offer. Yogwans are generally of a somewhat higher standard than yoinsooks but this isn't always the case. There is usually a posted price list in each room which indicates the basic cost of the room when it's singly occupied plus the smaller charges for each additional person. Proprietors will expect you to want to see the room and the bathroom facilities before you decide to stay but note that very few will speak any English at all. Never wear your shoes into the room – take them off and leave them outside.

Basic accommodation in these inns consists of a room provided with a thin mattress, known as the yo 요, a top cover, called the ibul 이불, and a hard pillow. The bedding is usually freshly laundered – if it looks grubby ask them to change it. In winter the rooms are kept warm by underfloor heating. The most commonly used fuel for this is coal which brings with it the danger of carbon monoxide poisoning due to small cracks in the floor so during winter you must make sure that the room is adequately ventilated. You can ignore this warning at your peril – every year hundreds of people die in poorly ventilated rooms! The above sort of accommodation will cost you between W4500 and W6000 – sometimes cheaper in country areas – and includes communal bathing facilities. These are not always adequate and in some cheaper places they'll consist only of a tap in the courtyard surrounded by several plastic bowls and buckets. If this is the case you're advised to watch a local get washed first before you attempt it as there is usually a ritual attached to which bowl you use for what and if you don't do it properly you can easily offend. Always rinse out any bowls you use with clean water when you're finished. You'll quickly get used to the copious quantities of water which Koreans get through when they're washing though initially it can be mind-boggling! Cold water is usually the rule for most of the year though in winter it will be heated. Naturally you can't strip off and have a complete shower in places like this and you'll have to make use of the public bathhouses known as mok yok tang 목욕탕. They're easily identified with the symbol ♨. At bathhouses you can rent towels and soap and bathe for as long as you like for around W800. Men and women have separate facilities. Many bathhouses also double as yogwans. For some obscure reason, many bathhouses close in summer. However, most good yogwan owners will heat up enough water for a quick but adequate shower if approached politely.

If you want your own bathroom in a yogwan then you will naturally pay more for accommodation – usually between W7000 and W8500. The price you pay will, to some extent, also reflect other facilities provided. Most rooms with attached bathroom will also have a wardrobe and table and frequently a television. Don't forget to bring your own lock with you as these are not normally provided though security is the very last of your worries. Koreans are an exceptionally honest people and you'd be extremely unlucky to have anything stolen anywhere.

If you're staying in the same area for a month or so it's well worth making enquiries about renting a flat or a room in a private home as this is going to work out much cheaper than staying in a yogwan on a day-to-day basis. Prices vary and if you don't speak Korean then you're going to need the help of someone who can. Expect to pay around W45,000 in Seoul and W35,000 or less in the countryside. Estate agents often have lists of flats available though they generally charge a commission of W5000.

Other travellers have suggested patronising a particular *tabang* (tea or coffee shop) in the area where you want to stay and asking the staff about the quality of the nearby yogwans. Most *tabangs* employ a girl to take coffee in a thermos and cups wrapped in large cloths to offices, shops and yogwans in the neighbourhood. As a result, they have an intimate knowledge of the yogwans in the area.

Most yogwans do not have their own restaurant but food can be ordered and eaten in your own room. Most yogwan owners will heat up water for you if you want to make tea, coffee or instant noodles in your room.

In addition to yogwans and yoinsooks there are a few Youth Hostels scattered around the country. They are located as follows:

Seoul
  Bando Youth Hostel, 60-13 Yeongsam-dong, Kangnam-ku (tel 57-2141/5)
Puyo
  105-1 Kygyo-ri (tel 3101/9)
Naksan
  30-1 Cheonjin-ri, Kanghyeon-myeon, Yangyanggun (tel Yangyang 2121/7)
Kyongju
  145-1 Kujeong-dong (tel 2-9991/8)
Aerin
  41, 1-ga, Posu-dong, Chun-gu Pasan (tel 27-222/7)

There's usually no need to book ahead for these places if you intend to stay in the dormitory rooms (six to eight bunks per room) which are the cheapest but during school holidays it might be a good idea to ring and confirm that they have a bed as they're used by youth parties. Bookings for the Puyo, Maksan and Kyongju hostels can also be made in Seoul by ringing the following numbers respectively – 778-0851/5, 70-7888 and 778-9906. Korean Youth Hostels bear little resemblance to their counterparts in Europe and America. They're usually huge places with incredible facilities and very well maintained. You can forget about spartan rooms, cleaning and cooking duties and all the other things you might associate with youth hostels elsewhere in the world. This is luxury at a bargain price if you don't mind dormitory rooms. The price for a bed varies between W2500 and W3000. They all offer private rooms in addition to the dormitories but these can be as high as W20,000 – Naksan is an exception in this respect and offers private rooms for W8000 (Korean-style) and W10,000 (Western-style). All the hostels have their own restaurants with meals available at very reasonable prices.

CURFEW

The 12 midnight to 4 am curfew which had been in force for 37 years was abolished in January 1982.

FOOD

There are four main types of food available in Korea – Korean, Chinese, Japanese and Western.

Korean food (han shik 한식). The basic Korean meal is known as pekpan 백반

which consists of rice 밥, soup 국, and side dishes. The number and variety of side dishes which you're served with varies from one restaurant to the next but at some you'll begin to wonder whether the table is large enough to hold them all! At one restaurant in Mogpo I was served with a total of 15 side dishes in addition to the rice and soup and all for W1000! No matter how many you're served with it will always include a dish of the national seasoned and fermented pickle known as *kimchi* 김치. The constituents and the taste of this dish varies from one place to the next and there are several varieties of it made with different vegetables. The most common variety is the one made with Chinese cabbage, ginger, garlic and chillis. Almost equally common is the side dish called *kakdu-gi* 깍둑기 one which uses radish as the basic ingredient. If you've never tasted it before you may need time to acquire a taste for it – from my own point of view I do think it is an acquired taste though once acquired I couldn't eat enough.

Pekpan is the basic meal and should cost you between W1000 and W1500 depending on where you eat. Another cheap,filling dish is called *bee bim pap* 비빔밥. If you want something more substantial which includes a meat or fish dish – and substantial is the word for these meals – then there's a wide range of possibilities. The main one is Pulgogi – the national dish. There are several varieties of this which, in order of descending cost are:

Thin sliced marinated beef (bulgogi) 불고기
Marinated ribs (bulkalbi) 불갈비
Unmarinated sliced beef (gu-ee) 구이
Unmarinated sliced pork (teji gu-ee) 돼지구이

Pulgogi is cooked at your table either over a gas ring or a coal brick heated brazier so if you want pulgogi don't forget to sit at a table which has the wherewithall to cook it. The most expensive variety will set you back W5000 and upwards but the least expensive can be had for W1500-W2000. It comes complete with side dishes.

The other main type of Korean dishes are various soups and broths (ji-gay) 찌게. These include fish soup (seng son ji-gay) 생선찌게, meat soup (kogi gee-gay) 고기찌게 with either beef (so-gogi) 소고기 or pork (teji-gogi) 돼지고기, bean curd soup (too-boo ji-gay) 두부 찌게 and fermented soy bean and vegetable soup (tenjang ji-gay) 된장찌게.

Chinese food (chung kuk um-shik 중국음식). Chinese restaurants are identified by two black swinging signs in Chinese characters above the entrance which are flanked by red streamers on either side. They're primarily designed for quick meals and often used by people looking for a quick lunch or breakfast. You shouldn't expect anything particularly special in the cheaper variety. They usually offer the following individual dishes:

Fried rice with egg (om rice) 오므라이스
Meat or seafood with vegetables in a soup (cham pong) 짬봉
Noodles with sauce (u-dong) 우동
Fried wontan (yakimandu) 야끼만두

Shared dishes include the following:
Sweet and sour pork (tang su-yuk) 탕수육
Deep fried battered pork with a spicy sauce (chajo-yuk) 자조육
Mixed seafood in sauce (chap tang) 잡탕
Fried noodles, meat and vegetables (chap che) 잡채
Egg soup (keran kook) 계란국

Japanese food (일식). Japanese restaurants are nowhere near as common as Korean and Chinese restaurants and food at one of them tends to be expensive for no obvious reason. Hot dishes at these restaurants include tempura (teegim) 튀김 – deep fried and battered dishes. The most usual are:

Shrimp tempura with vegetables (saoo teegim) 새우 튀김

Fish tempura (sengson teegim) 생선 튀김

Vegetable tempura (yache teegim) 야채튀김

The main cold dishes include:

Sashmi (raw fish) with hot mustard on rice roll (sengson chobap) 생선 초밥

Vegetables in rice roll wrapped with thin seaweed (known as kimpa) 김 밥

As above but wrapped in fried bean curd (yubu chobap) 유부초밥

Western food Probably the only western food you're likely to come across if you're on a budget and don't eat at a western-style hotel are the chicken and chips places (or the Korean equivalent – chicken and kimchi/grated cabbage salad). There are quite a few of these places popping up here and there though most of them are associated with a Crown beer stand bar. At these places a piece of chicken will cost W600 including salad/kimchi which is pretty good value if Colonel Sanders still lurks in your subconscious but one piece can't be considered much more than a snack so if you're hungry you could easily run up a bill of W2000.

Drinks

Koreans love their booze like they do their kimchi and there is no shortage of drinking establishments to suit every pocket and every taste. The traditional drink is makkoli 막걸리, a kind of rice beer, which is to Korea what beer is to Australia and Germany. It's the cheapest booze available but somewhat of an acquired taste whose colour and consistency varies widely from one place to the next. It's sold in places called Wang Tae Po 왕대포 – raucous beverage halls to be found all over Korea. If you drink makkoli on its own (without a meal), the person who takes your order will ask what *anju* 안주 you want. *Anju* are snacks which all Koreans eat with their drinks. They can be anything from a small packet of lightly fried *kim* (seaweed) to *ojing-o* (dried squid) to *tang kwong* (peanuts) to a saucer of chillied prawns depending on where you are but they're cheap.

Another very popular drink is called Soju 소주 which you'll often see Korean men drinking with a meal. It's the local firewater which contains between 20-35% alcohol (and, very improbably, according to a US Army base rumour, an opiate/barbiturate base). Like makkoki, it's cheap and goes down very smoothly – too smoothly in fact – leaving you totally disorientated and hung over the next day. After several sessions on it with various Korean hosts I resolved never to touch the stuff again! But maybe you'll like it – in moderation. Almost every restaurant sells it.

The other main alcoholic beverage is, of course, beer which here is called maekju 맥주. There are two varieties – OB and Crown. As a connoisseur of this elixir of life I'd say OB was the better of the two and comparable with Tooheys New (that's an Australian beer in case you didn't know). Over the last few years both the OB and Crown companies have set up stand bars all over the country furnished with stools and chunky pine furniture. You can't miss them. Most lay on music and are very popular with young people. They're not exclusively male bars by any means so women travellers need have no hesitation in using them. People who frequent them can be very friendly. The beer is sold in two sizes of glass – 500 cc and 1000 cc – and costs the same whether it's OB or Crown – W480 for the smaller glass and W940 for the larger. The only difference in Korea is that you pay for the suds as well as the liquid and the former takes up about one-third of the glass. You probably wouldn't go back to the same pub again if you were served beer like that in the west but here it's accepted. You can also buy bottled beer from corner shops – a large bottle should cost W550 (no deposit on the bottle). As in makkoli bars, the person who serves you will ask which *anju* you want though the choice is generally limited to *kim*, peanuts and dried squid.

For non-alcoholic beverages the most popular places are the *tabangs* or coffee shops which, like the bars, are found all over Korea. They're used by almost everyone to relax in, by businessmen wanting to talk and by young lovers looking for a quiet corner to exchange sweet nothings in. During the day they're always very busy and at lunchtimes you may be hard-pressed to find a seat. A coffee averages around W400 (or as low as W250 in the countryside) but, having bought one, you can sit there as long as you like. Many of these places cater for young people wanting to listen to the latest records and the waitresses may even bring you a record request slip with your coffee. But don't expect any heavy metal or anything vaguely progressive/punk/new wave. With the exception of one or two places it will be strictly *Stars on 45*, Abba, Leo Sayer and Elton John.

Though many *tabangs* also offer ginseng tea (*insam cha*), a better place to try this drink is at the special ginseng tea houses which are recognisable by the large picture of a ginseng root painted on the door or window. The tea at these places isn't particularly cheap at around W600 but it's made with good quality roots and sweetened with honey.

Korea – Getting Around

AIR
Korean Air lines (KAL) is the only domestic carrier and has a good network of flights connecting all the main cities and the principal tourist sites. Fares are very reasonable when compared to domestic flights in other neighbouring countries. The following flights are available:

From Seoul To Cheju-do (10 flights daily plus two extra on both Saturday and Sunday); To Chinju (one flight per day on Tuesday, Thursday and Saturday); To Kwangu (one flight daily); To Pusan (13 flights daily); To Sogcho (two flights daily); To Taegu (one flight daily); To Ulsan (two flights daily); To Yeosu (one flight daily).
From Pusan To Cheju-do (four flights daily plus extra flights on Monday (one), Tuesday (one), Wednesday (two), Thursday (two), Friday (one), Saturday (two) and Sunday (one); To Seoul (13 flights daily).
From Cheju-do To Chinju (one flight daily); To Kwanju (two flights daily); To Pusan (Six flights daily plus extra flights on Tuesday (two), Thursday (one), Saturday (one) and Sunday (one); To Seoul (10 flights daily plus extra flights on Monday (one), Wednesday (one), Thursday (two), Saturday (four) and Sunday (four); To Taegu (two flights daily); to Yeosu (two flights daily).
From Taegu To Cheju-do (two flights daily); To Seoul (one flight daily).
From Chinju To Cheju-do (one flight daily); To Seoul (three flights per week on Tuesday, Thursday and Saturday).
From Kwangju To Cheju-do (two flights daily); To Seoul (one flight daily).
From Yeosu To Cheju-do (two flights daily); To Seoul (one flight daily).
From Ulsan To Seoul (two flights daily).
From Sogcho To Seoul (two flights daily).

You must have your passport handy before boarding a domestic flight – you won't be allowed on the plane unless you have it. The authorities are also very concerned about espionage and, officially, you're not allowed to take a loaded camera on board. I had a huge altercation about this in Cheju-do at the check-in when they insisted I put the camera bag in the hold with the rest of the luggage. I naturally

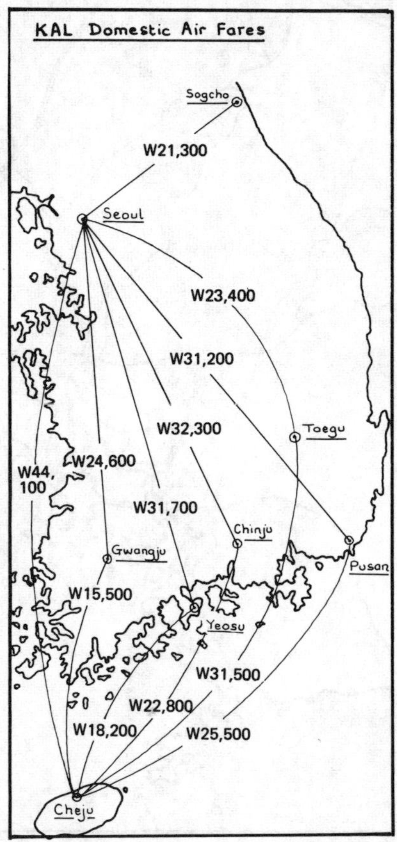

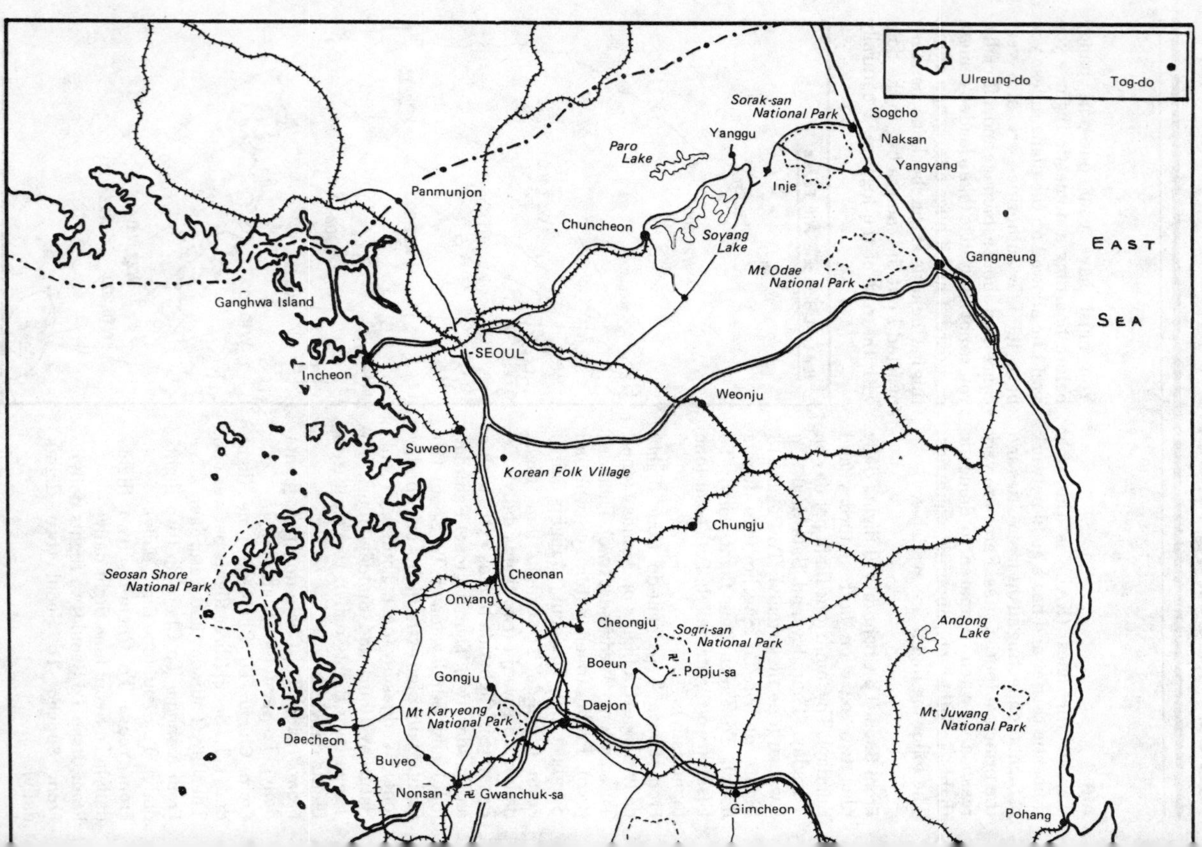
Ulreung-do
Tog-do
Sorak-san National Park
Sogcho
Naksan
Yanggu
Paro Lake
Yangyang
Inje
Panmunjon
Chuncheon
Soyang Lake
EAST
SEA
Gangneung
Mt Odae National Park
Ganghwa Island
SEOUL
Incheon
Weonju
Suweon
Korean Folk Village
Chungju
Seosan Shore National Park
Cheonan
Onyang
Cheongju
Sogri-san National Park
Andong Lake
Boeun
Popju-sa
Gongju
Daejon
Mt Karyeong National Park
Mt Juwang National Park
Daecheon
Buyeo
Nonsan
Gwanchuk-sa
Gimcheon
Pohang

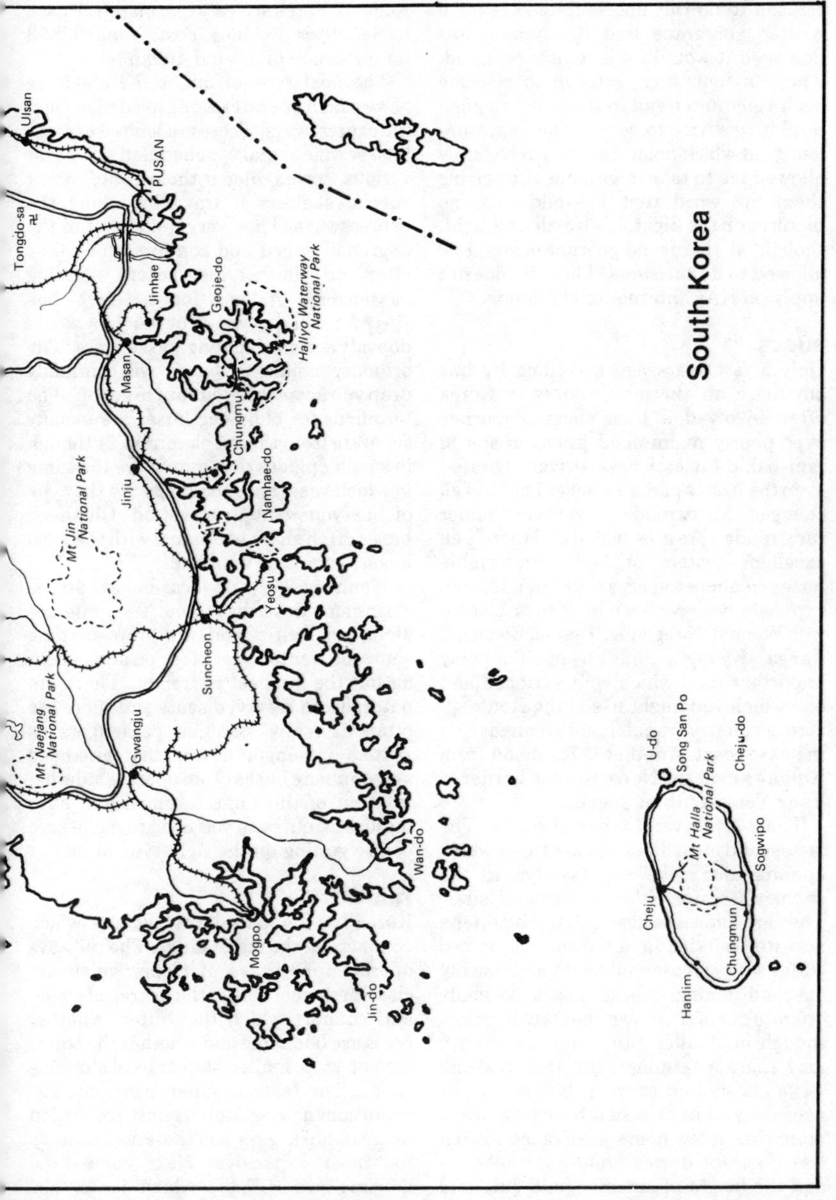
South Korea
Ulsan
PUSAN
Tongdo-sa
Jinhae
Geoje-do
Hallyo Waterway National Park
Masan
Chungmu
Jinju
Namhae-do
Mt Jin National Park
Yeosu
Suncheon
Mt Naejang National Park
Gwangju
Wan-do
Mogpo
Jin-do
U-do
Song San Po
Cheju-do
Mt Halla National Park
Sogwipo
Cheju
Chungmun
Hanlim

refused to do this unless they gave me a written guarantee that if anything was damaged it would be instantly replaced. They, in their turn, refused to give me such a guarantee and so stalemate reigned until it was time to go into the departure lounge at which point they very reluctantly allowed me to take it with me after giving them my word that I would take no pictures on the flight. It's worth a thought, though, as there's no guarantee you'll be allowed to do the same. This rule doesn't apply on KAL international flights.

BUSES

Only a few years ago travelling by bus anywhere off the main routes in Korea often involved a bone-shaking journey over poorly maintained gravel roads in ramshakle buses whose drivers ignored even the basics of road safety. That has all changed. Most roads – even very minor rural roads – are now sealed and there's an excellent system of fast, comfortable buses to almost everywhere. In addition, expressways have been built to link Seoul with Weonju, Kangnung, Taejon, Kwangju, Taegu, Kyongju and Pusan. The only important road which isn't surfaced and one which you might use is the Route 42 across country from Ichon to Tonghae on the east coast. Another is Route 56 from Kumhwa near the North Korean border to Yang Yang south of Sogcho.

There are several types of buses. The fastest and most luxurious are those which operate along the expressways to the country's major cities and tourist sites. They are known as kosok 고속 and offer a non-stop service (apart from one or two coffee stops), reserved seats and usually air-conditioning. These buses normally operate out of their own seperate terminal though in smaller cities and towns they may share a terminal with the chikheng 직행, or limited express, buses. It's not necessary to book a seat on kosok buses more than a few hours in advance – often less – except during holidays, weekends and the height of summer (mid July-mid August). Fares are very reasonable. Pusan to Seoul for instance, costs about US$8 for a journey of around 400km.

The next type of bus is the chikheng 직행 which operates along local roads and the expressways. These are limited express buses which make scheduled stops at various towns along their route or at special shelters if travelling along the expressways. They vary quite a lot in the degree of speed and comfort which they offer and whether they accept standing passengers. Asking for a dirct bus 직행차 will get you a better bus which doesn't accept standing passengers. The ordinary chikheng buses will normally drop you anywhere you care to get off. The terminals for chikheng buses are usually separate from the kosok terminals though in smaller places they may share the same in which case you should specify the type of bus you want to travel on. Chikheng buses often share a terminal with the local buses, known as wanheng.

Wanheng 완행 or local buses, are as their name describes them. They operate along set routes and will stop anytime someone wants to get off or on and accept all but the bulkiest of freight. There are naturally no reserved seats and there are often as many standing passengers as seated passengers. Note that chikheng and wanheng buses often operate side-by-side out of the same terminal and have duplicate routes so you need to make sure you're getting on the right type of bus.

TRAIN

Korea has a good railway network which connects all the major cities. The railways operate four types of trains which are classified according to the degree of speed and comfort which they offer, whether seats are bookable and whether the trains are non-stop, limited stop or local stopping trains. The fastest, super-luxurious, air-conditioned, non-stop trains are called saemaul-ho 새마을호 and these are naturally the most expensive. Next comes the mugung-hwa 무궁화 which is an air-conditioned, limited-stop train with dining car attached. There is also a non-air conditioned, limited stop train sometimes with a dining car attached known as the tongil-ho 통일호 . All the seats on the above trains are bookable but note that on the limited stop trains there are two types of seat – the 1st class 특실 and the economy class 좌석 – as well as standing tickets 입석 . At the bottom of the list are the local stopping trains known as wanheng 보통 . Seats on the local trains are not bookable and because of the frequent stops they are very slow.

As at most bus terminals, train schedules at stations will be entirely in Korean so you need to aquire a familiarity – at the very least – with the Korean characters for the main cities in Korea. Very few ticket clerks speak any English. If you're planning on using the railways to any extent to see Korea then it's well worth your while buying a copy of the booklet called 관광교통시각표 which is published monthly, costs W1000 and is available from most booksellers and stationers. It contains the complete air, train, bus and boat schedules for the entire country. Most of it is entirely in Korean except for the rail schedules which are in Korean and English.

TAXIS

In the cities taxis are metered and you'll never have to remind the driver that it's there. There is a basic charge of W600 for the first two km then W50 for each additional 400 metres. In the countryside, however, you won't come across meters so if you use taxis then you'll have to negotiate the fare before you set off.

SOUTH KOREAN RAILWAY TIMETABLES

A. Seoul-Taejon-Taegu-Pusan

Route: Seoul-Suweon-Pyeongtaeg-Cheonan-Jochiweon-Taejon-Yeongdong-Gimcheon-Gumi-Taegu-Samrangjin-Pusan

Train Type

Station	통	통	무	새	통	통	새	무	통
Seoul	0600	0700	0740	0800	0820	0840	0900	0920	0940
Suweon	0631	0731	0811		0850	0911		0950	1011
Cheonan	0707	0807	0847		0924	0947		1024	1047
Taejon	0800	0856	0936	0944	1010	1036	1044	1110	1136
Gimcheon		1002	1047		1112	1147	1147	1212	1247
Taegu		1054	1139	1125	1203	1239	1229	1303	1339
Pusan		1225	1305	1240	1325	1405		1425	1505

Train Type

Station	새	통	통	무	통	통	무	통	통
Seoul	1000	1020	1040	1100	1120	1140	1200	1220	1240
Suweon		1040	1111	1130	1150	1211	1230	1251	1312
Cheonan		1124	1145	1204	1224	1247	1304	1327	1347
Taejon	1144	1210	1234	1250	1310	1336	1350	1416	1436
Gimcheon		1312	1342	1352	1412	1442	1452	1521	1547
Taegu	1325	1403	1434	1443	1503	1534	1613	1613	1639
Pusan	1440	1525	1600	1605	1625	1700	1705		1805

Train Type

Station	새	무	통	새	무	통	새	무	통
Seoul	1300	1320	1340	1400	1420	1440	1500	1520	1540
Suweon		1350	1411		1450	1511		1550	1611
Cheonan		1424	1447		1524	1545		1624	1647
Taejon	1444	1510	1536	1544	1610	1634	1644	1710	1736
Gimcheon		1612	1647		1712	1747		1812	1847
Taegu	1625	1703	1739	1725	1803	1839	1825	1903	1939
Pusan	1740	1825	1907	1840		2005	1940	2025	2105

Train Type

Station	새	무	통	새	무	통	무	통	통	무
Seoul	1600	1620	1640	1700	1720	1800	1840	1940	2100	2140
Suweon		1650	1711		1750	1830	1911	2011	2139	2218
Cheonan		1724	1747		1824	1904	1947	2047	2224	2300
Taejon	1744	1810	1836	1844	1916	1950	2038	2140	2323	2359
Gimcheon	1843	1912	1947		2012	2052	2146	2247	0042	0118
Taegu	1929	2003	2039	2025	2103	2143	2239	2340	0148	0224
Pusan		2125	2205	2140	2225	2305			0334	0410

B. Pusan-Taegu-Taejon-Seoul

Train Type

Station	통	통	통	새	무	통	무	통	새
Pusan	0600	0640	0740	0800	0820	0840	0920	0940	1000
Taegu	0717	0801	0901	0913	0937	1006	1037	1101	
Gimcheon	0806	0854	0954		1026	1100	1126	1154	
Taejon	0907	0959	1102	1053	1126	1202	1226	1302	1253
Cheonan	0957	1051	1154		1217	1254	1317	1354	
Suweon	1032	1127	1234		1252	1332	1352	1432	
Seoul	1105	1200	1305	1240	1325	1405	1425	1505	1440

Train Type

Station	통	통	무	통	무	통	새	무	통
Pusan	1020	1040	1100	1140	1200	1240	1300	1320	1340
Taegu	1137	1201	1217	1301	1317	1401	1413	1437	1501
Gimcheon	1226	1254	1306	1354	1406	1454		1526	1554
Taejon	1326	1357	1406	1457	1506	1602	1553	1626	1702
Cheonan	1417	1449	1457	1549	1557	1654		1717	1754
Suweon	1452	1526	1532	1626	1632	1732		1752	1832
Seoul	1525	1600	1605	1700	1705	1805	1740	1825	1905

Train Type

Station	새	통	새	무	통	통	통	새	무
Pusan	1400	1440	1500	1520	1540	1620	1640	1700	1800
Taegu	1513	1601	1613	1637	1701	1737	1801	1813	1917
Gimcheon		1654		1726	1754	1826	1854		2006
Taejon	1653	1802	1753	1826	1857	1926	2002	1953	2106
Cheonan		1855		1917	1949	2017	2054		2157
Suweon		1932		1952	2026	2052	2132		2232
Seoul	1840	2005	1940	2025	2100	2125	2205	2140	2305

Train Type

Station	통	무	통	통	무	무	통
Pusan	1820	1840	2120	2140	2230	2300	2340
Taegu	1937	1957	2259	2319	0003	0033	0113
Gimcheon		2046	0009	0029	0113	0143	0223
Taejon	2121	2146	0122	0142	0225	0255	0335
Cheonan		2237	0226	0246	0329	0359	0439
Suweon		2312	0311	0328	0411	0441	0521
Seoul	2310	2345	0350	0412	0450	0520	0600

C. Seoul-Seodaejon-Iri-Mogpo

Route: Seoul-Suweon-Pyeongtaeg-Cheonan-Jochiweon-Seodaejon-Nonsan-Iri-Jeongeub-Song Jeong Ri-Yeong San Po (change here for Kwangju)-Mogpo

Train Type

Station	통	새	통	통	무	통	통
Seoul	0730	0910	1030	1130	1225	1310	1430
Soedaejon	0933	1057	1233	1335	1435	1506	1634
Nonsan	1018	1136	1318	1419	1519	1547	1720
Iri	1055	1205	1354	1456	1555	1619	1753
Yeong San Po	1303		1559		1757	1816	
Mogpo	1356		1654		1850	1906	

Train Type

Station	통	새	통	무	통	무
Seoul	1530	1710	1730	2030	2130	2310
Soedaejon	1735	1857	1933	2255	2356	0127
Nonsan	1819	1936	2017	2342	0044	0213
Iri	1855	2005	2053	0017	0120	0248
Yeong San Po	2101	2149		0228	0334	
Mogpo	2155	2238		0327	0434	

D. Mogpo-Iri-Soedaejon-Seoul

Train Type

Station	새	통	무	통	통	무	통	통
Mogpo	0840	1005	1105	1200	1405	1505	2020	2125
Yeong San Po	0928	1100	1155	1253	1458	1559	2017	2225
Iri	1113	1306	1351	1458	1659	1759	2329	0037
Nonsan	1142	1341	1426	1530	1732	1833	0006	0114
Soedaejon	1221	1426	1511	1615	1814	1916	0056	0202
Seoul	1409	1631	1713	1820	2021	2120	0330	0431

E. Seoul-Soedaejon-Chonju-Namweon-Yeosu

Route: Seoul-Suweon-Cheonan-Soedaejon-Nonsan-Iri-Chonju-Namweon-Suncheon-Yeosu

Train Type								
Station	통	무	통	통	새	통	무	통
Seoul	0830	1145	1410	1605	1810	2110	2210	1330
Soedaejon	1033	1348	1606	1810	2002	2335	0036	0152
Nonsan	1118	1432	1647	1854		0023	0124	0240
Iri	1154	1506	1721	1932	2108	0102	0202	0316
Namweon	1331	1644	1849	2109	2240	0249	0345	0501
Suncheon	1451	1804	2002	2228		0412	0508	0624
Yeosu	1540	1853	2045			0503	0600	

F. Yeosu-Namweon-Chonju-Soedaejon-Seoul

Train Type								
Station	통	통	통	무	통	통	통	통
Yeosu			0830	1055	1335	1940		2150
Suncheon	0635		0919	1134	1335	1940	2140	2242
Namweon	0754	0900	1038	1250	1541	2155	2301	0004
Iri	0932	1028	1217	1420	1727	2343	0047	0143
Nonsan	1007		1252	1453	1802	0021	0124	0221
Soedaejon	1055	1138	1337	1534	1847	0111	0213	0312
Seoul	1300	1330	1542	1736	2052	0340	0437	0538

G. Cheongryangri (Seoul)-Kapyong-Chuncheon

Train Type								
Station	통	통	통	통	통	통	통	통
Cheongryangry	0655	0830	1010	1210	1410	1555	1725	1930
Kapyong	0814	0951	1133	1330	1532	1717	1847	2053
Chuncheon	0850	1027	1209	1406	1608	1753	1923	2129

On Sundays and national holidays there are the following extra trains from Cheongryangry to Chuncheon: 0900 (arr 1100), 1015 (arr 1214), 1445 (arr 1640), 1715 (arr 1906) and 1955 (arr 2147).

H. Chuncheon-Kapyong-Cheongryangri (Seoul)

Train Type								
Station	통	통	통	통	통	통	통	통
Chuncheon	0705	0925	1105	1250	1455	1640	1835	1955
Kapyong	0741	1003	1145	1330	1531	1717	1913	2031
Cheongriyangri	0859	1121	1304	1451	1650	1835	2040	2152

On Sundays and national holidays there are the following extra trains from Chuncheon to Cheongriyangri: 0705 (arr 0856), 1215 (arr 1410), 1435 (arr 1634), 1705 (arr 1905) and 1945 (arr 2139).

I. Cheongriyangri-Wonju-Yongju-Kyongju-Pusan

Route: Cheongriyangri-Wonju-Chechon-Yongju-Andong-Yongchon-Kyongju-Ulsan-Pusan

Train Type							
Station	무	통	통	무	통	통	통
Cheongriyangri	0830	1030	1230	1630	2130		
Wonju	1022	1232	1434	1822	2331		
Yongju	1227	1455	1657	2028	0159	1021	1549
Kyongju	0702				0512	1318	1850
Ulsan	0805				0727		1932
Pusan	1017						2100

J. Pusan-Kyongju-Yongju-Wonju-Cheongryangri

Train Type						
Station	통	통	통	통	통	통
Pusan	0835	2055				
Ulsan	1001	2225				
Kyongju	1041	2307				
Yongju	1350	0218	0842	1042	1552	2337
Wonju		0448	1052	1305	1801	0210
Cheongriyangri		0700	1243	1515	1953	0415

K. Mogpo-Kwangju-Suncheon-Chinju-Masan-Pusan

Train Type								
Station	통	통	통	통	통	통	통	통
Mogpo	2155		0650	1050	1445	1830		
Kwangju	2329		0816	1216	1614	2002		
Suncheon	0153	0624						
Chinju	0340	0820					0850	1300
Masan	0509						1011	1417
Pusan	0642							

L. Pusan-Masan-Chinju-Suncheon-Kwangju-Mogpo

Train Type	통	무	통	통	통	통
Station						
Pusan	2015					
Masan	2141	0419	1742			
Chinju	2312	0544	1913	1945		
Suncheon	0056			2125	0730	
Kwangju	0322				0946	1255
Mogpo	0509					1421

Korea – Around the Country

SEOUL 서울

The capital of the nation with a population exceeding eight million, Seoul is a city of incredible contrasts, a fact which, despite its immense size, makes it one of the most fascinating cities in the world. It has risen from the dust and ashes of the Korean War, when it was flattened, to become a modern metropolis of high-rise buildings, 12-lane boulevards and non-stop traffic. Yet right beside this pulsing extravaganza of concrete, steel and glass, are centuries-old royal palaces, temples, pagodas and imposing stone gateways set in huge traditional gardens where you wouldn't know that the rest of the city existed. It's here that you can experience the timeless, almost eerie atmosphere, somehow Central Asian in origin, which endows this city with its unique character. And this same feeling permeates the narrow alleys and back streets below the skyscrapers and the few remaining traditional areas of the city which escaped destruction in the war.

Seoul hasn't always been the capital of Korea, indeed there have been several, the most famous being the Silla Dynasty capital at Kyongju (Gyeongju) in the south. Its origins go back to 1392 with the establishment of the Yi Dynasty which ruled Korea until 1910. It was during these many centuries, throughout which Korea remained largely a closed country to the outside world, that the palaces, shrines and fortresses which still stand today were constructed. Naturally, some things have disappeared such as the 10-mile wall which once surrounded the city, but five of the original nine gateways still remain and have been repaired by the government. This kind of funding for the repair and restoration of historic sites is one of Korea's outstanding features and explains why the very new and ancient continue to exist side by side in apparent harmony whereas in many other capitals around the world much that was of historic value has been swept aside to make way for new development.

It's more than likely you will enter Korea via Seoul and many travellers seem to get no further. The reasons for this are not hard to fathom. Seoul is a magnet which caters for every taste as well as being the cultural hub of this country. Public transport is excellent and it's easy to get around. You can still live very cheaply right in the centre of the city, and if you're short of money, even get a job teaching English (learning English could be classed as a national obsession). And, so long as you observe a few social rituals, people here can be disarmingly friendly and helpful. This is not a city where people, however busy, don't have the time of day to pass with you or, as in Japan and China, prefer to keep you at arm's length. It's worth staying in Seoul at least a week but at the end of that time making the effort to get down to Kangnam Express Bus Terminal on the other side of the Han River where you will find buses which will take you to the other magnificent places which Korea has to offer. Many travellers just never make it!

Orientation

Most travellers arrive in Seoul via Kimpo International Airport which is some considerable distance west of the city. Airport shuttle buses connect Kimpo with the city centre every 10 minutes from 7.40 am to 9.30 pm (from the city to the airport they run from 6 am to 8.10 pm). The fare is W500 and the journey takes about half an hour. The buses stop at Seoul Garden Hotel, Koreana Hotel, Plaza Hotel, KAL City Terminal, Tokyu Hotel, Hyatt Hotel and the Silla Hotel among others.

The budget hotel area is located at the back of the Sejong Cultural Centre on

Sejongro near the junction with Jongro where there is a huge archway over the road used to announce major current events. If you arrive by airport shuttle bus, get off at the Koreana Hotel, walk the 100 metres back towards the archway and cross the road via the subway. If you arrive by rail at Seoul Station, take the underground railway (subway) one stop to City Hall and walk towards the Koreana Hotel from there. If you arrive at Kangnam Express Bus Terminal on the other side of the Han River you need mini-bus No 731 which has a stop just outside the bus terminal. This will take you over the river, through one of the tunnels under Namsan Hill and eventually on to Jongro where you must get off. The fare will be W350. From where you get off it's a 5-10 minute walk back to the archway mentioned above. On the way there you should pass *Poshingak* – an ancient pavilion which houses a huge bell – on your left hand side. There is one other possible entry into the city which you will come across if you have taken the train from Chuncheon east of Seoul. In this case you will arrive at Cheongryangri station. From here, take the connecting link to the underground and railway (subway) and go six stops to Jong-gag. When you come out onto the street (Jongro) you will notice *Poshingak*. With the pavilion on your left-hand side walk down the street to the archway.

This budget hotel area is known as Dangju Dong and is very convenient for ancient royal palaces, the National Museum, the GPO, the Tourist Office, any of the embassies and airline offices and the shopping and entertainment area of Myeong Dong. It's also very convenient for many of the city's buses and mini-buses which stop outside the Sejong Cultural Centre or just over the road junction in front of the Gugje cinema. The fare on city buses is a standard W120 for any distance. Mini-buses cost more and the fare depends on the distance you go.

Information

Tourist Information There is a tourist information kiosk on the 1st floor of the terminal building at Kimpo International Airport. They have an excellent range of leaflets, booklets and street maps so make sure you call here before you board the airport shuttle bus.

In the centre of town at the back of City Hall is the main Tourist Information Centre (31 I-ka, T'aep'yongno, Chung-ku, tel 722-5765). They have the same range of promotional leaflets, booklets, street plans and maps of Korea as at Kimpo Airport but the receptionists, who speak English, can answer more specific enquiries from a loose-leaf file which they're strangely reluctant to get out. Copies of *This Week in Seoul* are also available here but it's hardly worth picking up a copy – most of it is in Japanese and Chinese. The one thing they don't have at this Tourist Centre are train and bus schedules in English. They work from a booklet called 관광 교통시각표 which is published in Korean once a month, costs W1000 and contains the complete air, boat, train and bus schedules (the only part of the booklet where the towns and cities are in English) and for the more obscure ferries which connect the islands off the west and south coasts to the mainland. It's available at most booksellers and stationers.

Note that the Korea Tourist Development Corporation, 3rd floor, Kuk-tong (Geugdong) Building, 60-1, 3-ka, Ch'ungmu-ro, Chung-ku (tel 261-7001/6) at the bottom of Namsan Hill isn't geared to cope with callers and anyway has no more information than the Tourist Information Centre.

The Tourist Information Centre can also arrange tours to the armistic village of Panmujon if you'd like to go there but their tours are considerably more expensive than those arranged by USO, 104 Gal-Wol-Dong, Yongsan-ku (tel 793 3478) just opposite Gate 21 of Yongsan US Army Base down the road past Seoul Railway Station. This latter, in case you're

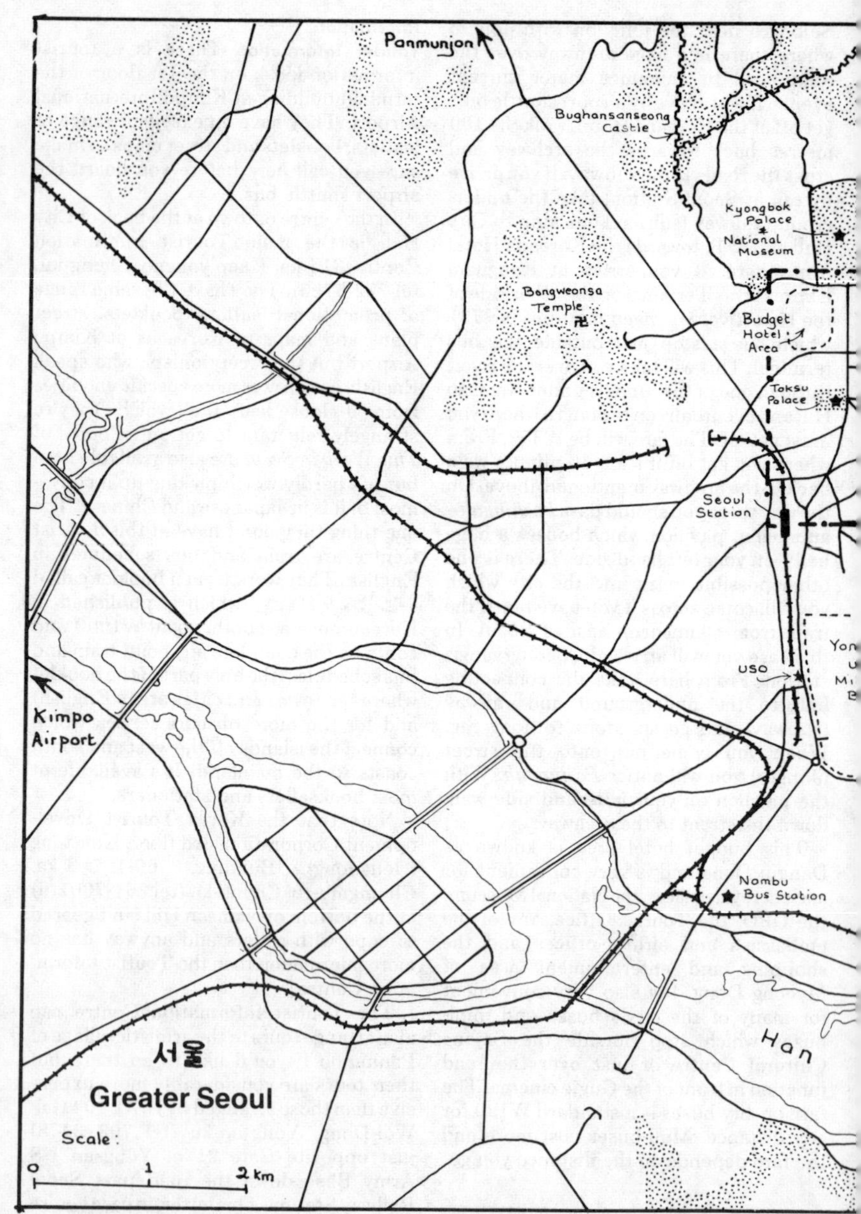
Panmunjon
Bughansanseong Castle
Kyongbok Palace
National Museum
Bongweonsa Temple
Budget Hotel Area
Toksu Palace
Seoul Station
USO
Kimpo Airport
Nombu Bus Station
Han
서울
Greater Seoul
Scale:
0
1
2 km

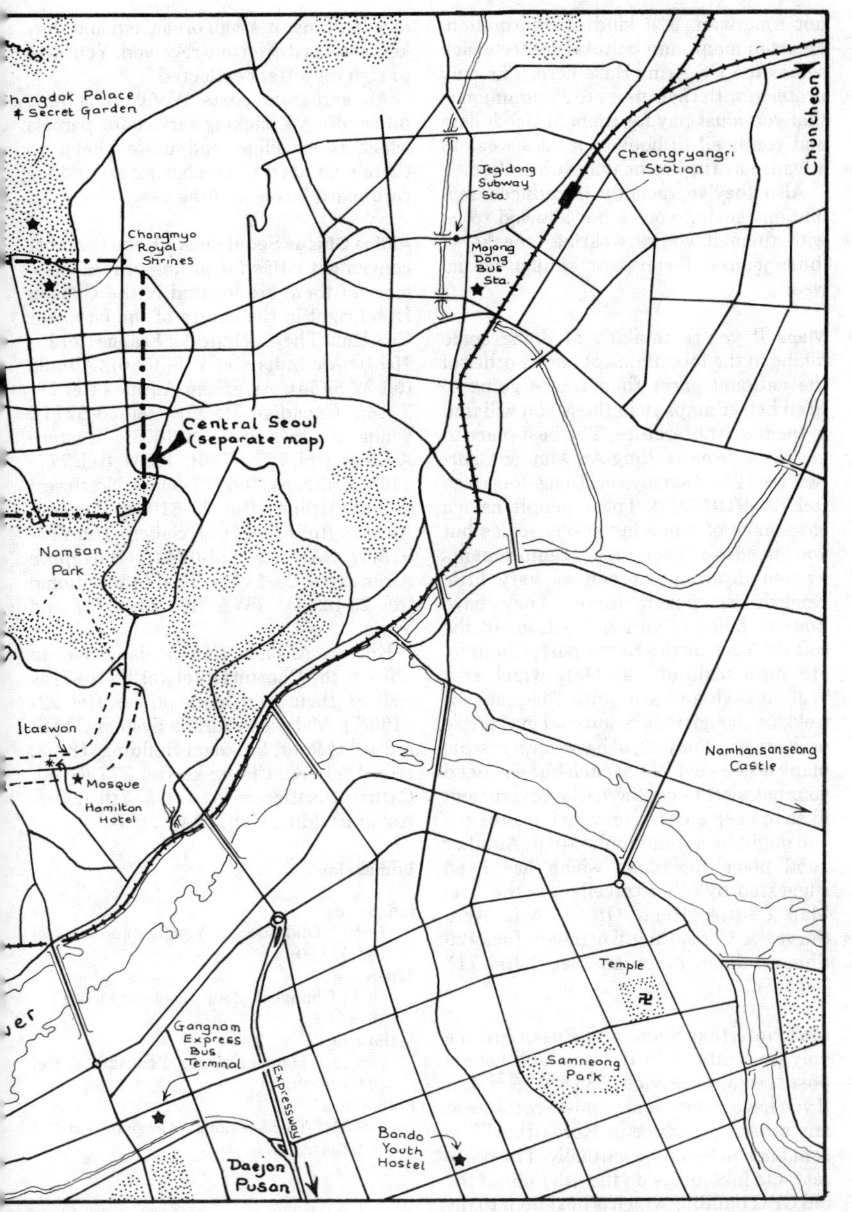
Changdok Palace
+ Secret Garden
Changmyo
Royal
Shrines
Central Seoul
(separate map)
Nomsan
Park
Itaewon
Mosque
Hamilton
Hotel
Jegidong
Subway
Sta.
Majang
Dong
Bus
Sta.
Cheongryangri
Station
Chuncheon
Namhansanseong
Castle
Temple
Samneong
Park
Gangnam
Express
Bus
Terminal
Expressway
Bando
Youth
Hostel
Daejon
Pusan

not American, is a kind of information, entertainment, and cultural centre which serves the US Army Base here. The only problem with their tours to Panmunjon is that you must pay for them in US dollars and you need to book at least a week in advance as they're heavily subscribed.

Also they've recently introduced regulations saying you're not allowed to go with them if you're wearing 'sneakers', 'blue jeans', T-shirts or similar casual wear.

Maps If you're thinking of doing some hiking in the mountains of one or other of the national parks then you're going to need better maps than those you will find in the tourist literature. The best place to get these from is Jung-An Map & Chart Service, 125-1 Gongpyeong Dong, Jongro-gu (tel 720-9191/2/3). These people have a vast range of maps in various scales but you need to have your requirements written down in Korean as very little English is spoken there. They have 'tourist' maps of various sections of the country such as the East Coast, Chejudo, etc, on a scale of 1:410,000 which cost W2000 each and are quite adequate for trekking though they're lettered in Chinese or Korean. They also have larger scale maps which cost W300 each but you need your passport to get them (the government likes to keep a check on who buys them – you might be a Communist spy!). Another good place for maps which has been suggested by other travellers is the Asia Map Centre, Head Office, Asia Aero Survey & Consulting Engineers Inc, 429 Shinsoo-dong, Mapo-ku, Seoul (tel 717 7511/5).

Mail Note that Seoul and Pusan are the only post offices in Korea which have a poste restante service 유치우편물교부 . If you have letters sent to poste restante at any other post office in Korea they'll be sent back to Seoul – eventually. The poste restante in Seoul is on the 9th floor of the old GPO building which is next door to the new building. It's well organised and they keep a record of letters received. You have to sign for letters collected.

An aerogram costs W350. The post office offers a packing service for parcels which is excellent and quite cheap so there's no need to go chasing around for cardboard boxes and the like.

Airline Offices Seoul must be one the most convenient cities for airline offices since most of them are located in the Chosun Hotel right in the centre of the city near City Hall. They include Air France (tel 23-1574), Air India (tel 778-3556), Alitalia (tel 22-8454), American Airlines (tel 28-3314), Canadian Pacific (tel 23-8271), China Airlines (tel 28-3678), Eastern Airlines (tel 777-9786), KLM (tel 777-2495), Lufthansa (tel 777-9655), Northwest Orient Airlines (tel 23-6106), Pakistan Airlines (tel 778-1161), Sabena (tel 777-9786), SAS (tel 23-0244), Singapore Airlines (tel 28-1226), Thai International (tel 23-0244), TWA (tel 23-8271) and Varig.

Korean Airlines (KAL) also have an office in the Chosun Hotel (tel 23-1067) as well as their own main offices (tel 22-2106/7). Malaysian Airline System (MAS) are at 1st floor, Paiknam Building, 188-3, I-ka, Ulchi-ro, Chung-ku (tel 777-6758). Cathay Pacific are at 1st & 7th floors, Kolon Building (tel 779-0321/9).

Embassies

Indonesia
: 1-887 Yoido-dong, Yongdungpo-ku (tel 782-5116/8).

Japan
: 18-11 Chunghak-dong, Chongro-ku (tel 73-5626/8)

Malayasia
: 726-115 Hannam-dong, Yongsan-ku (tel 794-72050).

Philippines
: 559-510 Yoksam-dong, Kangnam-klu (tel 58-9434).

Thailand
House 127, Namsan Village, Itaewon-dong, Yongsan-ku (tel 792-0197).
Republic of China (Taiwan)
83, 2-ka Myong-dong, Yonsan-ku (tel 776-2721/5). This embassy is just behind the GPO.

English-language Bookstores Probably the best of these is the huge bookshop in the Chongro Ilbunji Arcade in the basement of the Kyobo Building at the junction of Jongro and Sejongro. It's also worth checking out the Royal Asiatic Society, Korea Branch, Christian Centre Building, 136-46 Yunji-dong, Jongno-ku, which has the best selection of books in English on Korean subjects.

What to See

Kyongbok (Gyeongbog) Palace 경복궁
Located at the back of the Capitol Building at the end of Sejongro, this palace was first built in 1392 by the founder of the Yi Dynasty, King Taejo. It was burnt down during the Japanese invasion of 1592 and thereafter left in ruins until rebuilt in 1867 when it became the residence of the 26th ruler. The grounds of this palace contain some exceptionally beautiful buildings and a collection of ancient stone pagodas from other parts of the country, many of which were brought here by the Japanese during their occupation of Korea. Also in the grounds are the **National Museum** and the **National Folk Museum.** The collections in the National Museum are mainly of pottery and roofing tiles from the various Korean kingdoms but there's also an excellent section of stone and brass Buddhas and Bodhisattvas. Probably the most interesting of the two museums here, however, is the National Folk Museum which contains life-like recreations of traditional houses, festivals, clothing styles and agricultural implements. There's also a real surprise here in the form of a display of movable metal type which was invented and used in Korea around 1234 – two hundred years before Gutenberg's 'invention' of movable type printing in Europe! You'll probably need all day to see the palace and the two museums.

Kyongbok Palace is open daily from 9 am to 6 pm (April-October) and 9.30 am to 5.30 pm (November-March) and costs W550 entry. The museums are open daily except Monday from 9 am to 5 pm and cost W110 to the Folk Museum and W150 to the National Museum.

Chongmyo (Jongmyo) Royal Ancestral Shrines 종묘
This forested park near the centre of the city contains a collection of beautiful traditional Korean temples which house the ancestral tablets of the 27 Yi Dynasty kings and queens. The two main shrines, however, are only opened to the public on certain ceremonial days. The main one of these is on the first Sunday of May each year when the descendants of the royal family come here to honour the spirits of their ancestors in a very colourful Confucian ceremony which lasts six hours. On this day there's also traditional court dancing and music. It's something which shouldn't be missed if you're here at that time. Entry costs W550 and the park is open daily between 9 am and 6 pm.

Right at the top of **Chongmyo Park** is a bridge over the road to **Changgyongwon Zoo and Botanical Gardens** which contains the usual collection of bored and neurotic animals that can be seen in zoos all over the world if you like that sort of thing.

Changdok (Changdeog) Palace 창덕궁
Originally constructed in 1405 as an eastern detached palace, this is the best preserved of Seoul's five palaces and is still the residence of the remnants of the royal family. Like the other palaces in the capital it was burned down during the Japanese invasion of 1592 but rebuilt in 1611 and used as the official royal residence until 1867 when the king moved to Kyongbok Palace. The gateway to Changdok is a classic piece of traditional

Korean architecture and the oldest original gate in the city.

Changdok is also the site of the enchanting **Secret Garden (Piwon)**, a landscaped, wooded retreat which covers over 78 acres and was, during the days of the Yi Dynasty, reserved for members of the royal family and the king's concubines. This is Korean landscape gardening at its best. The garden contains over 40 pleasure pavilions as well as many ponds and stone bridges.

The palace and the Secret Garden are open daily but to see them you must join a tour group. These are fairly informal and it is possible to wander around on your own at various points. Each tour lasts about 1½ hours and costs W1200. Tickets go on sale half an hour before a tour starts. There are English tours at 10.40 am, 1.10 pm and 3.40 pm. Korean tours are at 9 am, 11.30 am, 2 pm and 4.30 pm. Japanese tours are at 9.50 am, 12.20 pm and 2.50pm.

Toksu (Deogsu) Palace 덕수궁

Located opposite Seoul Plaza Hotel right in the centre of the city, this palace was originally built as a royal villa towards the end of the 15th century. It became the official residence of the last of the Yi Dynasty kings, King Kojong, in 1897 following his year-long asylum in the Russian Legation. Kojong abdicated in 1907 but continued to live here until his death in 1919. After that, the palace was left to deteriorate until 1933 when it was restored by the royal family. Entry costs W400 and the opening times are the same as for Kyongbok Palace.

The grounds contain the Museum of Modern Art.

Other places

Two other places worth visiting in the centre of the city, both of them on Jongro, are **Pagoda Park** 파고다공원 which costs W150 entry and is famous for its 10-storied Koryo pagoda, and **Poshingak (Bosingag)** 보신각 or Bell Pavilion, which houses Seoul's city bell used in former times to announce dawn and sunset at which times the city gates were opened or closed. The bell is 2½ metres high and was cast in 1468. The street on which it stands – Jongro (Chongno) – translates into Bell street.

Further away from the centre of the city on the northern slopes of Namsan is **Korea House** 한국의집 which offers weekly programmes of traditional cultural activities such as dancing and music. They also put on films and displays. Many of the events put on here are well subscribed so check beforehand if seats are available. Every Saturday and Sunday at 3 pm there is a free display of Korean folk dances.

Namsan Tower is, of course, Seoul's most prominent landmark, siting on top of Namsan mountain between the centre of the city and Itaewon. There are superb views over Seoul and its environs from the top of this mountain if the weather is fine. You can either walk up there or take the cable car which operates every 5-10 minutes every day throughout the day and costs W550 single or W770 return. If you'd like to take the lift to the top of Namsan Tower this will cost you W1000 return. Note that no photography is allowed from the cable car or from Namsan Tower and if you go up the latter, cameras have to be left at the bottom.

Markets

Probably the best of these and the one where you're most likely to find bargains is Nadaemun of South Gate Market. This market spreads over many streets off the south side of Namdaemunro which is the road running from the GPO to Namdaemun, one of Seoul's ancient gateways about half-way between City Hall and Seoul station. There's an incredible variety of goods for sale here from bedrolls to turtles, laquer boxes inlaid with mother-of-pearl to cushion covers, clothes, brass-ware and exotic tropical fish. Bargaining is de rigeur, of course, and if you're in no hurry you should be able to knock up to

20% off the marked prices (though many things have no marked price). I personally felt that the laquered boxes inlaid with mother-of-pearl and the brocades were some of the best things on offer here. Beautiful stuff!

If you are hunting for brass Buddhas and the like then there are many shops on Jongro which specialise in these though prices are no longer cheap.

Note that the export of antiques from Korea is prohibited without prior permission from Customs and Excise. Also the export of ginseng – Korea's very first export – is severely restricted.

Entertainment

Most western travellers and GI's from the neighbouring Yongsan Camp head down to **Itaewon** on the south side of Namsan Mountain at least twice a week. It's an area of bars, music and dancing clubs (there's no entry fee as a rule), restaurants, brothels, shoe and clothes shops and many other things as well. The activities of the hookers here have to be seen to be believed. It's like a cattle market! You should expect to pay between W1200 and W1600 for a beer in these clubs which cater for all tastes in music. Just wander around and hop into any which take your fancy.

Many people head initially for the *Sportman's Club* though just why they do this isn't clear since I found the place very staid, expensive (a large beer and small orange juice cost W3800!!), and largely a meeting place for middle-aged American military officers. Much livelier and cheaper places include the *UN Tourist Club* (don't let the word 'tourist' put you off) – live bands, friendly place, small beers W500; *King Club* (good disco music and very popular, small beers W550), and *All That Jazz* on the same side as the Hamilton Hotel (excellent even if you're not normally a jazz fan but best on Sunday nights when black American GI's jam together, large beer and soft drink around W2000). *Heavy Metal*, across the street from the King Club has also been recommended. They have between 4000-5000 albums and happily take requests. None of the clubs have an entry fee but despite the fact that curfew was abolished in January '82 they still tend to close by 12 midnight.

To get from Itaewon from the budget hotel area you can take bus No 23 or 72 from outside the Sejong Cultural Centre (fare W120 or W110 if you buy a token beforehand) and get off at the Hamilton Hotel, or bus No 79 which is more frequent and goes over Namsan Mt. The main club area is a very short walk up the road from there. If you take a taxi from the Sejong Cultural Centre it will cost between W1000 and W1200. If you're taking a taxi back after 11.30 pm then you're likely to pay W2000 for the whole taxi, and, if there are spare seats, the driver may stop and pick up other people though you'll still have to pay W2000.

Another traveller has recommended the night market at Chongryangri which she described as '... a bit far, but I found the combination of neon, restaurants, food and clothing vendors and whores plying their wares out of tiny, pink-lit cubicles fascinating. No tourists or foreigners to be seen here.'

Another place which many travellers go to, especially on Sunday afternoons, is the *New Naija Hotel* which is connected with the USO. It's officially off-limits to anyone but American military personnel and their guests and there's a guard on the gate who may well stop you and ask for ID (meaning American servicemen's ID which, of course, you won't have). It's best to just keep on walking and mutter something about seeing 'Johnny' or some equally unlikely person or wave some official looking card. They're not very thorough. The bar here serves cheap drinks and can even get duty-free American cigarettes if you pretend to have an ID number (they keep a record of who buys them). In theory everything has to be paid for in cash US dollars though they will take won. There's also a restaurant here (serve yourself)

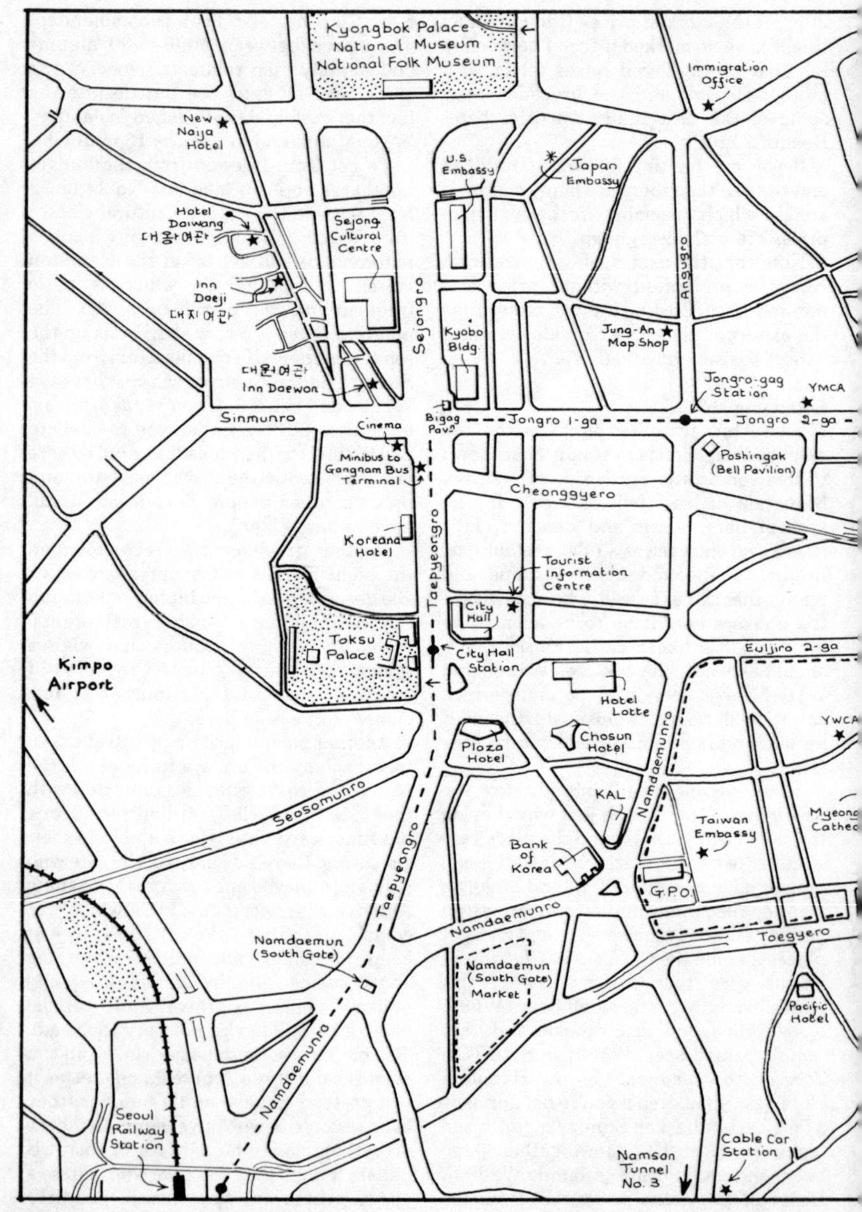
Kyongbok Palace
National Museum
National Folk Museum
Immigration Office
New Naija Hotel
U.S. Embassy
Japan Embassy
Hotel Daiwang
대왕여관
Sejong Cultural Centre
Inn Daeji
대지여관
Sejongro
Angugro
Kyobo Bldg.
Jung-An Map Shop
대원여관
Inn Daewon
Jongro-gag Station
YMCA
Sinmunro
Cinema
Bigag Pavn
Jongro 1-ga
Jongro 2-ga
Minibus to Gangnam Bus Terminal
Poshingak (Bell Pavilion)
Cheonggyero
Koreana Hotel
Taepyeongro
Tourist Information Centre
City Hall
Toksu Palace
City Hall Station
Euljiro 2-ga
Kimpo Airport
Hotel Lotte
Namdaemunro
YWCA
Plaza Hotel
Chosun Hotel
KAL
Seosomunro
Taiwan Embassy
Myeong Cathe
Bank of Korea
Taepyeongro
G.P.O.
Namdaemunro
Toegyero
Namdaemun (South Gate)
Namdaemun (South Gate) Market
Pacific Hotel
Namdaemunro
Seoul Railway Station
Namsan Tunnel No. 3
Cable Car Station

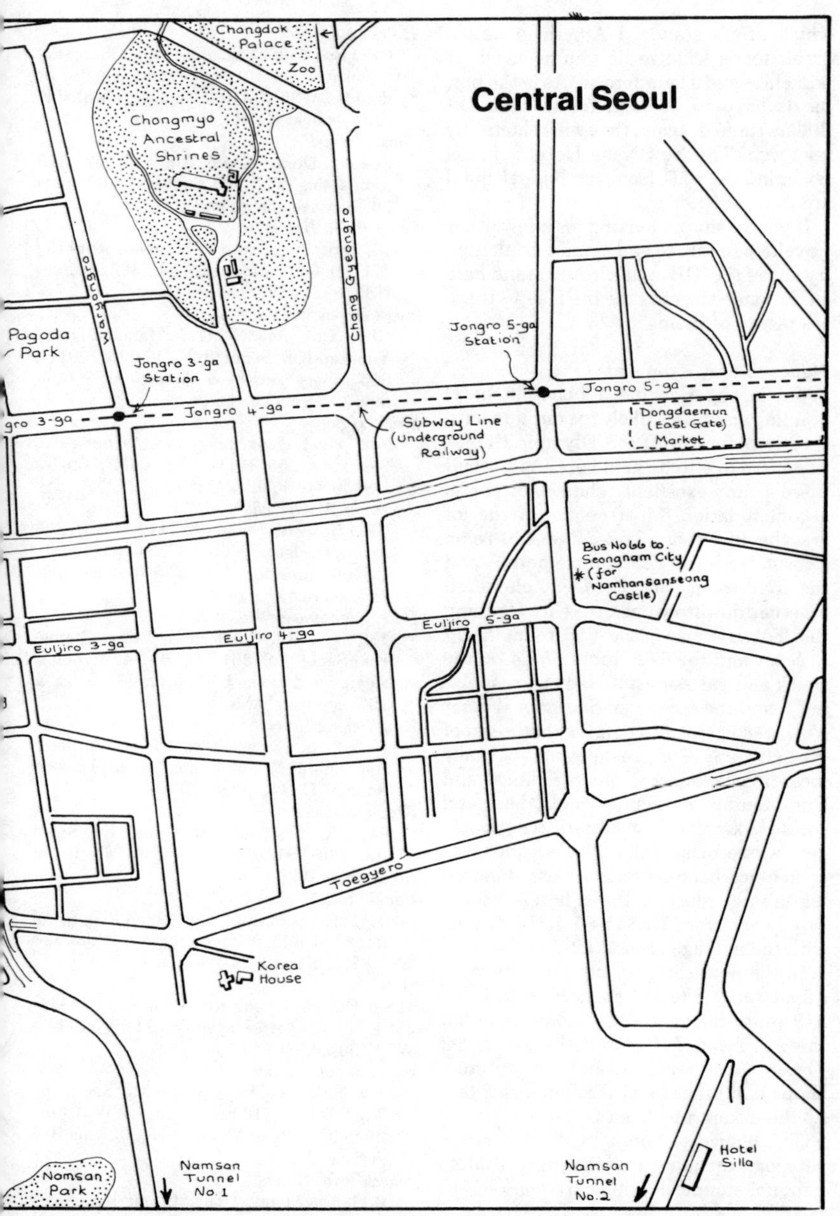
Central Seoul
Changdok Palace
Zoo
Chongmyo Ancestral Shrines
Wargongro
Chang Gyeongro
Pagoda Park
Jongro 3-ga Station
Jongro 5-ga Station
gro 3-ga
Jongro 4-ga
Jongro 5-ga
Subway Line (Underground Railway)
Dongdaemun (East Gate) Market
Bus No 66 to Seongnam City (for Namhansanseong Castle)
Euljiro 3-ga
Euljiro 4-ga
Euljiro 5-ga
Toegyero
Korea House
Namsan Park
Namsan Tunnel No. 1
Namsan Tunnel No. 2
Hotel Silla

which offers standard American fare – great for a change if you're tired of 'kimchi' – and a launderette. As in the bar, meals have to be paid for in cash US dollars though, again, they will reluctantly take won. The New Naija Hotel is just a few minutes' walk from the budget hotel area.

If you're simply looking for a few other travellers to talk to and a quiet drink then try any of the 'OB' and 'Crown' stand bars on the same street as the Inn Daeji – there are plenty of them.

Places to Stay – top end

Seoul is experiencing a boom in hotel building and this is likely to continue until shortly before the 1988 Olympic Games which are due to be held here. As a result there's an excellent choice of hotel accommodation. Most deluxe of the lot are the 956-room *Lotte*, the 470-room *Chosun* – Seoul's first deluxe hotel – and the 540-room *Seoul Plaza* clustered together downtown near to City Hall and the Toksu Palace; the 655-room *Hyatt Regency* and the 672 –room *Shilla* on the south and east sides of Namsan respectively; and the 806-room *Sheraton Walker Hill*, a resort/casino complex south-east of the city. Several restaurants (usually including Japanese, Korean, Chinese and Continental), swimming pools, bars and cocktail lounges, nightclubs, discos (usually very westernised), shopping arcades and conference/banquet facilities are standard features at most of these hotels. Room rates vary from US$45-85 for a double with the average around US$65.

In the next category are the 470-room *Ambassador*, the 410-room *President*, the 319-room *Royal*, the 217-room *Seoulin*, the 210-room *Tokyu* and the 245-room *Tower* most with several restaurants, shops and other facilities. The price of a double room runs from US$40-55.

The choice of hotels in the top range category includes the following ('international standard' hotels are marked *):

*Hotel Lotte**
CPO Box 3500, 1 Sogong-dong, Chung-ku, Seoul (tel 771-10), 956 rooms, singles or doubles, W35,700-46,200. This is probably Korea's best Hotel

*Chosun Hotel**
Sokong Dong, Seoul (tel 771-05), 470 rooms, singles US$65, doubles US$70 plus 10% service charge and 10% tax

*Seoul Plaza Hotel**
23, 2-ka, Taepung-ro, Chung-ku Seoul (tel 771-22), 540 rooms, singles US$62, doubles US$70 plus 10% service charge

*Hyatt Regency Seoul**
CPO Box 3438, 747-7 Hannam-Dong, Yongsan-Ku, Seoul (tel 795-0061/0041), 655 rooms, singles & doubles US$60-85 plus 10% service charge

*Shilla Hotel**
202 2-ga, Jangchung-Dong, Chung-Ku, Seoul (tel 255 3111), 672 rooms, singles US$36-41, doubles US$42-47

*Sheraton Walker Hill**
CPO Box 714, Seoul (tel 444 8211/9), 806 rooms, singles or doubles US$40 (standard), US$50 (superior) & US$55 (deluxe) plus 10% service charge

Hotel Ambassasor
186-54, 2-Ka, Changchung-Dong, Chung-Ku, Seoul (tel 261-1101/9), 470 rooms, singles & doubles US$55 plus 10% tax & 10% service charge

King Sejong Hotel
61-3, 2-Ka, Chungmu-Ro, Chung-Ku, Seoul (tel 766 4011), 350 rooms, singles US$33, doubles US$46 plus 10% tax

Koreana Hotel
61, 1-Ka, Taeypung-Ro, Chung-Ku, Seoul (tel 720 991/20), 281 rooms, singles & doubles W28,600

Pacific Hotel
31-1, Ka, Namsan-Dong, Chung-Ku, Seoul (tel 22 5100), 103 rooms, singles & doubles US$32 plus 10% service charge

Hotel President
188-3 Euljiro, Chung-Ku, Seoul (tel 232171/3131), 303 rooms, singles W19,500, doubles W26,400-29,300

Hotel Seoul Garden
169-1 Dowha-Dong, Mapo-Ku, Seoul (tel 713 9441-9), 410 rooms, singles W21,000-29,000, doubles W25,000-28,000 plus 10% service charge

Seoul Royal Hotel
6, 1-Ka, Myung-Dong, Chung-Ku, Seoul

(tel 771 45), 319 rooms, singles US$34, doubles US$42

Seoul Tokyu Hotel
120 5-Ka, Namdaemun-Ro, Chung-Ku, Seoul (tel 23 1151), 210 rooms, singles US$45, doubles US$48 plus 10% tax

Seoulin Hotel
149 Sorin-Dong, Chongro-Ku, Seoul (tel 72 0181/8), 217 rooms, singles US$29, doubles US$35

Tower Hotel
5-5 2-Ka, Changchung-Dong, Chung-Ku, Seoul (tel 253 9181/9), 245 rooms, singles US$20, doubles US$32

Places to Stay – mid-range

Central Tourist Hotel
227-1, Chang Sa Dong, Chong-Ro Ku, Seoul (tel 265 4121), 88 rooms, singles US$22, doubles US$27 plus 10% tax

Crown Hotel
34-69 Itaewon-Dong, Yonsang-Ku, Seoul (tel 792 8224/30), situated near US Army Headquarters Yonsang Compound. Singles & doubles US$25-36

Empire Hotel
63 Mugyo-Dong, Chung-Ku, Seoul (tel 777 5511/9), 120 rooms, singles & doubles US$30-37

Grand Hotel
17-12, 4-Ka Namdaemun Rd, Seoul (tel 23 0391), 51 rooms, singles US$ 14.50-15.50, doubles US$17-24 plus 10% service charge

Hamilton Hotel
119-25 Itaewon-Dong, Yongsan-Ku, Seoul (tel 794 0171/9), 139 rooms, singles US$16-19, doubles US$16-24. Like the Crown Hotel this one is situated near the US Army Headquarters Yongsan Compound

Lions Tourist Hotel
53-16 Chongmu-Ro, 2-Ka, Jung-Gu, Seoul (tel 266 1112-4), 87 rooms, singles & doubles US$20-22 but with some Korean-style rooms for US$12-23

Mammoth Hotel
620-29 Chonnong-Dong, Tongdaemun-Ku, Seoul (tel 435 3131/9), 219 rooms, singles US$26, doubles US$31

Metro Hotel
199-33, 2-Ka, Ulchi-Ro, Choong-Ku, Seoul (tel 776 6781-8), 83 rooms, singles US$24.50, doubles US$32.60

New Kukje Hotel
29-2, 1-Ka, Taepyong-Ro, Chung-Ku, Seoul (tel 72 0161), 139 rooms, singles US$23, doubles US$23-27

New Seoul Hotel
CPO Box 3385, 29-1, 1-Ka, Taepong-Ro, Chung-Ku, Seoul (tel 725 9071-9), 151 rooms, singles & doubles US$24

New Sky Hotel
108-2 Pyung-Chang-Dong, Chongro-Ku, Seoul (tel 75 5121), 140 rooms, singles & doubles US$24

Places to Stay – bottom end

There are two yogwans in Seoul where almost every budget traveller stays on first arriving in the city. Some people even become permanent fixtures while they raise money teaching English (or Spanish, or German, or whatever). They're both run by very friendly people and both are of the same quality. They are:

Inn Daewon 대원여관 Dang Ju-Dong, Jongro-Ku (tel 725 7891) 종로구 당주동 26 번지 Here you can have a room to yourself (if it's not full) or share with one or two others. The rooms cost W4000 or W2500 if you share. There's a communal shower, two toilets and basic cooking equipment. I found the rooms were not quite as pleasant as those at the Inn Daeji but this doesn't seem to matter too much when you're staying here.

Inn Daeji 대지여관 (tel 723 4659). This yogwan is just two or three minutes' walk from the Inn Daewon. It has a pleasant courtyard and more attractive rooms but suffers the disadvantage of having no shower or cooking facilities. The rooms here cost W4000-5000, the cost of which you can share with others as at the Inn Daewon.

Both the above places are excellent for meeting other travellers and for exchanging information. If you're looking for a job teaching English here in Seoul then these two yogwans are the places to enquire what's available, what the rates are and who to avoid. You can also find out all manner of other things here from where to sell your duty-free whisky to what's a good hotel in Ouagadougou.

If heaps of travellers give you the creeps then there are plenty of other simple yogwans – usually better maintained – in the alleys off the street on which the Inn Daeji is situated which will cost you about the same. If you'd prefer a yogwan with your own bathroom or at least with better bathing facilities (there's often a long queue for the shower at the Inn Daewon!) then try one or other of the bathhouses in this area. One of the slightly better yogwans which can be recommended in this area is the *Hotel Daewang* 대왕여관 서울 특별시 종로구 내수동 165-1 (tel 725 5395-6) which costs W6500 a double or W6000 if you stay over one week. The bathrooms here are clean and well maintained and the place is run by friendly people. Warm to hot water in the evenings and early mornings. Popular.

If you'd prefer to stay in the Itaewon area of town then a good yogwan is the *Sung Ji Hotel* 성지여관, 211-30 Itaewon-2 Dong, Yongsan-ku (tel 792 1691). Rooms here cost W9000 a double with own bathroom. It's very clean, friendly and recommended by many long stay travellers in Seoul.

Places to Eat

There are restaurants, cafes and bars all the way down the road on which the Inn Daeji is situated and many of them are very good so it's difficult to make recommendations but one which does deserve it is the fish restaurant called 삼 엇 next door to the 'OB' stand bar near the Inn Daeji. Here they offer fish fry (a whole fish), 'kimchi', seaweed, mussel soup and rice for W1000. They also have fried squid for W1000 and fried octupus for W1800 as well as 'Sundubu' – a strange concoction of pieces of octupus, chilli and other vegetables – for W700. In the mornings they offer western-style breakfasts (two-eggs, toast and coffee) for W600. The most popular place for these sort of breakfasts, however, is the cafe directly opposite. Their western-style breakfasts are a little more imaginative though it could be said that anyone who orders one of these breakfasts is unimaginative given that you can order a hearty Korean-style breakfast consisting of numerous tasty dishes for only W400 more.

Two or three doors down from the fish restaurant is an open sided cafe which offers pieces of chicken, fish pieces and fried potatoes. The food is good though perhaps a little greasy. Chicken costs W600 per piece, fish W100 per piece and fried potatoes W50 per portion. Roast chicken (which tends not to be so greasy) and coleslaw can also be bought at the Crown stand bars on this street – the price is the same at W600 per piece.

There are many other restaurants here which offer Korean and Chinese food and many of then are very popular with local people. You can eat well in most of them for W1500-2000 (more for 'bulgogi') but you need to have a translation of a typical Korean menu handy to make the best of them. Failing that, just wander in and see what other people are eating and tell them you want the same if you see something which looks good.

If you'd like some excellent western-style food in this same area the *Bibichoo Stand Bar & Restaurant* 비비추 (tel 722 3060) is the place to go. Their meals are fairly cheap, the helpings are large and the surroundings very pleasant and clean. Soup, hamburger steak with gravy, fish fillets, chips, dressed salad, rice & pickles cost just W2200. This place undoubtedly offers one of the best deals in western-style food in the whole of Seoul.

In Itaewon there are few restaurants which offer the same value as those around the back of the Sejong Cultural Centre and prices tend to be 60-100% higher for the same dishes. *Addone*, a restaurant diagonally opposite the Hamilton Hotel which calls itself 'Mexican' is a nice place but most definitely very American-ised and helpings are small. A decent meal here would cost you W2500-3000. The *Green Village Mexican Restaurant* next to (and, in fact, part of) the Hamilton Hotel is perhaps better value if you go for the daily 'specials' which run at around W3000-3500 and are not necessarily Mexican but if you go for a la carte take into consideration that they add 10% service charge and 10% tax to the prices on the menu. These taxes make meals here somewhat expensive though the food is very good. In the summer months you can eat from street stalls in Itaewon. One new place which has been recommended is *Popeye's*, a good outdoor cafe which is a great place to meet people, watch life go by and have a drink. It's right next door to *Colonel Sanders*.

Another good street for restaurants – many of them with set menus – is the one immediately behind the Kyobo Building opposite the Sejong Cultural Centre. This street is the first on the left hand side down Jongro. A range of different food is available at the restaurants here and you can eat well for W1000-1500.

Getting Around

The Subway (Underground Railway) The Seoul Subway is modern, fast, comfortable and cheap. It's an excellent method of getting from one place to another. A vast amount of construction work has been going on all over the city for a number of years now to extend the subway network and it's due for completion well before the 1988 Olympic Games. The network already connects all of Seoul's bus terminals and mainline railway stations as well as many points of interest in the city. You can also use it, without having to change trains, to get to Suweon.

Fares are based on the distance travelled but even the longest possible journey – from the centre of Seoul to Suweon – costs a mere W360 (about 50c). Subway trains have their destination in Korean and English on the front of the engines and all stations have their name in the same two languages at frequent intervals along the platforms so you can't get lost. Note that only in the centre of the city do the trains travel underground.

Bus The main bus terminal in Seoul is the Gangnam (Kangnam) Express Bus Terminal 영동선 호남선 on the other side of the Han River. To get there from the Sejong Cultural Centre (budget hotel area) you can either take the subway or mini-bus 41 from the Gugje cinema, fare is W350. If you take the latter then get off at the first stop across the Han River. The huge new complex next to the flyover is the terminal. It must have cost a fortune and is clearly designed for the 1988 Olympics which are to be held in Seoul. There's everthing here you could possibly want – restaurants, snack bars, coffee houses, pharmacies, bookstalls, even religious newsletter stalls! There is also an advance sales office 예매소 which is open daily from 9 am to 6 pm though it's most unlikely you'll ever have to use this facility – there are plenty of buses to get most places every-day. The terminal is very well-organised with signs in English and Korean over all the ticket offices and bus bays so you can't go wrong so long as you don't confuse places like Kongju, Kwangju and Kyongju.

To Chongju 청주 Every 10 minutes from 6 am to 8.30 pm. The fare is W3180.
To Iri 이리 Every half an hour from 6 am to 8.30 pm. The fare is W3130.
To Kangnung 강릉 Every 20 minutes from 6 am to 5.30 pm. The fare is W3350 and the journey takes about 3¾ hours.
To Masan 마산 Every 15 minutes from 6 am to 4.30 pm. The fare is W5070.
To Nonsan 논산 Every 50 minutes from 6.50 am to 7.30 pm. The fare is W2840 and the journey takes 3¼ hours.
To Pusan 부산 Every 10 minutes from 6 am to 4.30 pm. The fare is W5680 and the journey takes four hours.
To Puyo 부여 Every hour from 7 am to 4.30 pm. The fare is W3100 and the journey takes about 3¼ hours.
To Sogcho 속초 19 buses daily from 6.30 am to 4.30 pm. The fare is W4240 and the journey takes 5¼ hours.

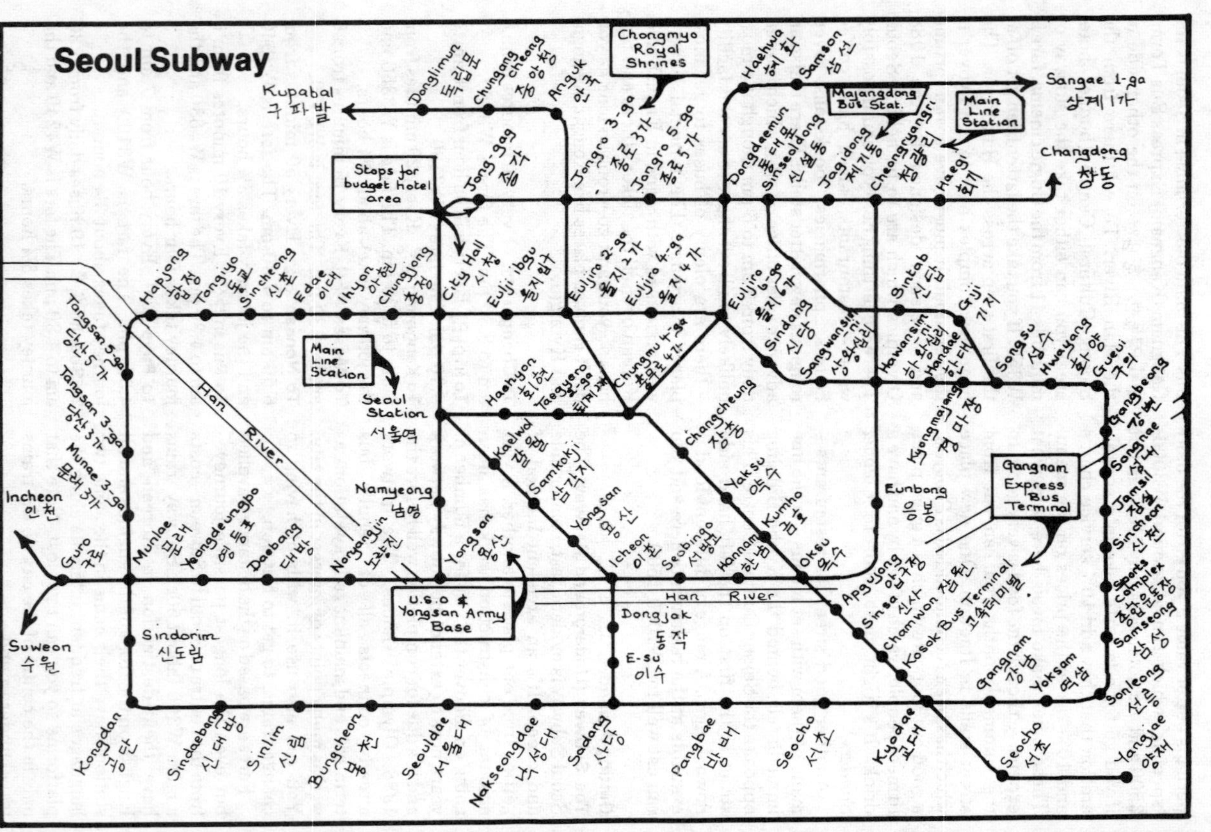
Seoul Subway
Kupabal 구파발
Donglimun 독립문
Chungang cheong 중앙청
Anguk 안국
Chongmyo Royal Shrines
Haehwa 혜화
Samson 삼선
Sangae 1-ga 상계1가
Majangdong Bus Stat.
Main Line Station
Changdong 창동
Stops for budget hotel area
Jong-gag 종각
Jongro 3-ga 종로 3가
Jongro 5-ga 종로 5가
Dongdaemun 동대문
Sinseoldong 신설동
Jagidong 제기동
Cheongryangri 청량리
Haegi 회기
Hapjong 합정
Tongiyo 동교
Sincheong 신촌
Edae 이대
Ihyon 아현
Chungjong 충정
City Hall 시청
Eulji ibgu 을지입구
Euljiro 2-ga 을지 2가
Euljiro 4-ga 을지 4가
Euljiro 6-ga 을지 6가
Sintab 신답
Giji 기지
Sindang 신당
Sangwansimni 상왕십리
Hawansimni 하왕십리
Handae 한대
Songsu 성수
Hwayang 화양
Gueui 구의
Main Line Station
Seoul Station 서울역
Haehyon 회현
Taegyero 3-ga 퇴계 3가
Chungmu 4-ga 충무로 4가
Changcheung 장충
Kyongmajang 경마장
Gangbeong 강변
Songnae 성내
Jamsil 잠실
Sincheon 신천
Sports Complex 종합운동장
Samseong 삼성
Sonleong 선릉
Gangnam Express Bus Terminal
Eunbong 은봉
Tangsan 5-ga 당산 5가
Tangsan 3-ga 당산 3가
Munae 3-ga 문래 3가
Han River
Namyeong 남영
Kaelwol 갈월
Samkokji 삼각지
Yongsan 용산
Yaksu 약수
Kumho 금호
Incheon 인천
Guro 구로
Munlae 문래
Yeongdeungpo 영등포
Daebang 대방
Nonyangjin 노량진
Yongsan 용산
Icheon 이촌
Seobingo 서빙고
Hannam 한남
Oksu 옥수
Apgujong 압구정
Sinsa 신사
Chamwon 잠원
Kosok Bus Terminal 고속터미널
U.S.O & Yongsan Army Base
Han River
Dongjak 동작
E-su 이수
Suweon 수원
Sindorim 신도림
Gangnam 강남
Yoksam 역삼
Kongdan 공단
Sindaebang 신대방
Sinlim 신림
Bungcheon 봉천
Seouldae 서울대
Nakseongdae 낙성대
Sadang 사당
Pangbae 방배
Seocho 서초
Kyodae 교대
Seocho 서초
Yangjae 양재

To Wonju 원주 Every 30 minutes from 6.30 am to 9 pm. The fare is W1210 and the journey takes 1¾ hours.
To Yosu 여수 Every hour from 6.30 am to 4.30 pm. The fare is W5810 and the journey takes seven hours.

From this part of the terminal there are other buses going to Dong Mae 동해, Gimje 김제, Gunsan 군산, Icheon 이천, Jecheon 제천, Nanweon 남원, Samcheok 삼척, Yongin 용인, Yeoju 여주, Yonmundae 연무대 and Yuseong 유성.

From the other part of the terminal there are the following buses:

To Cheonan 천안 Every 15 minutes from 6.30 am to 8.50 pm. The fare is W1190 and the journey takes one hour.
To Jinju 진주 Every 30 minutes from 6.20 am to 4 pm. The fare is W5530 and the journey takes five hours.
To Kimchon 김천 Every 40 minutes from 7 am to 4 pm. The fare is W3120 and the journey takes 2¾ hours.
To Kongju 공주 Every 40 minutes from 6.30 am to 7.20 pm. The fare is W2120 and the journey takes 2½ hours.
To Kwangju 광주 Every five minutes from 5.30 am to 5.40 pm. The fare is W4300 and the journey takes 4½ hours.
To Kyongju 경주 Every 40 minutes from 7 am to 4.10 pm. The fare is W4840 and the journey takes 4¼ hours.
To Mogpo 목포 Every 40 minutes from 6 am to 4.30 pm. The fare is W5250 and the journey takes nearly six hours.
To Onyang 온양 Every 20 minutes from 6.30 am to 8.40 pm. The fare is W1390 and the journey takes 1½ hours.
To Pohang 포항 Every 30 minutes from 6.30 am to 4 pm. The fare is W5300 and the journey takes five hours.
To Ulsan 울산 Every 20 minutes from 6.30 am to 4 pm. The fare is W5380 and the journey takes five hours.
There are also buses to Anseong 안성, Gumi 구미, Kumsan 금산, Pyeongtak 평택, Sangju 상주 and Yeongdong 영동.

The other bus terminal in Seoul is Majangdong, north-east of the city centre. It's within five to 10 minutes' walk of the Jegidong 제기동 subway station. As you come out of the station put the Midopa department store (opposite the station) on your left-hand side and walk to the first intersection. Turn right there and walk straight for 400-500 metres and you'll arrive at the bus station which is on your left.

Probably the only reason you'd come here for a bus was if you were heading to Chuncheon 춘천. There are many buses daily to Chuncheon which cost W1370 and take about two hours. All the timetables at this terminal and the notices above the ticket offices are in Korean and much of it is pretty near illegible so good luck finding the bus!

There's also a local bus terminal (called Sobu Bus Terminal) where you can get a local bus to Imsingak, near Panmunjon for just US$2.50 – even cheaper than USO though you may have to do a little walking. To get there from Namdaemun market take bus No 156.

AROUND SEOUL

Suweon 수원

Suweon is an ancient fortress city 48km south of Seoul and the provincial capital of Kyonggi province. The walls, which were constructed in the later part of the 18th century by King Congjo in an unsuccessful attempt to make Suweon the nation's capital, once surrounded the whole city but industrial and residential expansion in recent years has seen the city spill out beyond the enclosed area. The walls, gates, a number of pavilions and an unusual water gate have all been reconstructed recently along the original lines. It's possible to walk around almost all the wall but the best point of entry is South Gate 남문. Steps lead straight up to the pavilion at the top of Paltal Mountain 팔달산 from here. If you head off from here first to West Gate 서문 followed by North Gate 북문 and East Gate 동문

you'll see most of the principal features of the fortifications.

Getting There To get to Suweon from Seoul the easiest thing to do is to take the underground railway (subway) to the end of the line but make sure you get on the right train as the line branches at Guro 구로, one going to Suweon and the other to Incheon. The journey takes about 45 minutes and costs W360 one way. Subway trains have their destinations in Korean and English on the front of the engine.

Korean Folk Village 한국 민속촌

Someone is bound to accuse me sooner or later of having lost my sense of judgement but I think this place is excellent and well worth a day trip from Seoul. Most 'recreations' of traditional villages and the like that I've seen elsewhere in the world have mostly turned out to be disastrously kitsch. This is one place which doesn't fall into that category. It's obvious that a lot of effort, attention to detail and sensitivity have gone into creating this village and it's near to being authentic as the hundreds of tourists visiting it daily will allow. I loved it despite preconceived negative feelings about it though some of the credit for my enjoyment of it must go to the head monk, Yang Il, of the Kum Lyun-sa Buddhist temple here who showed me round. He also offered to put me up and feed me free of charge if I cared to stay – that's how kitsch it is.

The village has examples of traditional peasants', farmers' and civil officials' housing styles from all over the country as as craftsmen's work-shops, a brewery, Confucian school, a Buddhist temple and a market place. But it isn't just an empty museum – people live here and continue to practice traditional crafts though you shouldn't expect to see all the craftspeople hard at it when you visit. I went away feeling that it was a very good introduction to Korean culture and an experience which stood me in good stead for my subsequent travels around this country. If you enjoyed the National Folk Museum in the grounds of Kyongbok Palace in Seoul then you'll like this place. Entry to the village costs W2000 which includes a free bus to and from Suweon.

Getting There To get to the village, first go to Suweon at the end of the subway line. When you come out of the station go down into the subway straight in front of you and come back up on the opposite side of the road. On the left-hand side, several doors up there's an office for the Folk Village which has two mock totem poles decorating the doorway. It's here that you buy your ticket for the village and catch the free bus. Buses to the village go every hour on weekdays and every half hour on weekends from 9 am to 5 pm. The last bus back from the village is at 5 pm on weekdays and 6 pm on weekends and public holidays.

As an alternative to going by public transport, there are several bus tour companies in Seoul which will take you straight there and bring you back. One such is Eunma Kyotong Travel Co Ltd 은마관광(tel 722-2666) which is located next to the Gugje cinema (between the budget hotel area and the Koreana Hotel). They have daily buses at 10 am which cost W3200 plus you have to pay the entrance fee at the gate to the village but at the cheaper group rate of W1800.

Panmunjon 판문점

About 56 km north of Seoul lies the truce village of Panmunjon on the cease-fire line established at the end of the Korean War in 1953. It's in a building here that the interminable discussions go on about the re-unification of Korea and the violations of the cease-fire agreements. Personally, I felt that this was over-rated as a 'tourist attraction' though perhaps it's that element of danger that brings people here. Two American servicemen were hacked to death near here in 1976 by the North Koreans and, whilst I was there, tension was very high following the shooting of a South Korean soldier and the attempted

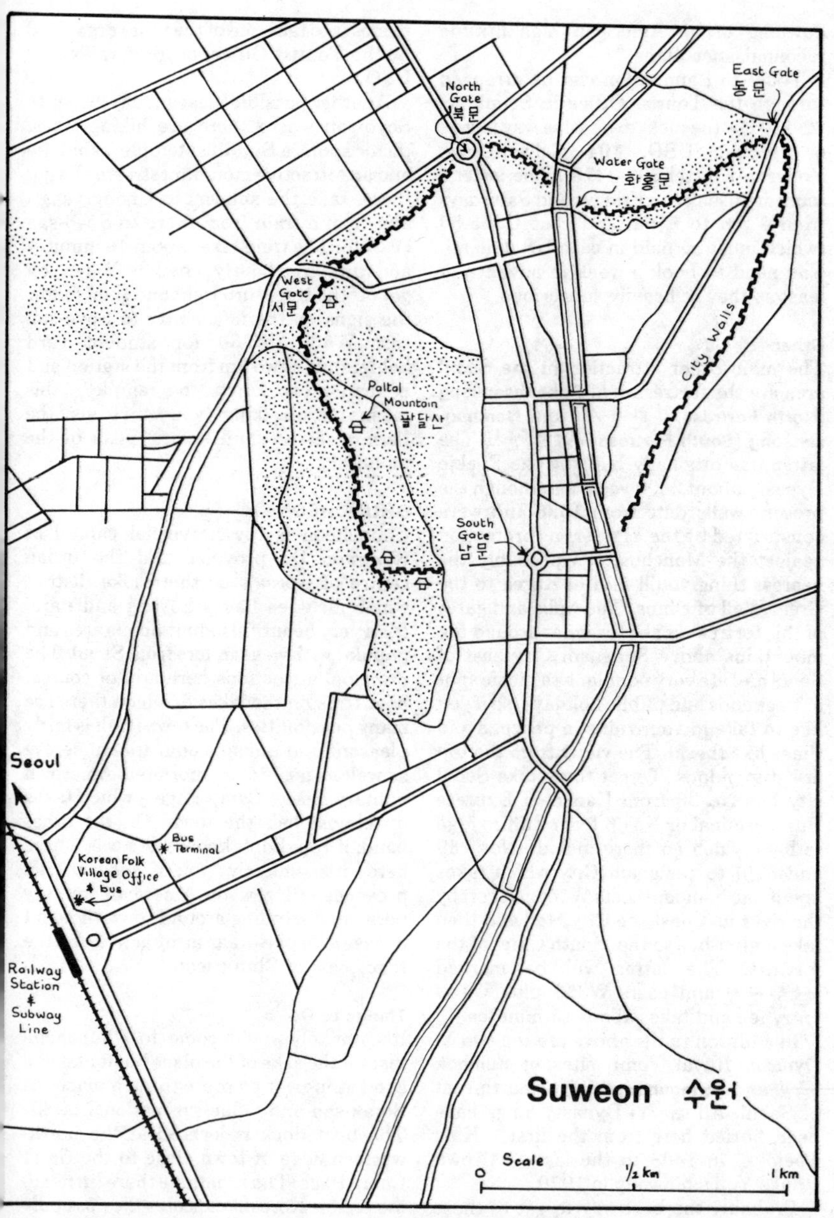
North Gate
북문
East Gate
동문
Water Gate
화홍문
West Gate
서문
Paltal Mountain
팔달산
City Walls
South Gate
남문
Seoul
Bus Terminal
Korean Folk Village Office & bus
Railway Station & Subway Line
Suweon 수원
Scale
0
½ km
1 km

downing of an American high-altitude reconnaisance plane.

Tours to Panmunjon can be arranged through the Tourist Office in Seoul (tel 72-1191) – the most expensive way to go – or through USO, 104 Galwol-Dong, Yongsan-Ku (tel 793-3478). The latter's tours are usually on Fridays and Saturdays from 8 am to 6 pm and cost US$5.50 (which must be paid in cash US dollars). You need to book a week in advance at least as they're heavily subscribed.

Other

The main other attraction in the Seoul area are the fortresses of **Pukhansansong (North Fortress)** 북한산성 and **Namhansansong (South Fortress)** 남한산성 The latter was originally built by the Paekje Dynasty about 2000 years ago though the present walls date from 1626 and were constructed by the Yi rulers as protection against the Manchus. It's probably the nearest thing you'll find in Korea to the Great Wall of China. The walls and gates of this fortress snake for miles around the mountains above Songnam City east of Seoul and are very popular as a picnic spot at weekends and public holidays (so if you like to take in your ruins in peace, avoid times like these). The views from the top are stupendous. To get there take Seoul city bus No 36 from Kangnam Express Bus Terminal or No 66 from Euljiro 5-ga (others which go there include Nos 239 and 570) to Songnam City which takes about one hour and costs W150. Get off by the river just past the City Hall and then take a mini-bus to the 'South Gate' of the fortress. The latter will be marked 남한산성 and costs W350 plus W150 entry fee and takes about 15 minutes.

In addition to the above are the two Yi Dynasty Royal Tomb sites of **Kumgok** 금곡 and **Tonggunung** 동구미 north-east of Seoul. All the Yi Dynasty kings have been buried here from the first – King Taejo — in 1408 to the last — Crown Prince Yongchinwang in 1970.

Probably the best way to get to these places is to take one of the tours organised by the Tourist Office, or, preferably, the USO.

Another possible pleasant day-trip is to Soyo-san where there are hiking trails, picnic spots, a Buddhist temple, campsite and an attractive mountain stream. To get there, take the subway to Chongryangri and then a train from there to Soyo-san (W360). The train takes about 40 minutes and runs on an hourly schedule. When you get off the train turn right and then follow the signs on the left. Entry to Soyo-san cost W600 (W350 for student card holders). It's two km from the station and a further two km to the temple – this means more walking if you want to visit the hermitages or climb to the peak of the mountain.

CHUNCHEON 춘천

Chuncheon is the provincial capital of Kangwon Do province and the urban centre of Korea's northern lake district which includes Lakes Soyang and Paro. It's a very beautiful mountainous area and popular with weekenders from Seoul. The principal attractions here are, of course, boat trips on the lakes of which there are many possibilities. The town itself is fairly pleasant and a major educational centre as well as host to an enormous American military base – Camp Page – which takes up almost half the town. On the other hand, if you didn't know there was a base here it's unlikely you'd suspect it's presence – I saw no American military personnel strolling around town though I did see a lot of Korean army activity on the roads east of Chuncheon.

Things to Do

It's unlikely you'd come to Chuncheon just for the sake of the place but it makes a good stop-over en route to such places as Sorak-san and Odae-san national parks. The boat dock is located at the north-western edge of town close to the tip of Camp Page. The timetable there (in none-too-legible Korean) indicates the possibilty

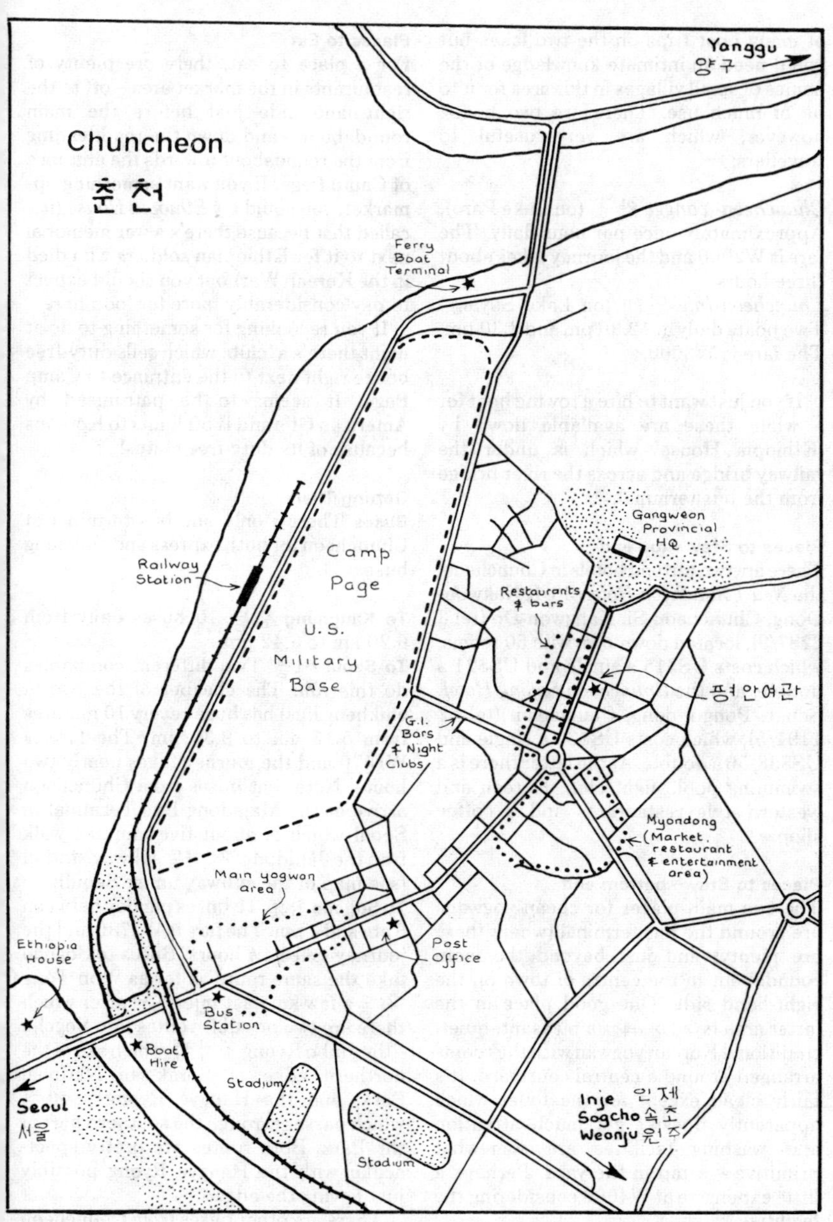
Chuncheon
춘천
Yanggu 양구
Ferry Boat Terminal
Gangweon Provincial HQ
Restaurants & bars
평안여관
Camp Page
U.S. Military Base
Railway Station
G.I. Bars & Night Clubs
Myondong (Market, restaurant & entertainment area)
Main yogwan area
Post Office
Ethiopia House
Bus Station
Boat Hire
Stadium
Stadium
Seoul
서울
Inje 인제
Sogcho 속초
Weonju 원주

of many boat trips on the two lakes but you'd need an intimate knowledge of the names of small villages in this area for it to be of much use. There are two boats, however, which are very useful to travellers:

Chuncheon-Yanggu 양구 (on Lake Paro). Approximately once per hour daily. The fare is W2000 and the journey takes about three hours.
Chuncheon-Inje 인제 (on Lake Soyang) Two boats daily at 12.30 pm and 2.30 pm. The fare is W3000.

If you just want to hire a rowing boat for a while these are available down by 'Ethiopia House' which is under the railway bridge and across the river bridge from the bus terminal.

Places to Stay – top end
There are two top end hotels in Chuncheon, the *New Chuncheon Hotel*, 30-1, Nakwon-Dong, Chuncheon-Si, Kangwon-Do (tel 3 2287/9), located downtown with 50 rooms, which costs US$15 a single and US$21 a double, and the *Chuncheon Sejong Hotel*, San 1, Pongui-dong, Chuncheon (tel 52 1191/5), which costs US$30 a single and US$38-56 a double. At the latter there is a swimming pool, night club, Korean and western-style restaurants and a coffee shop.

Places to Stay – bottom end
The two main places for cheap yogwans are around the bus terminal (where there are plenty) and just beyond the main roundabout in the centre of town on the right-hand side. One good place in the latter area is 평안여관 a pleasant, quiet, traditional Korean yogwan with the rooms arranged around a central courtyard. It's fairly clean except for the toilet which apparently doesn't get much attention and washing facilities are somewhat primitive – a tap in the yard. Perhaps a little expensive at W4000 considering the facilities.

Places to Eat
For a place to eat, there are plenty of restaurants in the market area – off to the right-hand side just before the main roundabout – and down the road leading from the roundabout towards the entrance of Camp Page. If you want something up-market, you could try *Ethiopia House* (it's called that because there's a war memorial next to it for Ethiopian soldiers who died in the Korean War) but you should expect to pay considerably more for food here.

If you're looking for something to do at night there's a 'club' which sells duty-free booze right next to the entrance to Camp Page. It seems to be patronised by American GI's and is off limits to Koreans because of its duty-free status!

Getting There
Buses There's only one bus terminal at Chuncheon for both express and chikheng buses.

To Kangnung 강릉 10 buses daily from 6.20 am to 5.42 pm.
To Seoul 서울 Two different companies do this run. The cheaper of the two (a chikheng bus) has buses every 10 minutes from 5.15 am to 9.30 pm. The fare is W1370 and the journey takes nearly two hours. Note that buses from Chuncheon arrive at the Majadong Bus Terminal in Seoul which is about five minutes walk fron the Jedidong 제기동 subway station (see map of the subway under Seoul).
To Sogcho 속초 10 buses per day between 6 am and 4 pm. The fare is W2730 and the journey takes 4½ hours. Buses to Sogcho take the same route as far as Won Tong 원통 a few km past Inje 인제 after which there are two possible routes into Sogcho – the Jinbo Ryong 진부령 which skirts the northern edge of Sorak-san National Park, and the Hangye Ryong 한계령 which passes through the southern part of the Park. Both routes are pretty spectacular with the Hangye Ryong possibly just having the edge.

There are other buses from Chuncheon

to Cheongju 청주 and Weonju 원주 among other places.

THE NORTH-EAST COAST

Sorak-san (Seolag) National Park 설악산국립공원 & Odae-san National Park 오대산국립공원

These two national parks between Kangnung (Gangneung) 강릉 are two of the most scenically beautiful areas in Korea with high craggy peaks, pine and mixed forests, tremendous waterfalls, boulder-strewn rivers with crystal-clear water, old temples and hermitages. They're at their best from mid to late-autumn when the leaves begin to turn and the mountainsides are transformed into a riot of colour but good at any time of the year. Nearby, on the coast, are some of Korea's best beaches. Sorak-san is the most popular of the two parks and an excellent place to go walking for a few days or even longer if you have camping equipment with you. Pick up a good map of the area in Seoul before you come here from Jung-Ang Map & Chart Service (see under Seoul for details). Probably the most useful is their *Tourist Map of East Coast*. Though most of the trails are well-marked you'll need a map if you intend to head out into the real wilderness beyond the more popular tourist area which is known as Outer Sorak 외설악.

Having said that, a word of warning is perhaps necessary. Sorak-san and particularly the area around Sorak-dong 설악동 the purpose-built tourist village at the end of the road into Outer Sorak, is extremely popular with school parties throughout the summer and autumn. Sixty bus loads of schoolkids and students on any one day is not unusual and you may literally have to queue to get on the various trails leading to the waterfalls and peaks. If you prefer to take in nature in more tranquil conditions then you have little choice but to head out into Inner Sorak 내설악.

Entry to Sorak-san National Park costs W440.

Places to Stay – top end

Except for one hotel near the hot springs all top end places are in Sorak-dong.

Sorak Park Hotel
74-3 Sorak-Dong, Kangwon-do (tel Sogcho 7711), doubles for US$47. There are no singles.

New Sorak Hotel
106-1 Sorak-dong, Sogcho, Kangwon-do (tel Sogcho 7131-50), 120 rooms, doubles for US$44. There are no singles.

Mt Sorak Tourist Hotel
170 Sorak-dong, Sogcho, Kangwon-do (tel Sogcho 7101/7105). 60 rooms, doubles for US$28-35. There are no singles.

At the Osaek mineral water and hot springs is the *Nam Solag Hotel*, 507 Somyon, Yangyang-kun, Kwangwon-do (tel Yangyang 2131/4), 80 rooms, singles & doubles US$20-25.

Places to Stay – middle and bottom end

Budget accommodation here is very difficult to find. Sorak-dong is an expensive place both for accommodation and food. If you stay here you're up for W12,000-14,000 per night though, if you're lucky and can find an empty hotel among the scores available here, you may be able to bargain them down to as low as W7000 (be warned that hardly anyone here speaks English so you'll need some familiarity with Korean to be able to do this). The alternatives to staying here are the Youth Hotel or beach houses at Naksan 낙산 nearby on the coast. Regular and frequent local buses connect Naksan with Sorak-dong. Otherwise, use Sogcho, equidistant from Sorak-dong as a base. Here there's a good choice of cheap yogwans and frequent buses to Sorak-dong. 내설악

Getting There

Entry to Sorak-san and the trails into the mountains is via Sorak-dong which is at the end of the road which branches off from the coast road about half way between Naksan and Sogcho. There are frequent buses both from Yang Yang 양양 a few km south of Naksan, and from

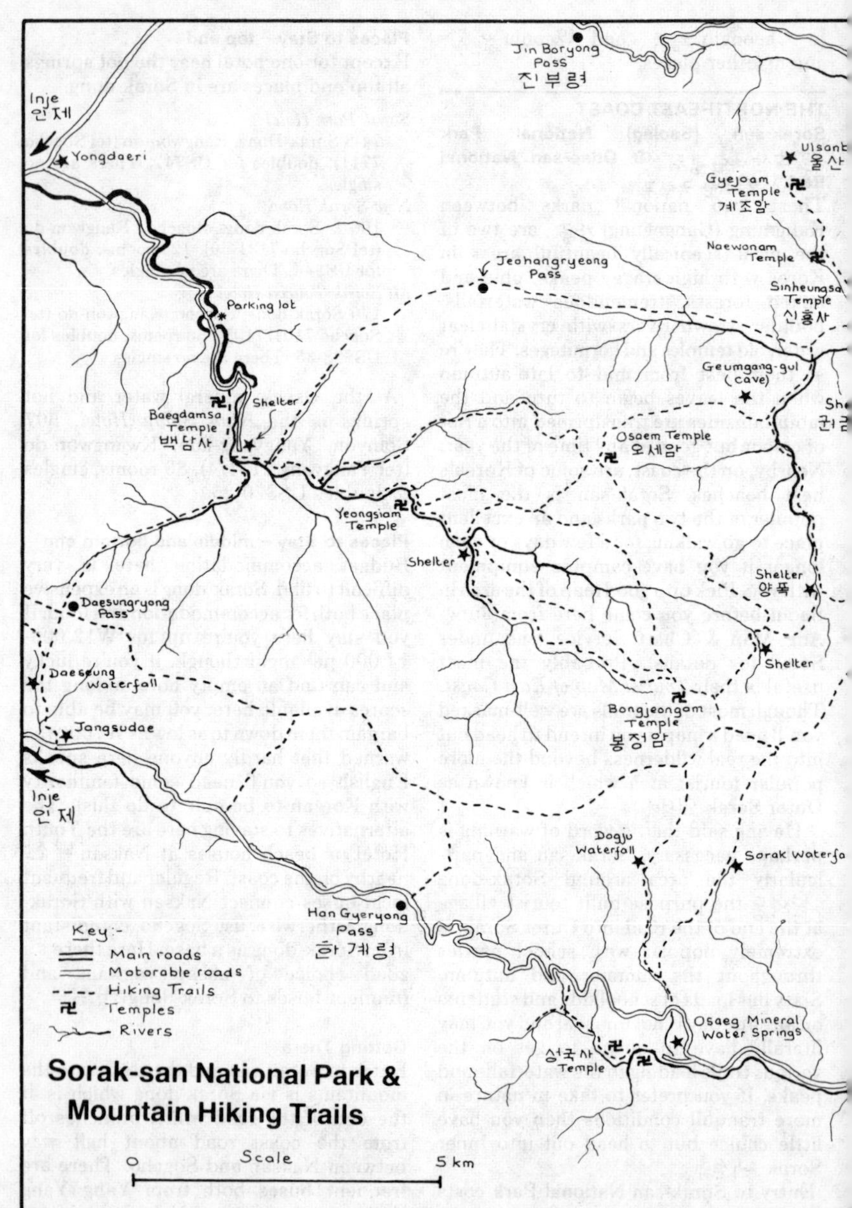

Sorak-san National Park & Mountain Hiking Trails

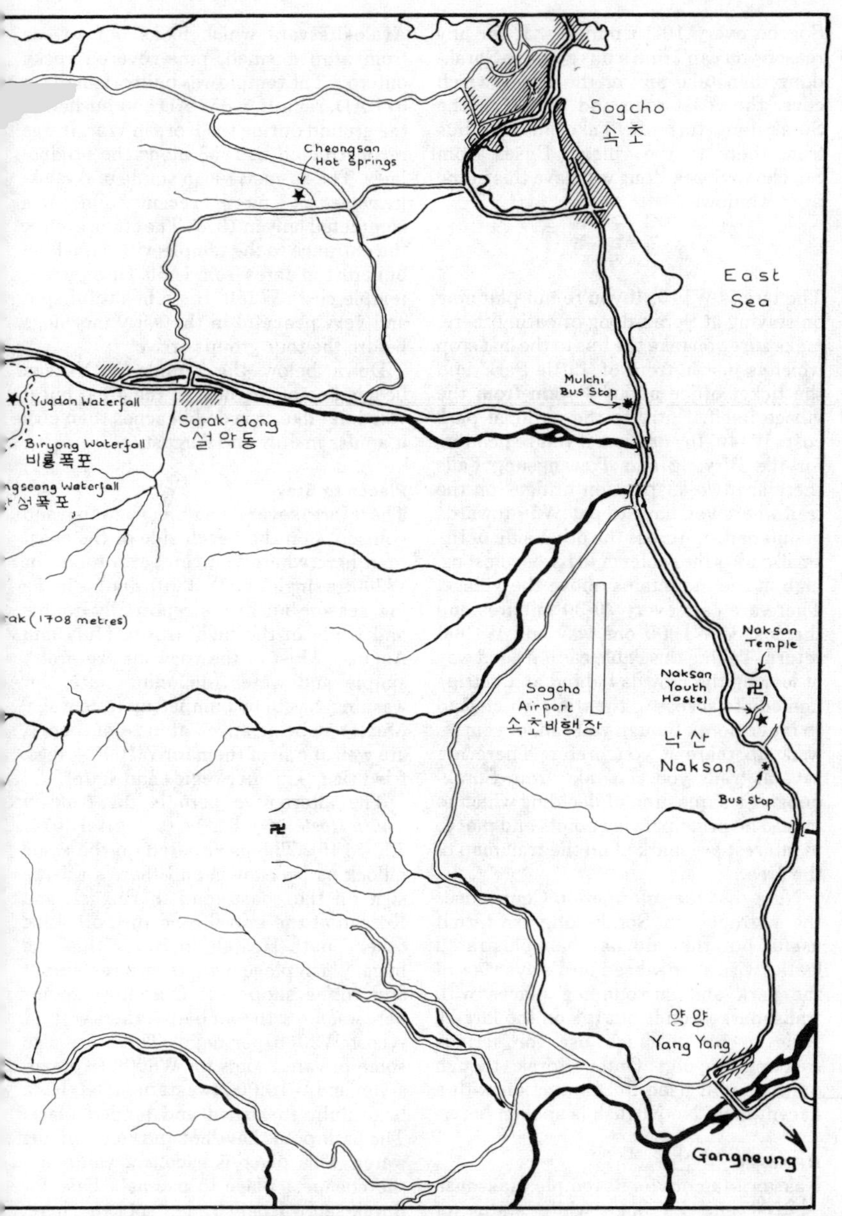
Sogcho
속초
Cheongsan
Hot Springs
East
Sea
Mulchi
Bus Stop
Yugdan Waterfall
Sorak-dong
설악동
Biryong Waterfall
비룡폭포
ngseong Waterfall
성폭포
rak (1708 metres)
Naksan
Temple
Naksan
Youth
Hostel
Sogcho
Airport
속초비행장
낙산
Naksan
Bus Stop
양양
Yang Yang
Gangneung

Sogcho every 10-15 minutes. If for any reason you can't find a bus going to Sorak-dong then take any of the buses which cover the coast road and get off at the Sorak-dong turn-off. Take another bus from there to the village. Buses from Sogcho to Sorak-dong will have this in the front window:

설악산 구단지 신단지 속초

The fare is W110. If you're not planning on staying at Sorak-dong or eating there, make sure you take the bus to the last stop which is just in front of 'Little Park' and the ticket office about 3½ km from the village itself. Entry to the national park costs W440. In addition, if you're heading for the Biryong and Towangsung Falls there are two suspension bridges on the trail where you have to pay W50 towards maintenance. Across the other side of the small park is the cable car to Kwongumsong, high in the mountains above the village. There are cars every 20-30 minutes and the cost is W1000 one way and W1900 return. Taking this cable car is a good way of leaving the crowds behind and getting immediate access to the trails which lead to Inner Sorak though you can, of course, walk up there if you prefer. There are several trails you can take from Sorak-dong. It's a question of deciding which to take. The principal viewpoints and places of interest are marked on the trail map of the area.

Note that the Information Centre near the entrance to Sorak-dong isn't that useful but they do have an illustrated leaflet with an idealised bird's eye view of the park and surrounding places with trails marked on it but it's on too large a scale to be of much use for serious trekking beyond Outer Sorak though quite good if used in conjunction with a decent map. No English is spoken here.

NAKSAN 낙산

Naksan is famous for its temple, Naksansa 낙산사 and its huge white statue of Avalokitesvara which looks out to sea from atop a small, pine-covered rocky outcrop. The temple was built originally in 671 AD, rebuilt in 858 AD and burned to the ground during the Korean War. It was reconstructed in 1953 along the original lines. The 15-metre-high statue of Avalokitesvara is more recent and was completed only in 1977. The stone arch at the entrance to the temple with a pavilion built on top dates from 1465. Entry to the temple costs W250. It's a beautiful spot and very peaceful in the early mornings before the tour groups arrive.

Down below the temple is Naksan beach, one of the best in the area, but if you don't like crowded beaches then give it a miss in July and August.

Places to Stay

There are several simple yogwans and yoinsooks on the beach side of the coast road here where you can get a room for W2000 a single and W3000 a double in the low season but prices reportedly double and triple in the high season (July and August). Most of the yogwans are pretty simple and water (including water for washing) has to be pumped up from wells. Meals can be arranged at most of them (I ate well at one of them for W1000 – eggs, fried rice, 'kimchi', vegies and soup).

The alternative here is the *Naksan Youth Hostel* 낙산 유스 호스텔 (tel 3071-723-6145). This is situated on the same hillock as Naksan-sa and there's a large sign on the coast road in English and Korean at the gravel road turn off. Like other Youth Hostels in Korea this is a huge, plush place with its own restaurant and coffee shop, etc. Dormitory rooms here – some with four beds, others with 14 – cost W2000 per night. There are also some private rooms for W8000 (Korean-style) and W10,000 (western-style). It's a beautifully furnished and tended place. The bathrooms have hot and cold running water. This place is excellent value and the cheapest place to use as a base for Sorak-san. English is spoken here.

Top: Sochul-ji pavilion & pond, Namsan Village, Gyeongji
Left: Huge concrete Buddha figure at Popju-sa Temple
Right: Bigag Pavilion reflected in the mirrored windows of the Kyobo Building, Central Seoul

Top: The old & the new, Namdaemun City Gate, Seoul
Bottom: Namhansanseong Fortress, Songnam City near Seoul

Getting There

Buses plying between Yang Yang and Sogcho Pass by Naksan. The bus will have the following in the front window:

속 낙 양
초 산 양

SOGCHO 속초

Sogcho is a quiet fishing town north of Sorak-san and the last major centre of population before the border with North Korea. There's not much of interest here for the traveller but it does have a lot of seafood restaurants and cheap yogwans which can be used for exploring Sorak-san if you don't want to stay at the Youth Hostel at Naksan.

Places to Stay

Most of the cheap yogwans are located around the chikheng bus terminal though there are others elsewhere in town which are indicated on the street map. At the smaller places a room will cost around W2000-3000 per night. If you'd like something slightly better then try the *Tong Hae* 동해여관 a new, two-storey building between the bus station and the seafront which has double rooms for W8000 with bath and TV. It's an excellent place with clean, pleasantly decorated rooms and spotless bathrooms and toilets. The staff are friendly and there is a Chinese restaurant downstairs. Just behind this place and reached by the alley beside the Chinese restaurant is the smaller, traditionally-built *Tong Ah* 동아여관 which was once popularised by the Peace Corps. It has been recently refurbished and is considerably cheaper at W4000 a double.

Most of the seafood restaurants are located in the streets between the main drag and the lagoon. Just wander around and take any which attract your attention.

Getting There

There are two bus stations in Sogcho located at opposite ends of the town to each other. The express bus terminal is situated at the entrance to town on the southern side of the lagoon. From here there are buses to Seoul 18 times daily from 6.30 am to 5.30 pm. The fare is W4240 and the journey takes five hours. These buses take the express-way via Kangnung and Weonju. Local buses to Sorak-dong, Naksan and Yang Yang stop outside here so if you're heading to any of those places there's no need to go right into town to find a bus.

At the chikheng bus terminal there are the following buses:

To Seoul 서울 Every 40 minutes from 5.50 am to 5.40 pm. The fare is W3810.

To Chuncheon 춘천 Eight buses daily from 6.20 am to 3.30 pm. The fare is W2730 and the journey takes about four hours.

To Kangnung 강릉 Every 10 minutes from 5.50 am to 8.30 pm. The fare is W1140 and the journey takes one hour and 40 minutes.

The chikheng buses from Sogcho to Seoul and Chuncheon take the Han Gyeryong Pass through the southern edge of Sorak-san National Park via Yang Yang and Won Tong. Another route, the Jin Boryong Pass, over the northern fringes of the park is planned but is still in the construction stage. When completed the Han Gyeryong Pass road will meet the Jin Boryong Pass road at Won Tong. After there the route is the same via Inje 인제 and Hungcheon 홍천. The route is scenically magnificent and sealed all the way.

In addition to the above buses from the chikeng bus terminal there are buses every hour to Inje from where you can catch a boat to Chuncheon (or continue by bus to Chuncheon). The boat offers spectacular lake and mountain views all the way to Chuncheon and is an excellent way of covering this stretch of the journey. Boat times are variable but they depart twice daily in either direction. The fare is W3000. Buses from Sogcho to Inje cost

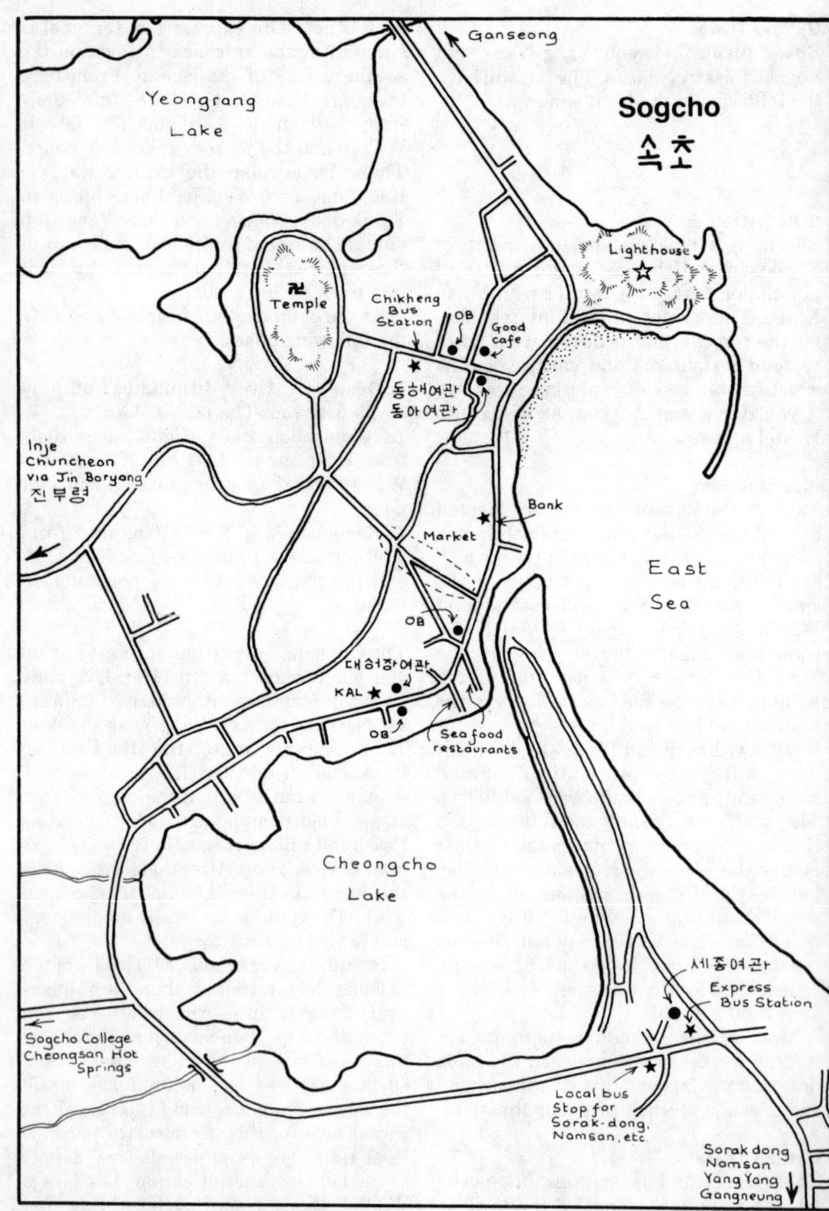
Ganseong
Sogcho
속초
Yeongrang
Lake
Lighthouse
Temple
Chikheng
Bus
Station
OB
Good
cafe
동해여관
동아여관
Inje
Chuncheon
via Jin Boryong
진부령
Bank
Market
East
Sea
OB
대하장여관
KAL
OB
Sea food
restaurants
Cheongcho
Lake
세종여관
Express
Bus Station
Sogcho College
Cheongsan Hot
Springs
Local bus
Stop for
Sorak-dong,
Namsan, etc.
Sorak dong
Namsan
Yang Yang
Gangneung

W1060 and take about 1½ hours. From there to Hungcheon the fare is W1040 and from Hungcheon to Chuncheon W540. All these buses from the chikheng bus terminal can also be caught at Yang Yang.

Local buses to Sorak-dong, Naksan and Yang Yang also start from the chikheng bus terminal. They're very frequent – every 10-15 minutes – and run from very early morning till late at night.

PUYO (BUYEO) 부여

Located south of a wooded hill around which the 백마강 (Paek Ma River) makes a wide sweep is Puyo, site of the last capital of the Paekje Kingdom 백제 . The capital was moved here from Kongju (Gongju) in 538 AD and flourished until destroyed by the combined forces of Silla and the Tang Dynasty of China in 660 AD. Today it's a quiet, very pleasant provincial town surrounded by wooded hills and paddy fields with a friendly and strongly traditionally-minded people. Of the Paekje ruins very little remains save for a few foundation stones of the army's arsenal and foodstore and a five-storey stone pagoda – only one of three surviving from the Three Kingdoms period. The main point of interest here is the museum, opened in 1971, which has one of the best collections of artifacts from the Paekje Kingdom you will find in Korea as well as other exhibits from later periods in the country's history.

Puyo National Museum

Open daily except Mondays from 9 am to 4.30 pm, the museum houses bronze spearheads, daggers, pottery and musical instruments from the 4-5th centuries BC, Paekje Dynasty jars, Buddha images and examples of roof tiles embossed with various designs and a collection of celadon vases, funeral urns and bronze bells dating fron the 6th to 14th centuries. There are also a number of interesting stone objects – baths, lanterns, Buddha images etc – in the gardens in front of the museum. Entry costs W50.

Buso San 부소산

The museum stands at the foot of Buso San, a pine-forested hill and focal point of Puyo which was once part of the royal palace grounds. It's now a popular park honeycombed with paths and roads and containing a number of very attractive temples and pavilions from some of which excellent views over the surrounding countryside can be had. Also on this hill is located the ruins of the Paekje army's food store where it's said to be still possible to find carbonised rice, beans and barley. Buso San is associated with the legend of the 3000 court ladies who threw themselves off a high cliff – known as Nakhwa-am – above the Paek Ma River onto the rocks below rather than be captured by invading Chinese and Silla warriors at the end of the Paekje empire. People come from all over Korea to see this spot. Strolling around this peaceful hillside is a very pleasant and relaxing way to spend a morning or afternoon combined with a visit to the museum. The park is open every day and costs W50 entry. There is a detailed map of the hill at the entrance though all the points of interest are marked in Chinese characters.

Other

Elsewhere in Puyo there is the small **Jeomgrim-Na** temple site near the centre of town which contains a five-storey pagoda dating from the Paekje period and a weather-beaten seated stone Buddha from the Koryo Dynasty period. This latter is one of the strangest Buddhas you're ever likely to see and bears an uncanny resemblance to the Easter Island statues. About a km further on down the same road is the **Gungnam Ji Pond and Pavilion** which was constructed by King Mu of the Paekje kingdom as a pleasure garden for the court ladies. Until a few years ago this place had been sadly neglected and had an air of dereliction about it but restoration has been done recently and the bridge which takes you across the pond to the pavilion is now in good repair. It's a beautiful place to sit and relax and watch the activity in the surrounding paddy fields.

Places to Stay

There are plenty of yogwans and yoinsooks around the two bus stations and across the main street near the large roundabout but my favorite was Kumgang Yogwan 금강여관(tel 2243), a charming, traditionally-built little place up the road towards the entrance to Buso San. Unfortunately, they want quite a lot of money for a room there these days and won't budge from W5000 per night. Quite close to this place is the *Puyo Youth Hostel* (부여유스호스텔), 105-1 Guyo-Ri, Buyeo-Eup (tel Buyeo 3791/2/3/4/5), a huge western-style building which seems to have precious little to do with either 'youth' or 'hostels' judging from the sort of people who stay there. Dormitory rooms (회운실) here cost W3500 with a YH card or W4235 without. Private rooms start at a staggering W19,800 for a single! It's a spotless place with excellent facilities including a bar, coffee shop and souvenir shop. Meals are served at a cost of W1900 (breakfast), W3800 (lunch), W5100 (dinner). All the above prices are plus 10% service and taxes. You may well find other travellers staying here.

Other than the above, a pleasant place to stay is the Myongsong Yogwan 명성여관 which has ondol rooms circling a kind of rock garden. The management is very friendly (but speak no English) and the rooms are very clean. Rooms around the garden cost W4000 (the first price quoted is W5200 a double but they're usually more than willing to drop this with minimal negotiation. There are also more luxurious rooms on the upper floor of the main building are W7000. It's a good place to stay and there's a makkoli den in the compound where you can join in that popular Korean custom of getting completely out of your head on this traditional jungle-juice and doing all manner of silly things you'll want to forget about in the morning unless alcoholic amnesia relieves you of this embarrassment.

Places to Eat

A meal in Puyo at most of the restaurants tends to be pretty expensive. If you want a no-frills Korean-style meal then there are a few cafes around the bus compound where you can eat well for W600-800. If you'd like something slightly better then try the restaurant just opposite the front entrance of Myongsong Yogwan where meals cost around W2000. One of the best restaurants I found with very reasonable prices was the *Chungnam Shiktang* 충남식당 which has a range of dishes from W1200 to W3500. For example omelette, rice with kimchi, soup and raw turnip here cost W1200 and was excellent. For a more substantial meal with beef or pork cooked at your table you would expect to pay between W2500 and W3500.

For a cheap beer, try the OB stand bar on the first street on the left-hand side down from the roundabout.

Getting There

There are two bus stations in Puyo, both located close to one another. The express bus terminal ('Kolon Express') is, in fact, just a patch of dirt but it's also where the buses to Kongju (Gongju) depart from.

To Seoul 13 buses daily, the first at 7.20 am and the last at 6.30 pm. The fare is W3100 and the journey takes about 3¼ hours. Booking in advance isn't really necessary.

To Kongju (Gongju) There are two sorts of buses to Kongju – local stopping buses and semi-express buses. There are 23 local buses per day, the first at 7.10 am and the last at 8.50 pm, and the fare is W550. There is a similar number of semi-express buses, the first at 6.40 am and the last at 6.40 pm, and the fare is W930. The journey time on the semi-expresses is about–3/4 hour. When trying to locate the

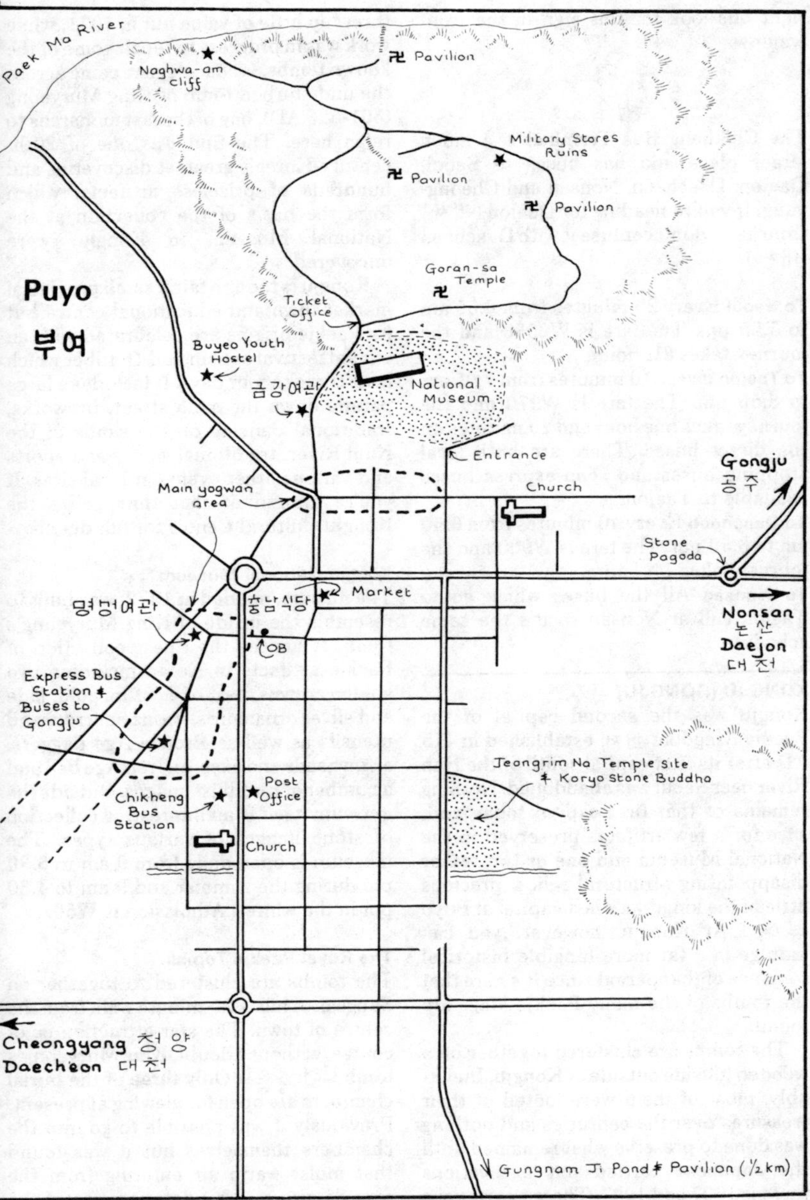

Paek Ma River
Naghwa-am cliff
Pavilion
Military Stores Ruins
Pavilion
Pavilion
Goran-sa Temple
Puyo
부여
Ticket Office
Buyeo Youth Hostel
금강여관
National Museum
Entrance
Gongju
공주
Church
Main yogwan area
Stone Pagoda
명성여관
충남식당
Market
OB
Nonsan
논산
Daejon
대전
Express Bus Station & Buses to Gongju
Jeongrim Na Temple Site & Koryo Stone Buddha
Post Office
Chikheng Bus Station
Church
Cheongyang 청양
Daecheon 대천
Gungnam Ji Pond & Pavilion (½ km)

right bus look for this sign in the front window:

공 종 청
주 치 주
　 원

The Chikheng Bus Terminal is a much larger place and has buses to Seoul, Daejon, Daecheon, Nonsan and Cheongyang. If you're heading for Daejon (대전) from here, don't confuse it with Daecheon (대천).

To Seoul Every 20 minutes from 6.55 am to 5.55 pm. The fare is W2530 and the journey takes 3½ hours.
To Taejon Every 10 minutes from 7.05 am to 8.55 pm. The fare is W970 and the journey takes one hour and 20 minutes on the direct buses. There are both local stopping buses and semi-express buses available to Taejon.
To Daecheon Every 40 minutes from 6.50 am to 6.50 pm. The fare is W900 and the journey takes 1¾ hours.
To Nonsan All the buses which go to Taejon call at Nonsan so it's the same schedule.

KONGJU (GONGJU) 공주

Kongju was the second capital of the Paekje Kingdom 백제 established in 475 AD after its first capital south of the Han River near Seoul was abandoned. Nothing remains of that first capital today and, save for a few artifacts preserved in the National Museum and one or two rather disappointing structural relics, precious little of the kingdom's last capital at Puyo 부여. At Kongju, however, you can indulge in a far more tangible historical romance of that period since it's here that the tombs of the many Paekje kings are found.

The tombs are clustered together on a wooded hillside outside of Kongju. Inevitably, most of them were looted of their treasures over the centuries and nothing was done to preserve what remained until the Japanese carried out excavations there is 1907 and 1933. These excavations threw up little of value but in 1971, while work was in progress to repair some of the known tombs, archaeologists came across the undisturbed tomb of King Muryeong (501-523 AD), one of the last monarchs to reign here. The find was one of 20th-century-Korea's greatest discoveries and hundreds of priceless artifacts, which form the basis of the collection at the National Museum in Kongju, were uncovered.

Kongju is today a fairly small provincial market town and educational centre but its Paekje origins are celebrated with an annual festival held in mid-October which lasts three to four days. It includes a large parade down the main street, fireworks, traditional dancing on the sands of the Kum River, traditional games and sports and various other events at local sites. If you're around at that time go to the Kongju Cultural Centre for full details.

Kongju National Museum

The musum, opened in 1972, was built to resemble the inside of King Muryeong's tomb. It houses the finest collection of Paekje artifacts in Korea including two golden crowns, part of a coffin, gold, jade and silver ornaments, bronze mirrors and utensils as well as Bronze Age daggers, arrowheads and axes, an Iron Age bell and a number of Buddhist images. Outside the museum itself is an interesting collection of stone images of various types. The museum is open daily from 9 am to 5.30 pm during the summer and 9 am to 4.30 pm in the winter. Admission is W50.

The Royal Paekje Tombs

The tombs are clustered to together on Sangsan-ri hill, a 20-minute walk from the centre of town. The star attraction is, of course, without a doubt, King Muryeong's tomb 무령 왕릉. Only three of the burial chambers are open for viewing at present. Previously it was possible to go into the chambers themselves but it was found that moist warm air entering from the outside was causing deterioration of the

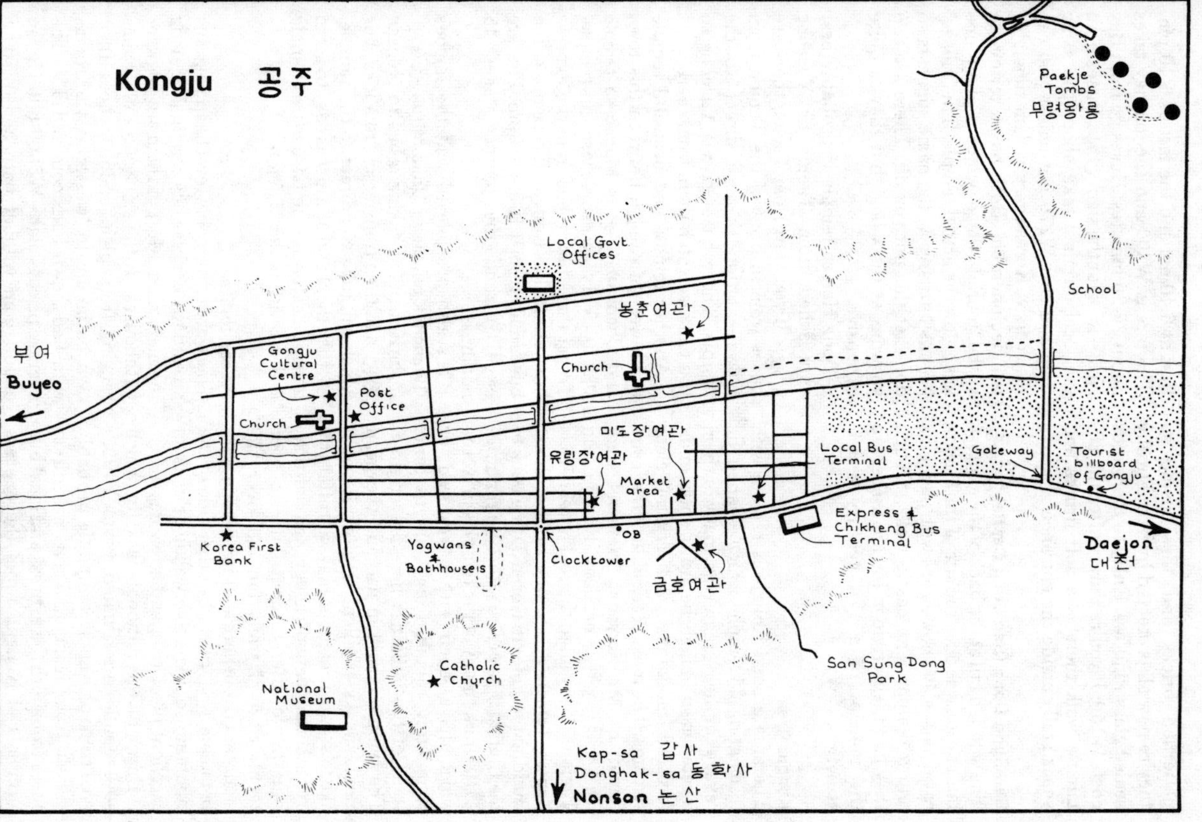

Kongju 공주
Paekje Tombs 무령왕릉
School
Local Govt Offices
봉춘여관
부여
Buyeo
Gongju Cultural Centre
Post Office
Church
Church
미도장여관
유림장여관
Market area
Local Bus Terminal
Gateway
Tourist billboard of Gongju
Express + Chikheng Bus Terminal
Daejon 대전
OB
Korea First Bank
Yogwans + Bathhouseis
Clocktower
금호여관
San Sung Dong Park
Catholic Church
National Museum
Kap-sa 갑사
Donghak-sa 동학사
Nonsan 논산

patterned bricks and tiles inside so they're now all protected by hermetically sealed glass windows. Entry to the tombs costs W150. If you're thirsty after the 20-minute walk there is a soft drinks and snack stall outside the entrance.

San Sung Dong (San Sung Castle) 산성동
The wooded hill at the back of the express bus station was once the site of the Paekje royal palace. It's now a park with pavilions and a temple. The castle walls, though they had their origin in Paekje times, are the remains of a 17th-century reconstruction.

Kongju Area
The area around Kongju is replete with fascinating old temples which escaped the ravages of the Korean War, many of them located in stunningly beautiful spots amid forested mountains and crystal clear streams. The most accessible of these are found in **Mt Keryeong National Park** 계룡산 국립공원 between Kongju and Taejon. To my mind the real jewel here is **Kap-sa Temple** 갑사, one of the oldest Buddhist temples in Korea dating back to the Unified Silla period (8th-10th centuries AD). Unlike many of the temples in Korea which have been either restored or completely rebuilt from time to time, some of the buildings here are original. The temple is still in use and the head monk speaks excellent English. If you'd like to stay overnight he may well offer you free accommodation (though, as a courtesy, you should offer to contribute to your keep). Several trails fan out over the mountains from here leading to **Dong Hak-sa temple** 동학사 on the other side of the mountain so if you like walking this is an excellent place to spend a few days.

Entry to the national park (in which both temples are situated) costs W400.

Getting to Kap-sa temple is probably easiest from Kongju. There are direct buses from both the express and local bus terminals in Kongju. From the express bus terminal there are 14 buses daily, the first at 6.40 am and the last at 6.40 pm. The fare is W300 and the journey takes about 25-30 minutes. Buses go from Bay No 3 – look for the sign: 갑사. Buses from the local terminal take about the same time and cost W270 but unless you can read cursive Korean very well the timetable is indecipherable. Both buses terminate at the 'tourist village' which is about one km below the actual temple. The 'village' isn't as intrusive as the name suggests so don't let this put you off. There are two yogwans at the village but they're quite expensive.

Dong Hak-sa temple is probably best approached from Taejon or Yuseong 유성. If you start from Taejon there are buses from in front of the Taejon main railway station that go direct to the temple. These buses go via Yuseong so you can also catch them from there.

Another remote and beautiful temple north-west of Kongju between this town and Cheonan 천안 is **Magog-sa temple** 마곡사. Very few people visit this temple. To get there take a bus from the express bus terminal in Kongju. There are seven buses daily from 9.10 am to 7 pm. The fare is W370 and the journey takes 45 minutes.

It's also possible to visit the famous **Gwanchuk temple** or **Unjin Miruk** 관촉사 from Kongju by taking a bus to Nonsan 논산 and then transferring to a local bus which will take you direct to the temple. On the other hand, it's just as easy to get to it using Taejon as your base so this temple is dealt with under 'Taejon'.

Places to Stay
There are remarkably few cheap yogwans around the express bus terminal or along the main road. Most of them are yogwan/bathhouses with a variety of rooms ranging from plain ondol without their own bathroom to 'western-style' rooms with beds, own bathroom and TV. The average price is high – W5000-6000 for an ondol room without bath and W7000-8000 for a western-style room with own

bathroom and TV. Try the Kum-ho Yogwan 금호여관. If you want something cheaper then try the yogwans and yoinsooks in the back streets near the river indicated on the street map. They're all pretty basic but OK for a night.

Places to Eat

A good place to eat is the Son-Mi Shiktang 선미식당 located on the main street between the Kum-ho Yogwan and the express bus terminal. You can get *bulgogi* here for W3000 which is excellent and served with a decent range of side dishes. If you're thinking of eating fried chicken at the cafes next to the express bus terminal make sure you don't order something you might not be anticipating like fried chicken heads (complete with beak!).

Getting There

The express bus terminal is well organised and you shouldn't have any difficulty finding the bus you want.

To Nonsan 논산 Every 30 minutes from 7.15 am to 8.25 pm. The fare is W570 and the journey takes 45 minutes.
To Puyo 부여 Every 20 minutes from 7 am to 9.05 pm. The fare is W550 and the journey takes 45 minutes.
To Seoul 서울 Every 10 minutes from 7.20 am to 7.20 pm. The fare is W1980 and the journey takes just over two hours.
To Taejon 대전 Every 20 minutes from 6.55 am to 6.32 pm. The fare is W610 and the journey takes 45 minutes.

DAEJON (TAEJON) 대전

Daejon is the capital of Chung Cheong Nam province and a major industrial centre. For the traveller, there's little of interest in the city itself but it is an excellent base from which to explore nearby temples and national parks since transportation facilities from here are very good. You'll also come here if you're heading south to Mogpo 목포 by rail and from there to Cheju-do 제주도.

Information

Tourist Information There is a kiosk in the forecourt of the railway station staffed by no less than four apparently very bored people but unless you speak fluent Korean you can disregard this place completely as a source of information.

Changing Money If you're staying in the centre of town near the railway station and need to change travellers' cheques, the Hanil Bank opposite the Daejon Hotel doesn't offer this service and will refer you to the Bank of Korea which is some distance away. The alternative, if you don't mind a slight loss, is the Daejon Hotel itself. They'll change travellers' cheques at approximately 1% below the bank rate. They also won't give you change under W100 unless hassled.

Places to Stay – top end

There are no top end hotels in Daejon but there are a number of middle range hotels which are quite adequate if you're looking for a western-style hotel. They include:

Taejon Tourist Hotel
20-16 Won-Dong, Daejon (tel 253 8131), 30 rooms, singles & doubles US$17-28 plus 10% service charge and 10% tax. Located opposite the post office and very close to the railway station.

Joong Ang Hotel
318 Chung-Dong, Tong-ku, Daejon (tel 253 8801), 75 rooms, singles & doubles US$34.

Yousung Tourist Hotel
480 Bongmyong-Ri Yousung-Eup, Taedok, Chungnam Province (tel 4 0811), 57 rooms, singles & doubles US$19-20. Located about 10 minutes by car outside the city.

Places to Stay – bottom end

For some reason there are very few yogwans in the centre of Taejon and most double as bathhouses. Prices are relatively high, averaging about W5000 a single and W6000 a double including own bathroom but without hot water and to get these rates you need to do a little bargaining (most will initially quote higher rates). One of the better ones is the *Yongsong*

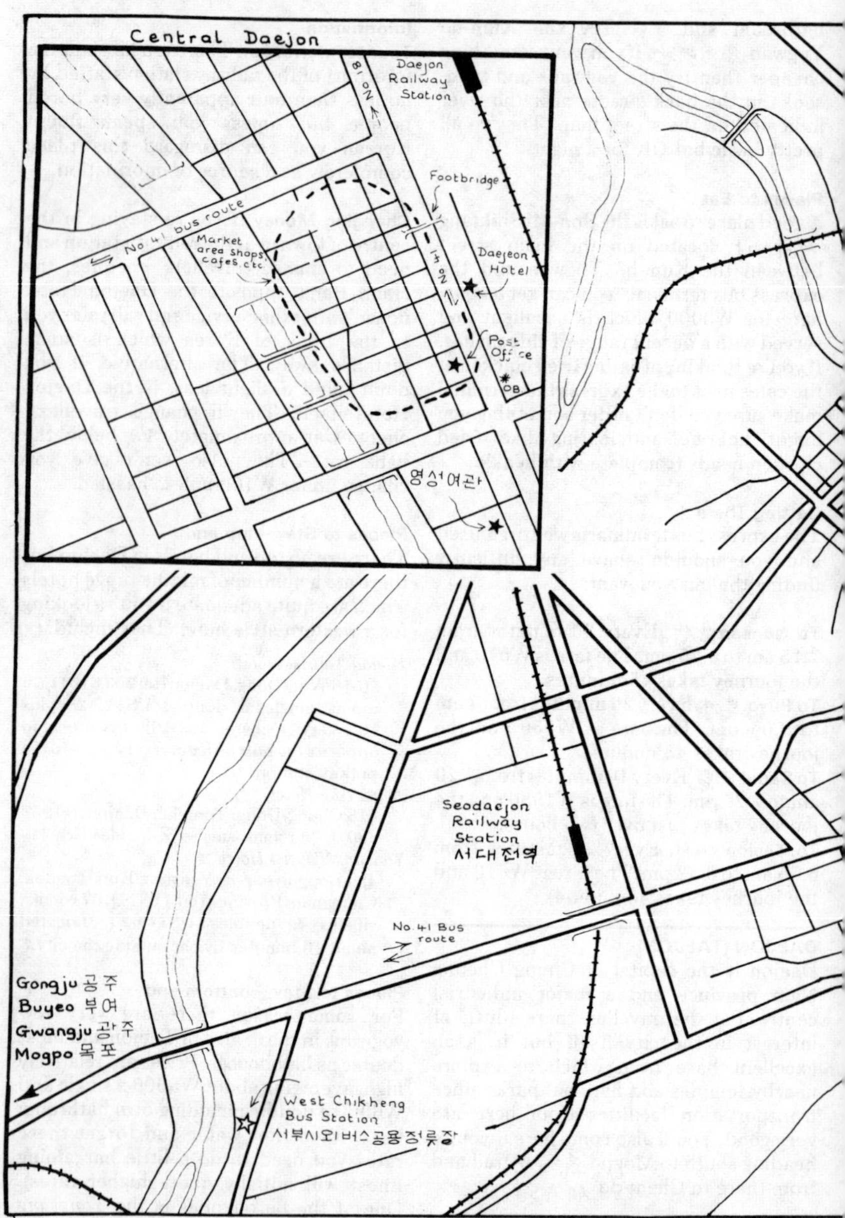
Central Daejon
Daejon Railway Station
No 18
Footbridge
No 41 bus route
Market area Shops, cafes etc
No 41
Daejeon Hotel
Post Office
OB
영성여관
Seodaejon Railway Station
서대전역
No.41 Bus route
Gongju 공주
Buyeo 부여
Gwangju 광주
Mogpo 목포
West Chikheng Bus Station
서부시외버스공용정류장

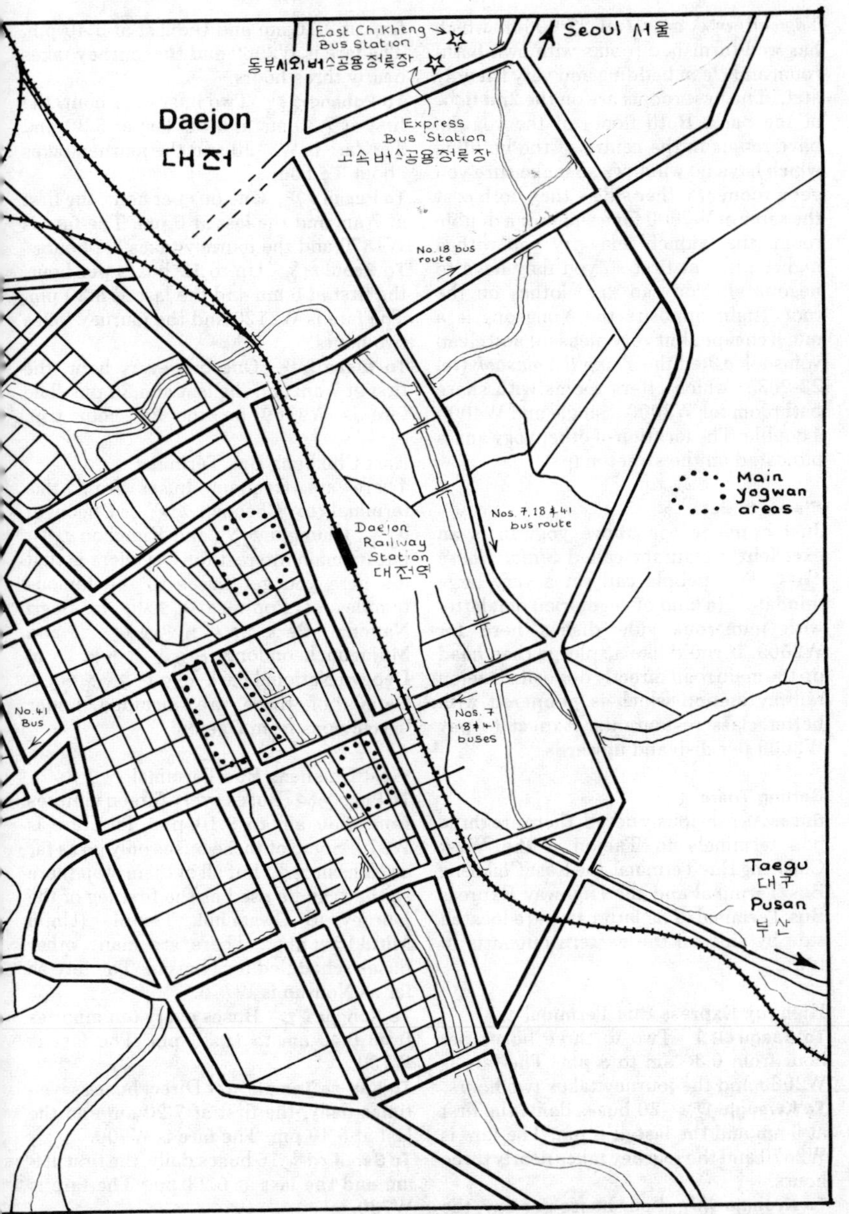
East Chikheng
Bus Station
동부시외버스공용정류장
Seoul 서울
Daejon
대전
Express
Bus Station
고속버스공용정류장
No. 18 bus
route
Main
yogwan
areas
Nos. 7, 18 & 41
bus route
Daejon
Railway
Station
대전역
Nos. 7
18 & 41
buses
No. 41
Bus
Taegu
대구
Pusan
부산

Yogwan 영성 여관 (tel 22-9060), which has well-furnished rooms with own bathroom and clean bedding and very friendly staff. The best rooms are on the 2nd floor at the back. Both floors of the yogwan have rooms in the centre of the building which have no windows so make sure you get a room at either side – they both cost the same at W7000 for a single or a double room (the 'ajimah' may try you with a higher price at first so you may have to negotiate). You can dry clothes on the roof. Right opposite the Yongsong is a much cheaper but very pleasant and clean yoinsook called the *Yoing Il Yoinsook* (tel 23-2035) which offers rooms with share bathroom for W3000 a single and W4000 a double. The location of other yogwans is indicated on the street map.

Places to Eat

Just opposite the above yogwan is an excellent restaurant called *Shilbi House* 실비집 Two people can eat a very large 'pindatok' (a kind of vegetarian omelette) with numerous side dishes here for W2600. If you'd like a splurge then head up the main road directly opposite Daejon railway station which is peppered with better class restaurants. Expect to pay W2000 per dish and upwards.

Getting There

Buses As previously noted, there are three bus terminals in Taejon – the West Chikheng Bus Terminal, the East Chikheng Bus Terminal and the Highway Express Bus Terminal. The latter two are located side by side on the eastern outskirts of town.

Highway Express Bus Terminal

To Taegu 대구 Two to three buses per hour from 6.30 am to 8 pm. The fare is W2060 and the journey takes two hours.

To Kwangju 광주 20 buses daily, the first at 6 am and the last at 8 pm. The fare is W2570 and the journey takes nearly three hours.

To Kyongju 경주 Four buses per day, the first at 7.10 am and the last at 5.40 pm. The fare is W2960 and the journey takes nearly three hours.

To Pohang 포항 Two buses per hour, the first at 7.30 am and the last at 5.30 pm. The fare is W3420 and the journey takes about 3½ hours.

To Pusan 부산 One bus per hour, the first at 7 am and the last at 6 pm. The fare is W4370 and the journey takes 3½ hours.

To Seoul 서울 Up to 12 buses per hour, the first at 6 am and the last at 8.30 pm. The fare is W2120 and the journey takes two hours.

To Ulsan 울산 One bus every hour, the first at 7 am and the last at 5.30 pm. The fare is W2960 for the 3½ hour trip.

East Chikheng Bus Terminal

There are frequent buses from this terminal to Cheonan 천안, Cheongju 청주, Chungju 충주 and Kimchon 김천 but its main interest for travellers is that it's here you get buses to the famous temples of Popju-sa 법주사 in Sogri National Park 속리산 국립공원 and Mujuguncheondong 안국사 구천동 in Deogyu National Park 덕유산 국립공원. Details of these are included under 'Excursions from Daejon'.

West Chikheng Bus Terminal

To Puyo 부여 Buses every fifteen minutes from 6.30 am to 9.10 pm. The fare is W970. Some of these buses only go as far as Nonsan 논산 but all of them stop there so they can be used as the first leg of the journey to Gwanchuk Temple (Unjin Miruk) 은진 미륵. There are many other buses scheduled for Nonsan. The fare as far as Nonsan is W770.

To Kongju 공주 Buses every ten minutes from 6.40 am to 10.30 pm. The fare is W730.

To Kap-sa Temple 갑사 Direct buses seven times daily, the first at 7.20 am and the last at 5.40 pm. The fare is W900.

To Seoul 서울 16 buses daily, the first at 8 am and the last at 6.23 pm. The fare is W730.

Trains Note there are two railway stations in Daejon. Daejon Railway Station in the centre of the city serves the main line between Seoul and Pusan and all trains en route to either of those cities stop here. The other station on the west of town is Seodaejon Railway Station. This station serves the line to Mogpo via Nonsan, Iri and Kwangju though if you're heading for Kwangju you must change at Yeong San Po.

Getting Around

The most important city bus, as far as the traveller is concerned, is No 41 which connects the West Chikheng Bus Terminal 서부시외버스 공용 정류장 with Seodaejon Railway Station 서대전역, Daejon Railway Station 대전역 and the East Chikheng Bus Terminal/Highway Express Bus Terminal 동부시외버스 공용정류장 / 고속버스 공용 정류장. Two others of use are Nos 7 and 18 both of which connect Daejon Railway Station with the East Chikheng Bus Terminal/Highway Express Bus Terminal. The fare on local buses is W120 regardless of distance.

AROUND DAEJON

Gwanchuk Temple (Unjin Miruk) 관촉사

This old Buddhist temple just outside Nonsan is famous throughout Korea for possessing the largest stone Buddha in the country. It has some unique features, the likes of which you won't see elsewhere in the country, and is well worth a visit. The statue was built in 968 AD during the Koryo Dynasty and stands 18 metres high. It's made out of three pieces of granite – one piece for the face and body and two others for the arms. The courtyard in which it stands is surrounded by typical Korean temple buildings. If you're lucky, you may come across a small festival going on here. Admission costs W200 or W150 with student card.

Getting There There are two ways to get to Gwanchuk, one of them considerably easier than the other. The easiest way is to take a bus from Daejon to Nonsan (W350, 45 minutes). When you arrive there you will find yourself at the Chikheng bus terminal 직행. From there walk towards the railway station, cross the tracks, and carry on a further 200 metres down the same street on which the station building is located. On the left-hand side you will find the local bus terminal 완행. From here there are buses every 15-20 minutes which will take you direct to the temple – look for 관촉사 on the destination board in the front window of the bus. The fare to the temple is W130.

The other way to get there if you don't mind a short walk is to take the same bus to Nonsan from Daejon as above but show the ticket office the name of the temple (in Korean). They'll sell you a ticket for W670 and direct you to bay No 15 (the bus will have 관촉사 on its destination board as well as Nonsan). The place where you must get off at is called Naedong Li 내동리 where there's a large billboard with a painting of the statue on it and a soft drinks cafe. Make sure they don't put you off at Gyochon Li 교촌리 which they tend to do, otherwise you'll find yourself walking three times as far! From Naedong Li it's a two km walk to the temple along a gravel road. There's a fork in the gravel road about half way there – take the left hand fork.

Coming back from Nonsan, there are buses to Taejon every 5-10 minutes which cost W770 and take about 1½ hours. If you'd like to stay near the temple for the night there is a small yogwan just below the temple entrance.

Popju-sa Temple 법주사 & Sogri-san National Park 속리산 국립 공원

Popju-sa is one of the largest and most famous temple sites in Korea and an absolute must for all travellers. It's also very popular as a weekend picnic destination with Koreans so if you're not keen on hoardes of people and prefer to enjoy your temples in relative peace and quiet then go during the week. Entry to the park costs W800 or W600 with a student card.

The temple was begun as early as 553 AD during the Silla Dynasty which was when the Daeongbo-Jeon Hall with its enormous golden Buddhas and the five-roofed Palsang-Jeon Hall were constructed. At the time it was one of the largest sanctuaries in Korea. Repairs were undertaken in 776 AD but in 1592 it was burned to the ground during the Japanese invasion. Reconstruction began in 1624 and it's from this time that the present Palsang-Jeon Hall dates making it one of the few wooden structures at Popju-sa to survive since the 17th century. Most of the others were constructed or reconstructed towards the end of the Yi Dynasty. Popju-sa is, however, famous for yet another reason. It has the largest Buddha statue in Korea – possibly in the whole of North-East Asia. The 27-metre (88 feet)-high statue of the Maitraya Buddha dominates the temple compound. It is made of poured concrete and took 30 years to build being completed only in 1968. Photographs of this Buddha are on all tourist blurbs.

There are many other interesting features at Popju-sa including stone lanterns, a rock-cut seated Buddha, a huge bell and an enormous iron cauldron cast in 720 AD which was used to cook rice for the 3000 monks who lived here during its heyday.

As though the magnificence of the temple buildings themselves were not enough, Popju-sa is surrounded by the luxuriously-forested mountains of Sogri-san National Park which, although at its best in the autumn, is beautiful at any time of the year. There are many hiking trails in the mountains above the temple – all well marked – and several hermitages where you may be able to stay for the night. If you have the time, several days' hiking here is highly recommended.

There is a *Youth Hostel* at Sogri-san village as well as plenty of yowans and yoinsooks though the average price of the latter is around W9000-10,000.

Getting There Direct buses to Popju-sa from Taejon depart from the East Chikheng Bus Terminal. There are buses every 15 minutes, the first at 6 am and the last at 8.10 pm. The fare is W1050 and the journey, over an exceptionally scenic route, takes 1¾ hours. Buses depart from Bay No 12 – look for the Sogri-san 속리산 and Boeun 보은 destination sign in the front window. The buses terminate at Sogri-san village about a km before the temple.

Leaving Sogri-san, there are buses to the following places:

To Taejon 대전 Buses every 10 minutes, the first at 7.20 am and the last at 8.25 pm. The fare is W1050.

To Taegu 대구 Four buses daily, the first 6.40 am and the last at 5.55 pm. The fare is W2310.

To Seoul 서울 Buses every 15 minutes, the first at 7.50 am and the last at 6.15 pm. The fare is W2810.

To Suweon 수원 One bus every hour, the first at 8.15 am and the last at 5.40 pm. The fare is W2350.

There are also buses to Cheongju 청주

Mujuguncheondong 안국사 구천동 & Deogyu National Park

If Popju-sa whets your appetite for magnificent old temples set in beautiful surroundings then you might also like to visit this one and because it's not as famous as Popju-sa it tends not to get so crowded here on weekends. Buses for Mujuguncheondong depart from Taejon's East Chikheng Bus Terminal every 30 minutes from 6.20 am to 6.10 pm. The fare is W1770 and the journey takes about 2¼ hours.

Kap-sa Temple 갑사 & Dong Hak-sa Temple 동학사

If you haven't yet visited one or other of these two tranquil and very old temples in Mt Keryeong National Park west of

Taejon then remember that they're well worth it. It's probably easiest to get there from Konju and to combine a visit to one or other of these places with Konju (see 'Konju' for transport details from there). You can also get there from Taejon's West Chikheng Bus Terminal. There are seven buses daily from 7.20 am to 5.40 pm. The fare is W900 and the journey takes one hour and 20 minutes.

MOGPO (MOKPO)

Located at the end of the railway line near the south-western tip of mainland Korea is the fishing port of Mogpo. It's from here that the cheapest ferries to Cheju-do depart. The town itself is of little interest and you'll probably only stay overnight here but if you have time to spare it's worth wandering along the waterfront near the ferry terminal to see the incredible number of octopii that are for sale – all kept alive in aerated plastic tubs and bowls! It's also worth climbing up to the top of the rocky hill at the back of town for the views and sunsets.

Places to Stay

The yogwans and yoinsooks here fall into two categories as far as price goes. The simpler ones offering Korean-style rooms with common bathroom go for W2000-3000 a single and W3000-3500 a double. They vary considerably; some are excellent, others leave much to be desired. The best are on the side streets off the road directly opposite the railway station immediately to the left of the footbridge which goes across the main road. They include the Seoul Yogwan 서울 여관, Kwangyong Yoinsook 광영 여인숙, Kukdo Yoinsook 국도 여인숙 and Taesong Yoinsook 태성여인숙. There are others in the roads further over to the left of the railway station but if you go there it's suggested you avoid You-Il Yoinsook 유일여인숙 as it's the same price but very dingy.

If you're looking for something better – a Korean-style room with some furnishings, a TV and own bathroom then you're up for a hefty W8000-8400 a double. Yogwans in this category are often called 'hotels'. They all offer much the same facilities and there's little to choose between them but the most convenient are the Tongmyong Yogwan 동명여관, Taehwajang Yogwan 태화장여관 and Tongyang Yogwan 동양 여관.

Places to Eat

Of all the cafes in the streets around the railway station the one I'd nominate as best for value and quality of food is the Yonghwa Um Shiktang 영화 음식점. Two can eat 'pekpan' here for W2000 which includes soup and rice plus 15 other plates per person (!!) of mussels, fried fish, crab with sauce, kimchi (of course!) and other vegetables. You'd find that hard to beat anywhere in Korea and the staff are very friendly.

If you're a fried chicken fiend then try the *Broasten Chicken House* (that's the way it's spelt in English) which offers somewhat expensive fried chicken with salad and kimchi. Slightly cheaper chicken pieces with salad can be found in the 'Crown' beer house opposite the YMCA.

If you're looking for somewhere to go in the evening, or whenever, try the 'Coffee and Music' Chongye 청예 place which has a DJ there all day with an astonishing collection of LPs. Coffees cost W300 and the waitress will bring you music request slips. The 'OB' stand bar indicated on the street map is also a good place to meet local young people and have a cold beer.

Getting There

Buses The Chikheng Bus Terminal/Express Bus Terminal is a considerable distance from the centre of town. Take local bus No 1 to get there.

To Kwangju 광주 Buses every 15 minutes from 5.30 am to 9.15 pm. The fare is W1140.

To Seoul 서울 Several buses daily from 6 am to 5 pm. The fare is W4860.

There are other buses to Kwangju which

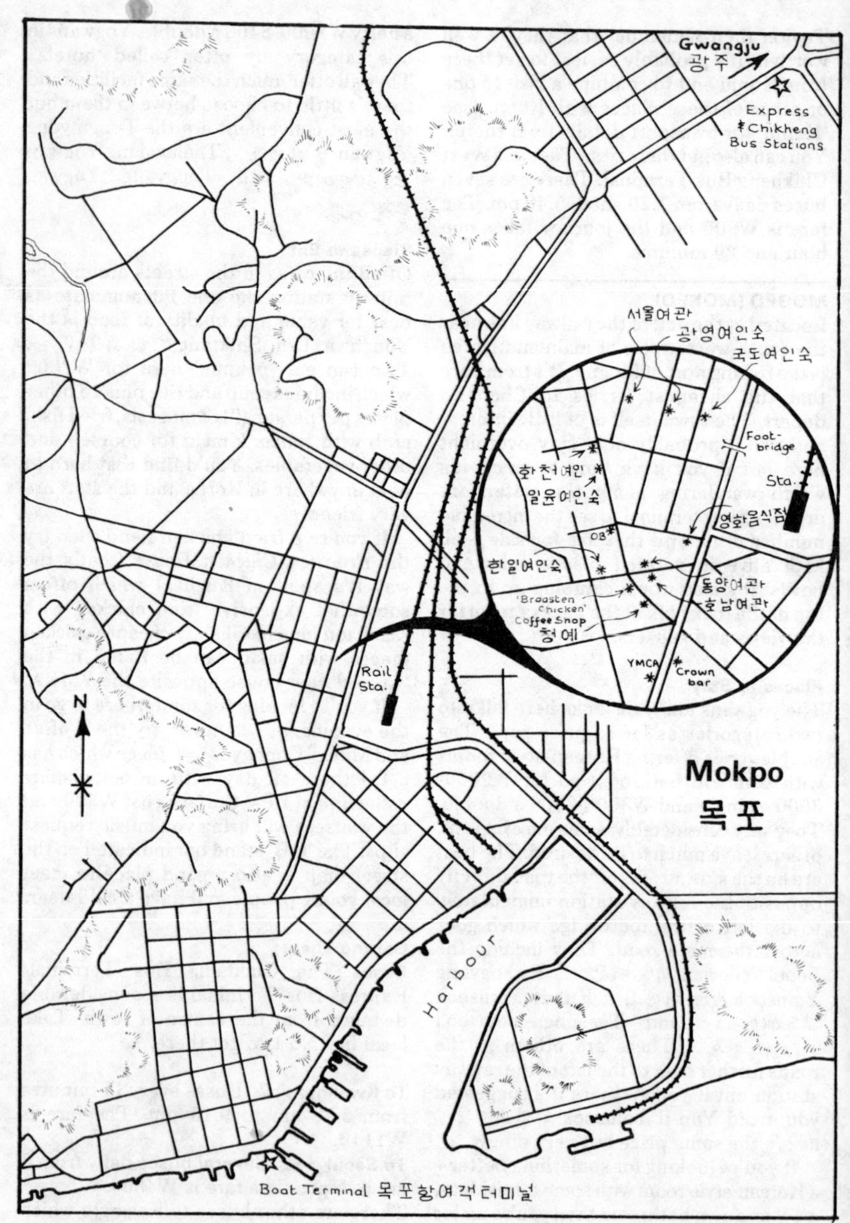
Gwangju
광주
Express
& Chikheng
Bus Stations
서울여관
광영여인숙
국도여인숙
Foot-
bridge
Sta.
화천여인
일윤여인숙
영화음식점
OB
한일여인숙
동양여관
호남여관
'Broasten
Chicken'
Coffee Shop
청예
YMCA
Crown
bar
Rail
Sta.
N
Mokpo
목포
Harbour
Boat Terminal 목포항여객터미널

go via less direct routes. If you'd like to visit the island of Wando 완도 which is connected to the mainland by bridge, then first take a bus to either Yeongsanpo 영산포 (for W740) or to Naju 나주 (for W780). At Naju change for another bus to Wando. There are buses from Naju to Wando every half hour from 5.30 am to 6.50 pm and the fare is W1730.

Boats There's a relatively new boat terminal 목포항 여객 터미널 at Mogpo which now handles all the ferry departures and arrivals. In the terminal are the ticket offices, a coffee shop, pharmacy and snack bars. It's from here that you take the ferry boats to Cheju-do 제주도.

There are two passenger ferries to Cheju-do per day at 10 am and 4 pm except on Sundays when there's only the 10 am boat. The 4 pm ferry is also a car ferry. During the summer holidays there may be three per day. The fares on the 10 am boat are W4300 (3rd class), W6410 (2nd class B) amd W9570 (2nd class A). The morning ferry is supposed to take about seven hours but if the sea is at all rough it can take over nine. From personal experience of this boat, I would never again go in 3rd class. Koreans, it seems, do not make good sailors in general so if the sea is rough you can guarantee that 3rd class (which is always crowded) will be awash with vomit. At least in 2nd class B which is a carpeted, communal cabin you can get away from this to a large extent.

The fares on the 4 pm boat are W6980 (3rd class), W9180 (2nd class B) and W14,250 (2nd class A). The journey takes about 5½ hours.

Booking in advance for these ferries isn't really necessary. Just go down to the boat terminal about two hours before the ferry is due to sail.

There are many other local ferries from Mogpo to the islands west and south of here but if you're thinking of making a trip around the islands you really need a copy of the national bus, boat, rail and flight timetables and prices booklet which is published every month and is for sale at most bookshops and stationers for W1000 (관광 교통 시각표). To work out a route you need to sit down for a couple of nights with this booklet and a map in Korean and English as the former is entirely in a mixture of Korean and Chinese (though mostly Korean). Perhaps the one you might be most interested in is the service to Wando 완도 because from here you can get another ferry to Cheju-do. There is a ferry every day from Wando to Mogpo at 8 am. The trip takes about six hours.

There are also ferries from Wando to Cheju-do but only during the summer. At this time there are two ferries a day at 12 noon and 4 pm. The 12 noon ferry takes just over two hours and costs W6570 (2nd class) and W7860 (1st class) but it only operates in April (1st-5th and on 31st), July 21st, August 20th, October (1st-11th and on 30th). The 4 pm ferry takes three hours and costs W6570 (2nd class) and W8840 (1st class). There is no 4 pm ferry on the first and third Wednesdays of the month.

Getting Around

Two local buses of use are No 1 which connects the Chikheng Express Bus Terminal with the railway station and the ferry terminal. The fare is W110 for any distance. A taxi from the railway station to the bus terminal will cost about W700.

CHEJU-DO (JEJU-DO) 제주도

Eighty-five km off the southern-most tip of the peninsula lies Korea's windswept island of myth and magic. It is to Korea what Crete is to Greece, what Mustang is to Nepal and what the Icelandic Sagas are to Denmark – something which blossomed from the same flower but which developed its own uniquely different hues. Isolated for many centuries from mainland developments, it acquired its own history, cultural traditions, dress, architecture and even language. The latter, for instance, though classified only as a dialect, was the result of the island's occupation between

1276 and 1375 by the Mongols and is as different from Korean as Provencal is from French. Mainlanders have great difficulty understanding what is being said here. Then there is the enigma of the 'harubang', or grandfather stones, carved from lava rock whose purpose is still debated by anthropologists. Certainly parallels are easily drawn between these and the mysterious statues found on such places as Easter Island and Okinawa, yet debates about whether they once represented the legendary guardians of the gates to Cheju's ancient towns seem largely irrelevent as you stand next to them in the gathering twilight at Seong Up, Cheju's ancient capital. Seong Up is today preserved in traditional style as a national monument.

None of this is to suggest that Cheju is somehow chafing at the bit for independence from the mainland. There are no similarities here between the Wales of Great Britain or the Quebec of Canada nor much place for such thoughts in a land sandwiched between three giants. The island is indisputedly part of the Korean cultural tradition and seen as such but its differences are sufficiently evocative to draw people here in search of legend from all over the world. Things are certainly changing here and have been for the last two decades since the government realised its tourist potential, and the island's supposed matriarchal society, exemplified by the skin-diving women who are the subject of folk songs, trinkets and photographs in tourist literature, is on the wane. Nevertheless, Cheju remains, along with Seoul and Kyongju among the 'musts' of all travellers to Korea.

Its people remain exceptionally friendly, unassuming and largely unaffected by all the 'development' and, outside of Cheju city itself, the tranquil, rural atmosphere is timeless. And, if all this sounds like tired tourist literature plagiarism, then you'll be pleased to discover that Cheju also offers some of the most outstanding geographical features you're likely to come across in this part of the world. The island is dominated by the almost 2000 metres (6560 feet) high extinct volcano of Mt Halla, the highest mountain in South Korea, with its own crater lake and several well-marked hiking trails which explore its forested slopes. From the summit you will be rewarded with incomparable views if the clouds are kind to you. Then there are the beaches dotted around the island; the impressive Chongbang Falls at Sogwipo on the south coast reputed to be the only waterfall in Asia which plunges directly into the sea; another spectactular, but smaller, volcanic cone at Songsanpo on the eastern tip of the island, and the Mang Jang Caves whose humid, 9°C average temperature will not only make you wish you were back in the balmy warmth on the surface but which is the longest known lava tube in the world.

So if you're time is regrettably short in this fascinating country, Cheju-do should be on your short-list of priorities. No wonder Koreans choose it for their honeymoons!

CHEJU CITY 제주

The island's capital has the most easy-going and festive atmosphere of any city you're likely to encounter in Korea. It's small, compact, everything except the bus terminal is within easy walking distance of anywhere else, and, despite the amount of construction which has gone on here recently, you'll still run into many gems of traditional Cheju-style houses made of lava stone with thatched roof and high surrounding dry-stone wall. Right in the centre of town you'll find Cheju's oldest building, the 15th-century **Gwandok-jok-dong Pavilion**, complete with 'harubang' and, nearby, an interesting and extensive daily market which sells everything from clothes to Chinese herbs to fish to the pineapples, citrus fruits and apples which are grown on Mt Halla's southern slopes.

Most of the places worth visiting are outside of Cheju city itself but whilst you're there make sure you see Gwandokjok-dong pavilion 돌할으방 the **Samsonghyol Museum**, and **Yongdu-am** or Dragon's Head Rock 용두암 on the shore between the city centre and the airport.

Orientation

If you arrive by air, the airport is about two km west of the city. Local buses are available into the centre of town – frequent service. Arriving by boat, there's no need to take a taxi or bus since all the cheap yogwans and yoinsooks are only a few minutes' walk from the ferry terminal. If you need to go the the Korean Airlines office (tel 2-6111), this is located opposite the KAL Hotel – Cheju's only high-rise building. Bus No 3 goes past the office.

Places to Stay – top end

There used to be only four top-end hotels on Cheju, three in Cheju City and one in Sogwip on the other side of the island. But with recent construction on the edge of the city there's more choice now.

Chuju KAL Hotel
: 1691-9,1 Dong, 2-Do, Cheju (tel 22 7250), 310 rooms singles US$30 and doubles US$45 plus 10% service charge and 10% tax (foreigners excluded from latter charge). This is Cheju's original high-rise and conveniently close to the city centre.

Cheju Grand Hotel
: PO Box 45, Cheju (tel 7 2131), 552 rooms, singles US$35 doubles US$52-63 plus service charges and taxes. A new hotel on the outskirts of Cheju City.

Hotel Paradise Cheju
: 1315, 1-Dong, 2-Do, Cheju (tel (3) 0171), 57 rooms, doubles US$36 plus 10% service charge and 10% tax..

Hotel Seohai
: 291-30 Yon-dong, Cheju, PO Box 99 (tel 7-4111/40), doubles for US$48 plus service charges and taxes.

Hotel Paradise Sogwipo
: 674-1, Sogwi-Ri, Sogwi-Up, nam cheju Gun, Cheju-do (tel Sogwipo 2161), 59 rooms, singles and doubles US$38-51 plus service charges and taxes.

Places to Stay – bottom end

You'll have no problem finding accommodation in Cheju. The number of yogwans and yoinsooks is legion so you'll literally be spoilt for choice except perhaps between mid-July and mid-August when it gets quite crowded (also prices tend to be a little higher at this time). Most of the places are located on or off Sanji Ro and between this road, Kwan Deck Ro and the sea front. If you arrive by boat you'll probably be met by people from the various yogwans offering you a room and to show you the way there. If you think what you're being offered sounds like a good deal then go and have a look but my own favourite was the Yangsan-do Yoinsook 양산도 여인숙 only a stone's throw from the boat terminal next to the police station (?) and another yoinsook with the name of Hanil Yoinsook 한일 여인숙 which has a Chinese cafe on the ground floor. The rooms here are W2000 for singles and W2400 for doubles. Ask for a room on the top floor which has an open flat roof, good views and is quiet. Also, out of the tourist season, you'll probably have the communal bathrooms all to yourself though this doesn't matter a great deal as they're kept very clean anyway. The staff here is exceptionally friendly and I noticed from the register that quite a few other travellers stay here.

If you prefer to live in a room around a traditional courtyard then there are a number of similarly priced yogwans and yoinsooks just a few metres further on, on the left-hand side. For something of above-average quality, for which you'll pay considerably more, then walk up to the first road junction where there's a white monument in the middle of the road. From here, take either the first or the second road on the right-hand side and you'll instantly be spoilt for choice.

Places to Eat

As with yogwans, so with restaurants, there are literally hundreds of them. Just along Sanji Ro alone (the road leading from the ferry terminal to the first junction) there are Korean, sea food,

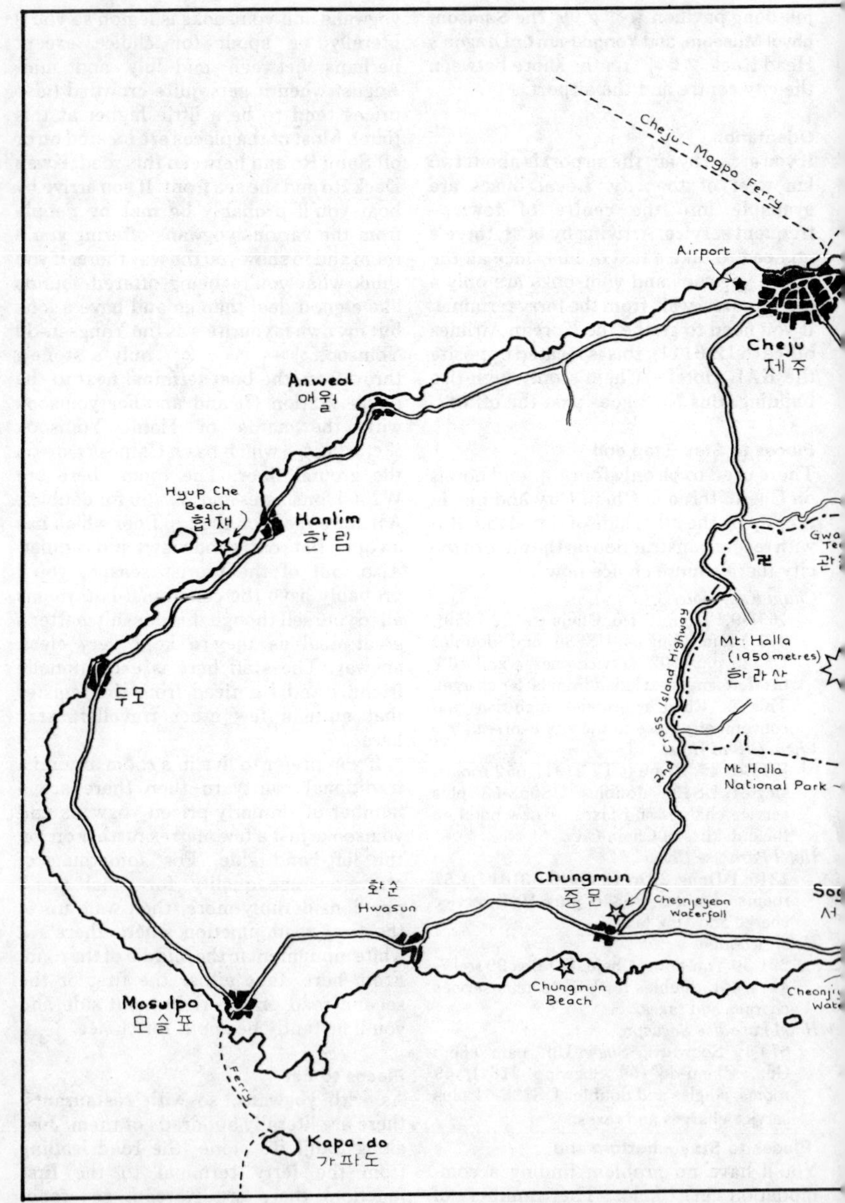
Cheju – Mogpo Ferry
Airport
Cheju
제주
Anweol
애월
Hyup Che
Beach
협재
Hanlim
한림
두모
Mt. Halla
(1950 metres)
한라산
2nd Cross Island Highway
Mt. Halla
National Park
Chungmun
중문
Cheonjeyeon
Waterfall
화순
Hwasun
Chungmun
Beach
Mosulpo
모슬포
Ferry
Kapa-do
가파도

Yeosu Ferry
Pusan Ferry
Hamdok
함덕
Man Jang
Caves
만장굴
Pyeongdae
Udo
우도
Ferry
Song San Po
성산포
Songsanilchubong
성산일출봉
Seong Up
성읍
Pyosun
표선
Namweon
남원
5.16 Cross Island High
Cheong Bang
Waterfall
정방
Sogwipo – Pusan
Ferry
제주도
Cheju-do (Island)
0
10 km

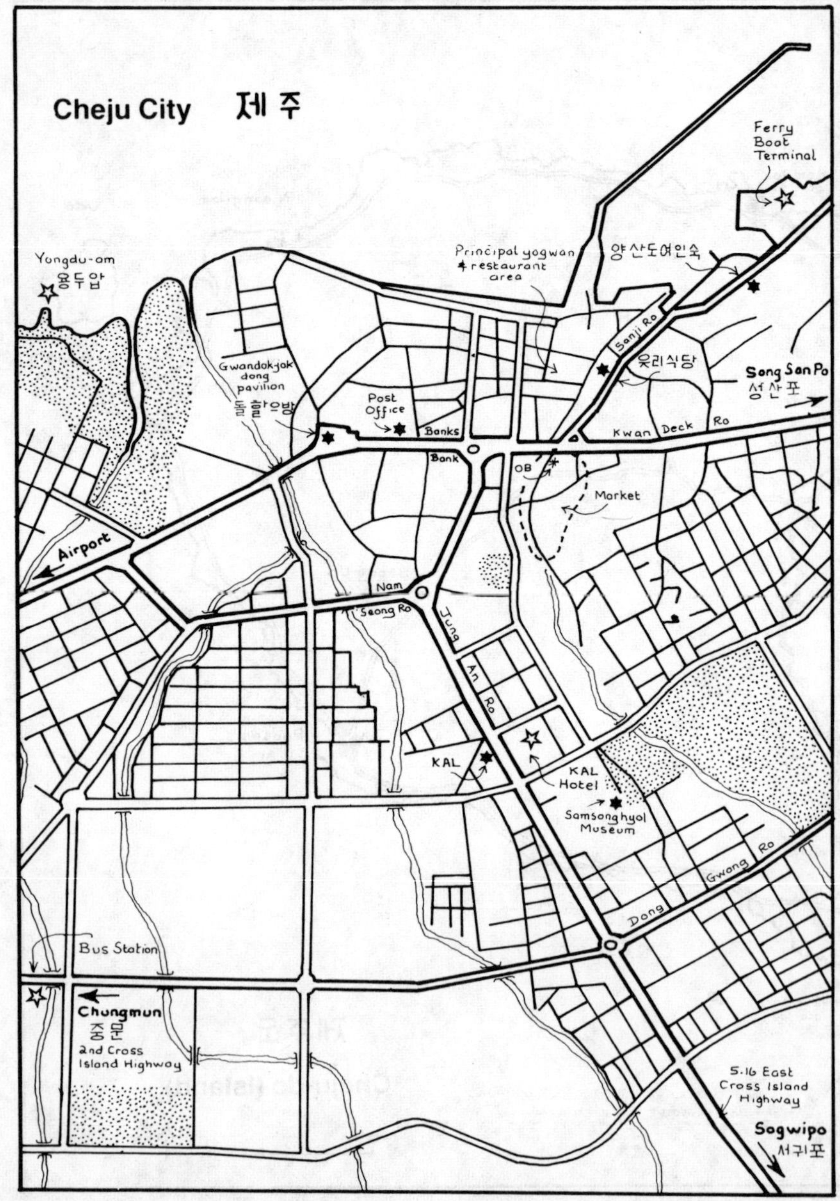
Cheju City 제 주
Ferry Boat Terminal
Principal yogwan & restaurant area
양산도여인숙
Yongdu-am
용두암
Sanji Ro
우리식당
Song San Po
성산포
Gwandokjok dong pavilion
돌하루방
Post Office
Banks
Kwan Deck Ro
Bank
OB
Market
Airport
Nam
Seong Ro
Jung
An
Ro
KAL
KAL Hotel
Samsonghyol Museum
Gwong
Ro
Dong
Bus Station
Chungmun
중문
2nd Cross Island Highway
5.16 East Cross Island Highway
Sogwipo
서귀포

Chinese, Japanese and western-style, fried chicken restaurants all of which, except the fried chicken place, you can eat well at for between W1500 and W2000. They're all pretty good and it's impossible to recommend one in preference to another but if you're looking for a 'bulgogi' then try the Yuri Shiktang 유리 식당 about half way up Sanji Ro on the right hand side as you come from the ferry terminal. Excellent food and plenty of it for W2000 as well as very friendly staff.

A good place to meet local young people and students in the evenings is the 'OB' stand bar just where the market starts at the junction of Sanji Ro and Kwan Deck Ro. If you get talking to people there they'll probably invite you along to whatever is happening that evening, especially at weekends.

If you're looking for a splurge then try one or other of the restaurants along Jung An Ro which is the road which leads from the centre of town up the hill and past the KAL Hotel. Expect to pay between W3000-4000.

Getting Around

You probably won't have to use Cheju city buses at all except to get to the airport (two km) or to the Chikheng bus terminal (about a km). Buses to the former you can find outside the GPO. Buses to the latter are a little more tricky since most of them are not numbered but you can find them at the bottom of the hill in the centre of town (Jung An Ro) – keep asking the conductors/conductresses and the other people waiting at the stop. The alternative is to take the No 3 to the big junction past the KAL Hotel and then take another bus along Dong Gwang Ro on which the terminal is located.

There are plenty of buses from the terminal to most places of interest around the island and so long as you have your destination written down in Korean characters to show the ticket clerk and the people who check your ticket before you board the buses then you'll never get on the wrong bus. The people here are very helpful. There is a timetable but unless you're very familiar with Korean you'll have difficulty reading it as it's not been written very carefully. In any event, there are only four main roads which lead out of the city and they all go to Sogwipo 서귀포 on the southern coast of the island.

The coast road going west will give you the best selection of beaches on the island which include Hyup Chemun 협재 , just past Hanlim 한림 , and Chungmun 중문 , on the southern coast, which is being developed as a tourist resort. At Hanlim there is also the famous wool sweater and tweed factory opposite the Isadora Clinic which is the only place in the East where you can buy sweaters woven to traditional Irish designs! The coast road going east from Cheju city will take you to Gim Nyeung 김녕 and the Man Jang Caves 만장굴 the volcanic cone of Song San Po 성산포 and then round the coast to Pyson 표선 and Sogwipo. 서귀포

The other two main roads are the cross-island highways which skirt the slopes of Mt Halla and are the ones you will need if you're going to climb the mountain. The one which skirts the eastern side of the mountain is known as the '5.16' and buses taking this route will have 제 5.16 횡단 in the front window. The road passes three points at which you can start the trek to the peak of Mt Halla and ends up at Chungmun 중문 . The fares on the buses which take these two mountain routes are more than those which follow the coast roads – about double. The reason for this as far as I can make out is that only mini-buses do the cross-island routes and it's a long 1st/2nd gear crawl to the top which obviously uses more gas.

There is one other minor route which will be of interest and this is the road from Poysun 표선 to Seong Up 성읍 . It continues on past Seong Up to join the '5.16' on the lower northern slopes of Mt Halla. This is the road you take to see Cheju's ancient city capital.

A few examples of schedules and fares are:
Cheju City-Sogwipo (via 2nd cross-island highway) Every 20 minutes from 5.20 am to 9.40 pm. The fare is W1420 and the journey takes nearly two hours.
Cheju City-Sogwipo (via the 5.16 cross-island highway) Every 12 minutes from 6.40 am to 9.20 pm. The fare is W810 and the journey takes one hour and 10 minutes.
Sogwipo-Pyosan Frequent schedule throughout the day and evening. Costs W400 and takes about half and hour.
Cheju City-Man Jang Caves Direct buses to the caves (which are about 2.5 km from the main coast road) depart about once per hour during the hours of daylight. The fare is W410 and the journey takes about 45 minutes.
Cheju City-Song San Po Frequent services throughout the day and evening. The fare is W680 and the journey takes about 1½ hours.

Boats There are frequent ferries from Cheju City to Mogpo 목포, Wando 완도, and Pusan 부산 daily. There's also a daily ferry from Sogwipo 서귀포 on the southern coast of Cheju-do to Pusan.

To Mogpo Two passenger ferries per day (sometimes three in the summer months) at 7 am (except on Mondays) and 9 am. Fares are W6980 (3rd class), W9180 (2nd class B) and W14,250 (2nd class A) on the 7 am boat. The journey takes about 5½ hours. The fares on the 9 am boat are W4300 (3rd class), W6410 (2nd class) and the journey takes about seven hours but can take nine if the sea is rough. Note the warning about travelling in 3rd class given under 'Boats' in the 'Mogpo' section.

To Wando There are two ferries to Wando at 7.20 am daily and 3.30 pm but the 3.30 pm ferry only operates from 1 April to 31 May, 20 July to 20 August and 1 October to 30 November. Fares on the 7.20 am ferry are W6570 (2nd class) and W7860 (1st class) and the journey takes 3½ hours. The fares on the 3.30 pm ferry are W6750 (2nd class B), W8840 (2nd class A) and W14,670 (1st class). The ferry journey is nearly two hours.

To Pusan There are four different ferries to Pusan. Three of the ferries leave from Cheju City and the fourth from Sogwipo. The cheapest is the passenger ferry from Cheju City which departs daily except Saturday at 7 pm, takes about 13 hours and costs W6340 (3rd class), W9490 (2nd class B) and W14,200 (2nd class A). The next cheapest is the ferry from Sogwipo to Pusan which departs daily at 4 pm, takes about 15 hours and costs W6680 (3rd class), W9980 (2nd class B) and W14,930 (2nd class A). The last two ferries from Cheju City cost the same and leave at 7 pm daily except Saturday and 7.30 pm daily except Sunday. The 7 pm ferry takes 10 hours and the 7.30 pm ferry takes 11 hours. The fares are W10,340 (3rd class), W13,630 (2nd class B) and W19,390 (2nd class A). The 7 pm ferry is a car ferry which is operated by Hanguk company.

The seas in the straits between Cheju-do and the mainland are often quite rough so if you're not a good sailor then it might be worth your while thinking about taking one of the faster ferries or even flying. The cheapest flight to the mainland is Cheju-Yeosu. There are two daily flights at 9.50 am and 2.40 pm which cost W14,900 (about US$21). It's a 45 minute flight.

AROUND THE ISLAND

Chungmun Beach 중문

This is probably the best and longest beach on the island but it's in the process of being developed into a tourist resort. All the same, it will be several years before the process is over-done. Yogwans are available in town. To get there take one of the mini-buses which go along the 2nd (ie west) cross-island highway and get off at Chungmun. The buses will have 제2횡단 in the front window.

Sogwipo 서귀포
The main attraction in Sogwipo is the 23-metre (75 feet) high waterfall of Jeong Bang 정방 , the only waterfall in Asia which falls directly into the sea. It's a very impressive sight and only a 10-15 minute walk from the centre of town. Just off the coast from here can be seen several small, partially forested and very rocky islands. Entry to the falls costs W500. To get to Sogwipo, take one of the mini-buses which go along the 5.16 (east) cross-island highway. The fare is W810 and the journey takes just over one hour.

There are plenty of yogwans in Sogwipo if you care to stay the night or, if you set off early enough from Cheju, you could combine a visit to Jeong Bang with one to either Chungmun, west of Sogwipo, or to Seong Up, north of Pyosan, and be able to get back to Cheju by nightfall. There are plenty of buses connecting Sogwipo with the other towns on the south coast.

Seong Up 성읍
Located only a short bus ride north of Pyosun is Cheju's ancient capital founded in the early part of the 15th century. Today it's just a quiet, small village but full of interesting things to see and well worth spending several hours wandering through it since the whole village has been preserved in traditional style. The old Confucian school in the centre of the village has been reconstructed and it's here, of course, that many of the 'harubang' or grandfather stones are to be seen. There are plenty of well illustrated bill-boards describing (in English and Korean) the main features and history of the principal sites and no-one here is going to rush out and hassle you to buy tourist trash. It isn't that sort of place.

You can get here directly from Cheju City by taking a bus to Pyosun. There are thirteen buses daily, the first at 6 am and the last at 8 pm. The journey takes about 45 minutes. The bus you want is the one with the 표선행 sign in the front window. Alternatively, if you're on the southern coast, go first to Pyosun and then take another bus to Seong Up. If you're heading back to Cheju City after visiting Seong Up the last bus back from the village comes through about 8 pm but is frequently late (the bus due at 7 pm arrived around 7.35 pm).

Man Jang Caves 만장굴
East of Cheju and about 2½ km off the coast road from Gim Nyeong (Kim Kyong) 김녕 are the Man Jang Caves. The main section of the caves is 6.978 km long (!!) with a height and width varying from three to twenty metres. It is the longest known lava tube in the world and if you've never seen one of these then make sure you visit these caves. Take a sweater with you and a reasonable pair of shoes – it's damp down there (87-100% humidity) and the temperature rarely rises above a chilly 9°C. The cave is well lighted as far as a huge lava pillar (about a km from the entrance) which is as far as you're allowed to go without special permission. The caves are open every day and entry costs W800.

There are direct buses to Man Jang Caves from Cheju City which cost W410 and take about 45 minutes to get there but they're not very frequent. If you get stuck waiting for a bus at Man Jang then take a taxi to the main road or hitch. You can easily combine a visit to Man Jang with one to Song San Po and get back to Cheju by nightfall if you want.

Song San Po 성산포
Song San Po is the town at the extreme eastern tip of Cheju-do nestled at the foot of the spectacular volcanic cone of Songsanilchubong 성산 일출봉 whose sides plunge vertically into the surf and around which – if conditions are favourable – you can watch Cheju-do's famous diving women searching for seaweed, shell-fish and sea urchins. It's an excellent place to watch the sun rise if you care to stay overnight in one of Song San Po's yogwans. Unlike Mt Halla, there's no longer any crater lake on the summit and

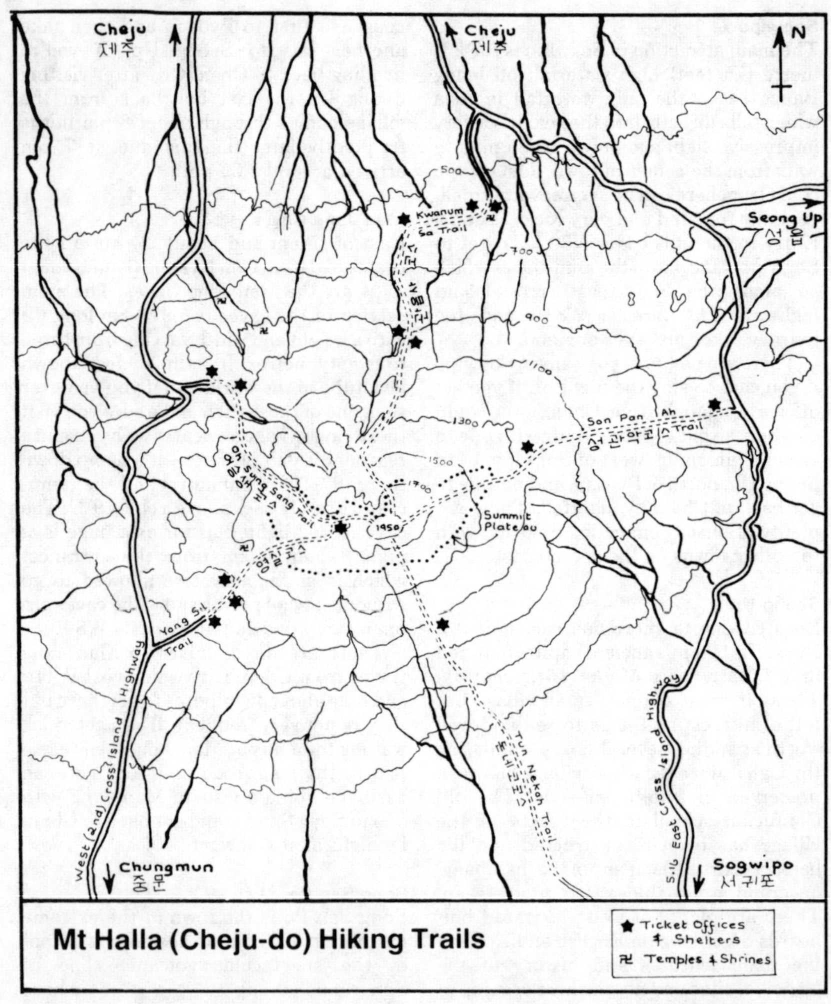

Mt Halla (Cheju-do) Hiking Trails

the area below the jagged outer edges of the peak is continuously harvested for cattle fodder (it supports luxurious meadows. Here is one of Cheju-do's most scenically beautiful areas.

Also, north-east of here, just off the coast, is the island of U-do which is still very rural and where there are no cars. It's about as far as you can get from civilisation in this part of the world – worth a visit if you have the time. There are ferries from Song San Po.

Buses to Song San Po from Cheju are frequent and cost W680. The journey takes about 1½ hours. There is no entry fee to Songsanilchubong but if you're on a budget then give the restaurant and soft drink stalls at the start of the walk a miss as prices are double what they are anywhere else. You may come across some enterprising local youths about half way up to the summit offering jogging shoes and a shoe-shine service in exchange for high-heel shoes and W500 (ever seen well-dressed Korean ladies in anything other than high heels?). They do a roaring trade. It's also possible to rent horses.

Trekking on Mt Halla

Walking to the top of Mt Halla is one of the highlights of a visit to Cheju-do but make sure you get off to an early start. No matter how clear the skies may look in the morning, the summit is often obscured by cloud in the early afternoon which is when you should be on the way down. Anyone can do this trek. No experience is necessary and no special equipment required. Just make sure you have a decent pair of jogging/hiking boots and something warm (it gets chilly up there at nearly 2000 metres). There are five well-marked trails – three coming in from the east and two from the west and they all connect with one or other of the two cross-island highways. The whole area is now a National Park and entry to it costs W200. Detailed trail maps are available free of charge at all the ticket offices which are located at the beginning of the trails.

The two shortest trails are the ones coming in from the west side – the Oh Sung Sang 어승생 코스 and the Yong Sil 영실코스. It takes the average person about 2½ hours to climb to the summit along either of these and about two hours to get back down again. Coming from the east side you should plan about four or five hours to the summit. If you have camping equipment available there are several sites where you can erect a tent. Close to all the ticket offices are places where you can buy soft drinks, snacks and even soju. There's also quite a large and active Buddhist monastery close to the Kwanum-sa trail 관음사 코스.

To get there from Cheju City simply decide which trail you want to start off on and then take the appropriate mini-bus along either the 5.16 or the 2nd cross-island highway. Tell the driver or his assistant which trail you want to go on and they'll make sure you're put down at the right spot.

YEOSU 여수

Yeosu lies about half way along the mountainous and deeply indented southern coastline of Korea. It's a spectacularly beautiful area peppered with islands and peninsulas and large parts of it between Yeosu and Pusan now make up the Hallyo Waterway National Park. One of the most popular trips in this part of the country is to take the hydrofoil from Yeosu to Pusan (or vice versa) via Namhae, Samcheonpo, Chungmun and Seongpo.

Yeosu's most famous historical associations are with Admiral Yi who routed the Japanese navy on several occasions in the 16th century following the introduction of his highly manoeuverable iron-clad war ships or 'turtle ships'. These ships have lent their name to that popular brand of Korean cigarettes – 'Geobugseon' – and you can see a full-size recreation of one of them here at Yeosu. From being a naval base in the 16th century, Yeosu is now an expanding industrial and resort city which is worth spending a day or two exploring.

Orientation

Because of the mountainous terrain of the peninsula on which Yeosu stands the city is divided into a number of distinct parts. Only the ferry terminal and railway station are within walking distance of each other. The express and chikheng bus terminals are way across the other side of town. To get from one to the other or into the centre of town you'll need to use public transport. City bus Nos 3, 5, 6, 7, 8, 9, 10, 11, 13 and 17 go past the two bus terminals but probably the most useful is No 11 which connects the bus terminals with the railway station via the centre of town. If you arrive by air, the airport is about seven km out of town but served by local buses. There's no need to take a taxi – simply walk the few metres from the terminal buildings to the road and wait for a bus which will have 여수 in the front window. The fare is W290 and the journey takes about 40 minutes ending up at the chikheng bus terminal.

Things to See & Do

Right in the centre of town stands the **Jinnamgwan Pavilion** 진남관, one of the longest pavilions in Korea. It's a beautiful old building originally constructed for receiving officials and holding ceremonies and later used as military quarters. High up on the hill which overlooks the area between City Hall and the railway station is the **Chungmin-sa Shrine** 충민사 dedicated to Admiral Yi and built in 1601 by another naval commander, Yi Si-eon, though it has been renovated since then. There are excellent views over Yeosu and the harbour area from here but it's a steep climb.

Another popular spot in Yeosu is **Odong-do** 오동도, an island which is linked to the mainland by a 730-metre-long causeway. It's a craggy, tree and bamboo-covered island with a lighthouse and picnic spots and well-marked walking trails. The best time to see the island is in spring when it's covered in camellia blossoms.

If you're up to a more substantial trek there is **Hansan-sa Temple** 한산사 high up on the wooded mountain slopes to the west of Yeosu. The temple was built in 1194 AD by a high priest named Bojo during the reign of the Koryo king Myeongjong. The trail up to the temple is well-marked and the views are superb.

Places to Stay

The majority of yogwans and yoinsooks here are clustered between the city hall and the railway station, the cheaper ones being near the railway station. There are a few others just outside the gate to the hydrofoil jetty; a few more in the centre of town just below the Jinnamgwan pavilion, and others outside the bus terminals.

There are no top-end hotels in Yeosu as such but there is the adequate middle-range *Yeosu Tourist Hotel*, 766 Konghwadong, Yeosu (tel 2 313115), with 50 rooms which cost US$18/23 for singles/doubles. Korean-style rooms cost US$14/26 for singles/doubles. Another yogwan which has been recommended here is the Sam Song Yogwan 삼성여관 near the docks.

Getting There

Buses The express and chikheng bus terminals are next to each other on the western side of the city on the road out to Suncheon and the airport.

To Pusan 부산 There are 14 buses daily, the first at 6 am and the last at 5.30 pm. The fare is W3110 and the journey takes about 4½ hours.

To Seoul 서울 There are nine buses daily, the first at 6.30 am and the last at 4.30 pm. The fare is W5110 and the journey takes about seven hours.

Boats

Yeosu-Pusan via Hallyo Waterway National Park 한려 해상 국립공원

The hydrofoil, *Angel*, operates out of the new port at the back of the railway station. Except during the holiday season (July and August) it isn't necessary to book in advance. If you want to check whether there is room before you go down to the port then ring (2)-3617 (English is spoken). The hydrofoil is operated by the Hanryeo Development Co Ltd. Departure times and fares are as follows:

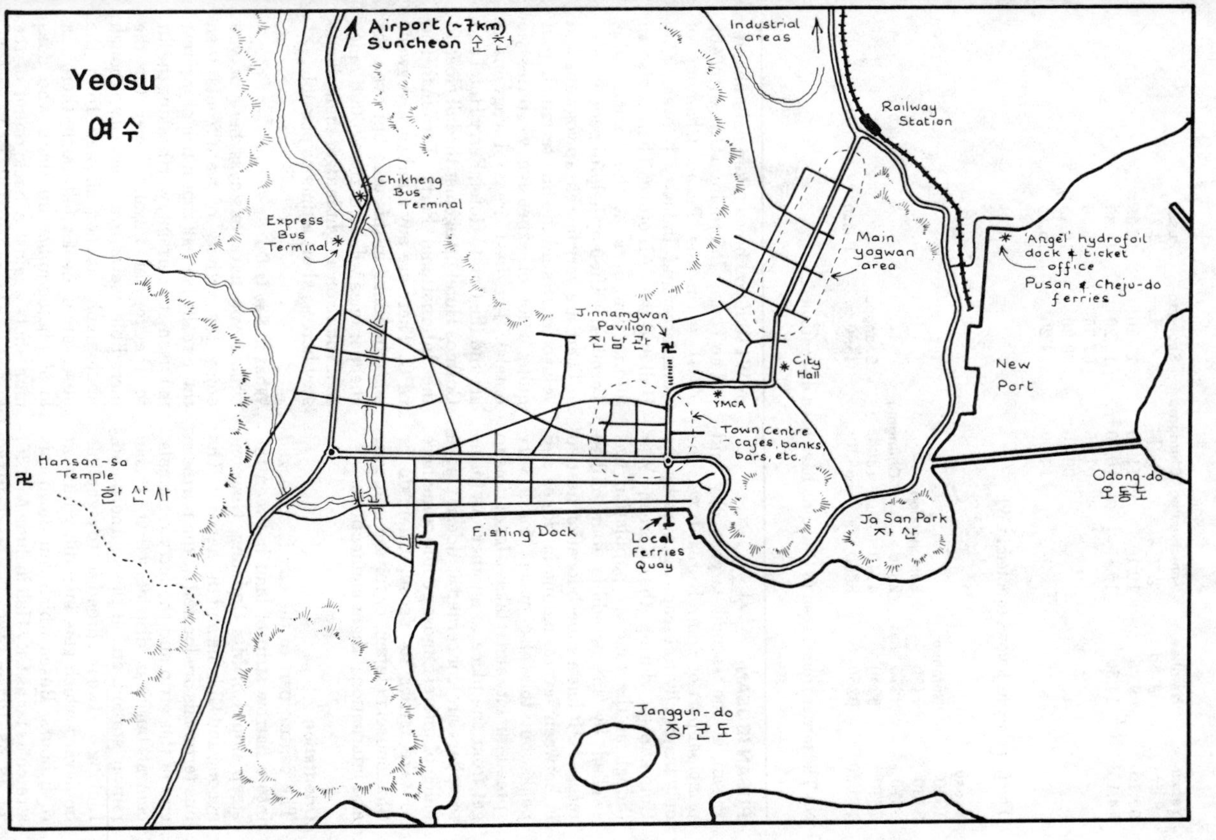
Yeosu 여수
Airport (~7km) Suncheon 순천
Industrial areas
Railway Station
Main yogwan area
'Angel' hydrofoil dock & ticket office
Pusan & Cheju-do ferries
New Port
Odong-do 오동도
Ja San Park 자산
City Hall
YMCA
Town Centre - cafes, banks, bars, etc.
Jinnamgwan Pavilion 진남관
Local Ferries Quay
Janggun-do 장군도
Fishing Dock
Chikheng Bus Terminal
Express Bus Terminal
Hansan-sa Temple 한산사

Yeosu 여수	Namhae 남해	Samcheonpo 삼천포	Chungmu 충무	Seongpo 성포	Pusan 부산
09.10	09.45	10.10	11.00	11.20	12.35
14.15	14.50	15.15	16.00	16.20	17.35
			07.15	07.35	08.50
			09.10	09.30	10.45
			14.00	14.20	15.35

The fares are as follows (quoted in W):

Yeosu					
1910	**Namhae**				
3430	1450	**Samcheonpo**			
6370	4270	2890	**Chungmu**		
7670	5240	4140	1300	**Seongpo**	
11,630	9250	8330	5830	4590	**Pusan**

NB The ferries from Yeosu to Cheju-do have been discontinued.

PUSAN (BUSAN) 부산

Pusan is the second largest city and principal port of South Korea. It was the only major city to escape capture by the Communists during the Korean War though at the time its population was swelled by an incredible four million refugees. It has a superb location nestled in between several mountain ridges and peaks but this also makes for a very spread-out city and it takes a lot of time to get from one place to another. As far as travellers are concerned it doesn't have much of interest, most people come here to take ferries to Yeosu, Cheju-do or Shimonoseki (Japan) or for the domestic and international flight connections.

Orientation

The central part of the city is squeezed into a narrow strip of land between the steep slopes of Mts Gudeong, Goweon-gyeong and Gubong and the harbour. The bus terminals are located at the northern end of this strip and the ferry terminals, central business district, GPO, Pusan railway station, etc, at the southern end. Linking the two is a broad six to eight lane boulevard which gets incredibly busy at rush hours. Buses which run down this stretch as far as City Hall include Nos 26, 34, 42, 55, 127 and 139. The fare is W120 or W110 if you buy a token beforehand.

The Tourist Information Office (tel 462 9734) is in the Pusan Chamber of Commerce and Industry between City Hall and the JAL office. There's also an information desk at the Express Bus Terminal staffed by helpful people.

There are very few cheap yogwans and yoinsooks around the bus terminals (but quite a lot of expensive western-style hotels). The best area for yogwans is around the Bando Hotel, Ferry Hotel and Cosmos Hotel up against the hill close to the International Ferry Terminal and GPO. There are any number of yogwans and yoinsooks in this area but even the cheaper ones will be in the W6000 range so if you're on a tight budget then plan to stay here as short a time as possible.

What to See & Do

Unless you have business here or you enjoy the activity of waterfronts then there really isn't all that much of interest in Pusan. It's certainly worth taking the lift to the top of Pusan Tower for the incredible views over the city, though photography is not allowed from the observation decks (although there's a local photographer up there who does mug shots against a background of the harbour so I wonder who's fooling who?).

The return fare in the lift is W690. Coffee and soft drinks are available at the top but there's no restaurant.

If you're looking for something to do on an evening most of the bars and cocktail lounges around the Hotel Royal on the bottom side of the Pusan Tower cater for Korean businessmen and are, hence, expensive. In many of them you are obliged to buy a 'snack' with your first drink and that can cost you anything from W3000-5000! For something more down to earth head for 'Texas Street' opposite Pusan railway station (it's the first street parallel to the main boulevard). This is Pusan's answer to Seoul's Itaewon – an area of music clubs, bars and pick-up joints that attracts GIs and travellers. It hasn't got the same range as Itaewon but at least a few beers won't burn a large hole in your pocket.

Places to Stay – top end

Pusan's top hotels are located in two clusters, one around the Express Bus Terminal and the other around the Pusan Tower in the centre of the city. Which one you choose will depend on whether you intend to stay a few days or simply overnight. They include the following:

Hotel Crown
830-30 Pomil-dong, Tong-ku, Pusan (tel 69 1241/7), 5-star, 135 rooms, no singles, doubles US$35-38, western, Japanese, Chinese and Korean restaurants, night club, bars, sauna, etc

Hotel Commodore
743-80 Yongju-dong, Chung-ku, Pusan (tel 44 9101/7), 5-star, 325 rooms, no singles, doubles US$42-61, western, Japanese, Chinese and Korean restaurants, night club, bars, game room, sauna, etc.

Kukje Hotel
830-62 Pomil-dong, Pusan (tel 642 1330/4), 5-star, 139 rooms, singles US$30, doubles US$40-43, Korean, western, Chinese and French restaurants, night club, game room, sauna, etc

Hotel Sorabol
37-1 1-ka, Taechong-dong, Chung-ku, Pusan (tel 463 3511/9), 5-star, 152 rooms, Korean, western, Japanese and Chinese restaurants, night club, bars, sauna, etc

The Westin Chosun Hotel
737 Uil-dong, Haeundae-ku, Pusan (tel 72 7411/20), at Haeundae Beach, 5-star, no singles, doubles US$52-65, western, Japanese, Korean and French restaurants, disco club, bars, swimming pool, etc

Busan Tourist Hotel
12 2-ka Tongkwang-dong, Chung-ku, Pusan (tel 23 4301/9), 4-star, 288 rooms, singles US$30, doubles US$32-34, Korean, western, Japanese and Chinese restaurants, night club, disco club, bars, sauna, etc

Hotel Busan Arirang
1204-1 Choryang-dong, Tonk-ku, Pusan (tel 463 5001/8), 4-star, 121 rooms, singles US$25, doubles US$36-38, western, Korean and Japanese restaurants, night club, disco club, bar, etc

Ferry Hotel
37-16 4-ka Chungang-dong, Chung-ku, Pusan (tel 463 0881/90), 4-star, 122 rooms, no singles, doubles US$31-34, Korean, western and Japanese restaurants, night club, night club, bars, sauna, etc

Hotel Kukdong
1124 Chung-dong, Tongrae-ku, Pusan (tel 72 0081/90), at Haeundae Beach, 4-star, 107 rooms, singles US$34, doubles US$39-40, Korean, western, Japanese and Chinese restaurants, night club, bar, sauna, etc

Hotel Phoenix
8-1 5-ka Nampo-dong, Chung-ku, Pusan (tel 22 8061/9), 4-star, 120 rooms, no singles, doubles US$36, western and Korean restaurants, night club, bar, game room, sauna, etc

Places to Stay – middle

Bando Hotel
36 4-ka Chungang-dong, Chung-ku, Pusan (tel 44 0561/9), 3-star, 146 rooms, singles US$22, doubles US$ 30-31, western, Korean and Japanese restaurants, night club, game room, sauna, etc

Busan Plaza Hotel
1213-14 Choryang-dong, Tong-ku, Pusan (tel 463 5011/9), 3-star, 123 rooms, no singles, doubles US$25-28, Korean and western restaurants, night club, game room, etc

Busan Royal Hotel
2-72 2-ka Kwangbok-dong, Chung-ku, Pusan (tel 23 1051/9), 3-star, 112 rooms, singles

US$27.50, doubles US$34.50, Korean, western and Japanese restaurants, night club, game room, etc

Moon Hwa Tourist Hotel
517-65 Pujon-dong, Pusanjin-ku, Pusan (tel 66 8001/7), 3-star, 80 rooms, singles US$23, doubles US$33-40, western and Korean restaurants, game room, sauna

Hotel Tong Yang
27 1-ka Kwangbok-dong, Pusan (tel 22 1205/7), 3-star, 64 rooms, singles US$23.50, doubles US$32-39, Korean and western restaurants, bars, game room

Tourist Hotel UN
335-5 Amnam-dong, So-ku, Pusan (tel 26 5181/4), 3-star, 50 rooms, singles US$18, doubles US$27-36, Korean, western and Japanese restaurants, night club, bar

Busan Tower Hotel
20 3-ka Tongkwang-dong, Chung-ku, Pusan (tel 23 5151/9), 3-star, 108 rooms, no singles, doubles US$26-30, western and Korean restaurants, night club, bar, game room

Tongnae Hotel
212 Onchon-dong, Tongrae-ku, Pusan (tel 53 1121/5), 3-star, 64 rooms, no singles, doubles US$20-24, western and Korean restaurants, night club, bar, game room

Paradise Beach Hotel
1408-5 Chung-dong, Haeundae-ku, Pusan (tel 72 1461/8), 2-star at Haeundae Beach, 50 rooms, no singles, doubles US$24-38, Korean, western, Japanese and Chinese restaurants, casino, night club, bar, tennis court, game room

Places to Stay – bottom end

The cheapest are the yogwans and yoinsooks near the Express Bus Terminal. A good one is *Yongung Yoinsook* 용궁 여인숙, which is an excellent little place tucked away down an alley. It's quiet, has clean rooms and communal bathrooms with a friendly *ajimah.* Rooms are W3000/3600 for single/double. The scruffier *Lagwon Yoinsook* 락원 여인숙 is opposite. If you want a bathroom try the *Kyongdong Yogwan* 경동 여관 which is a modern, very clean place with rooms for W7000 a double though you may initially be asked for W8000.

Most of the cheap yogwans and yoinsooks in the downtown area near the ferry terminals are located around the Ferry and Bando Hotels. There are plenty to choose from and the one you stay at will probably be decided by whether you want your own bathroom or not. An average place without own bathroom will cost W6000-7000 and one with a bath W8000-9000. There are also a number of very basic yoinsooks which cost around W3000-4000 but they're definitely very basic. One yogwan which can be mildly recommended is the *Chong Hwa-Jang Yogwan* 정화장 which costs W8000 a double with own bathroom. It's quiet and very clean but otherwise probably no better than many others in the same price range.

Places to Eat

The number of places to eat cheaply around the bus terminal area is limited. The small Chinese cafe round the corner from the Yongung Yoinsook does reasonable 'om rice' and 'kimpa' and you can eat well for around W1000-1500. Nearby is a fried chicken cafe which offers good but greasy pieces of chicken (W600 per piece) with shredded cabbage and ketchup if that takes your fancy.

A much better selection of cafes can be found in the downtown area though, naturally, prices are higher there. One exception is a small fish restaurant housed in a shack half-way up the steps which lead to the south side of the Pusan Tower from the main street below (these steps take a tortuous route over the roofs of the buildings which cling to the side of the hill and they go past a billiard hall). A whole side of fried fish here cost W1000 with kimchi. A really good place to eat is the Japanese-style restaurant called *Hae Chun Jip* 해춘집 just down the street from the Bando Hotel. You can't miss the place with its external and internal pine-timbered decor. Here you can get excellently cooked food at very reasonable prices (W1500-2000). It's very popular at lunch times with office workers.

Top: Muyol group of Silla Royal Tombs, Gyeongju
Left: Pavilion on Buso-san in Buyeo the former capital city of the Paekje Kingdom
Right: Temple eaves, Pulguk-sa Temple, Gyeongju

Top: Sorak-san National Park
Left: Jeong-Bang Waterfall, Sogwipo, Cheju-do 'falls directly into the sea'
Right: Songsanilchubong Volcano, Cheju-do

Getting There

Buses

The following buses are available from the Express Bus Terminal:

To Kwangju 광주 Every 20 minutes from 6 am to 6.30 pm. The fare is W3670 and the journey takes 4¼ hours.
To Kyongju 경주 Every 30 minutes from 7 am to 7.30 pm. The fare is W1100 and the journey takes one hour.
To Seoul 서울 Every 10 minutes from 6 am to 6.30 pm. The fare is W5680 and the journey takes 5½ hours.
To Taegu 대구 Every 10 minutes from 6 am to 9 pm. The fare is W1880 and the journey takes nearly two hours.
To Taejon 대전 Every 50 minutes from 6 am to 6.30 pm. The fare is W3830 and the journey takes 3½ hours.
To Yeosu 여수 Every 50 minutes from 6 am to 6.10 pm. The fare is W3110 and the journey takes 3¾ hours.

Boats

Pusan-Shimonoseki (Japan)

The ferry between Pusan and Shimonoseki is the cheapest way of getting between the two countries but not by a great margin (the cheapest flight available is Pusan-Fukuoka which operates daily and costs about US$52 which is only US$12 more than the cheapest passage available on the ferry). The ferry departs daily except on Saturdays at 5 pm from both Pusan and Shimonoseki and arrives the next day at 8.30 am. In Pusan the ferry leaves from the International Ferry Terminal. The fares are W51,300 (US$63) (1st class A); W44,900 (US$55) (1st Class B); W37,700 (US$46) (2nd Class A); W30,600 (US$37) (2nd Class B and C). If you have a student card then you're entitled to a discount of 20% in 2nd Class bringing the fare to W25,000 (US$30). There is a departure tax of W1000 to pay in addition to the fare. If it's the Japanese boat you are going to be taking then make sure you spend the last of your Korean won (eg in the duty-free shop) before boarding as they don't accept won on the boat for anything.

Pusan-Yeosu via Hallyo Waterway

The journey between Pusan and Yeosu via the Hallyo Waterway National Park on the *Angel* hydrofoil is a popular trip in this part of Korea. The ferry is operated by the Hanryeo Development Co Ltd. There's usually no need to book in advance but if you want to know if there's room before you go down to the dock then ring 44 3851/3 (English is spoken). The schedule is as follows:

Pusan	Seongpo	Chungmu	Samcheonpo	Namhae	Yeosu
09.10	10.30	10.55	11.40	12.05	12.35
14.00	15.20	15.45	16.30	16.55	17.25
07.15	08.35	08.50			
11.20	12.40	12.55			
16.10	17.30	17.45			

The fares are as follows:

Pusan					
W4590	**Seongpo**				
W5830	1300	**Chungmu**			
W8330	4140	2890	**Samcheonpo**		
W9250	5240	4270	1450	**Namhae**	
W11,630	7670	6370	3430	1910	**Yeosu**

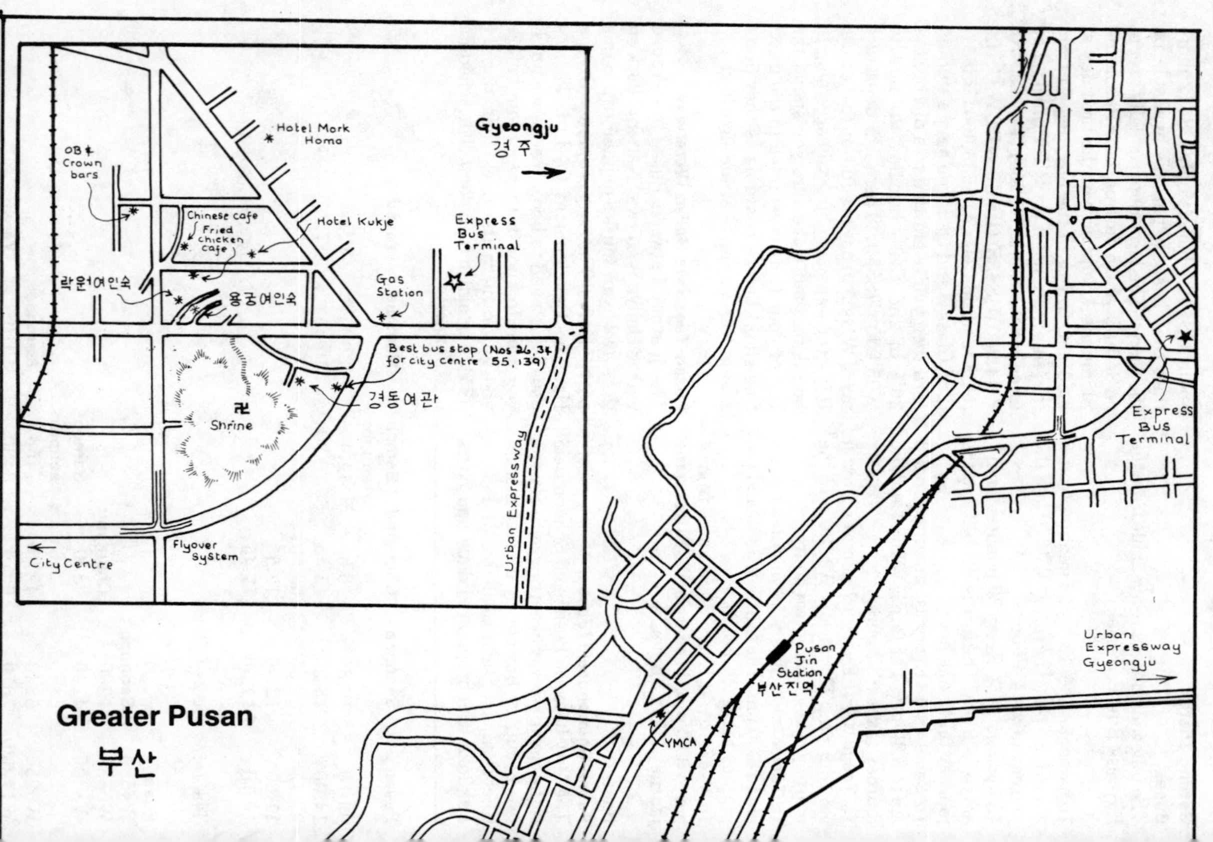
Greater Pusan
부산
Gyeongju
경주
Hotel Mork Homa
OB + Crown bars
Chinese cafe
Fried chicken cafe
Hotel Kukje
Express Bus Terminal
락운여인숙
용궁여인숙
Gas Station
Best bus stop (Nos 26, 34 for city centre 55, 139)
경동여관
Shrine
Urban Expressway
Flyover System
City Centre
Express Bus Terminal
Pusan Jin Station
부산진역
YMCA
Urban Expressway Gyeongju

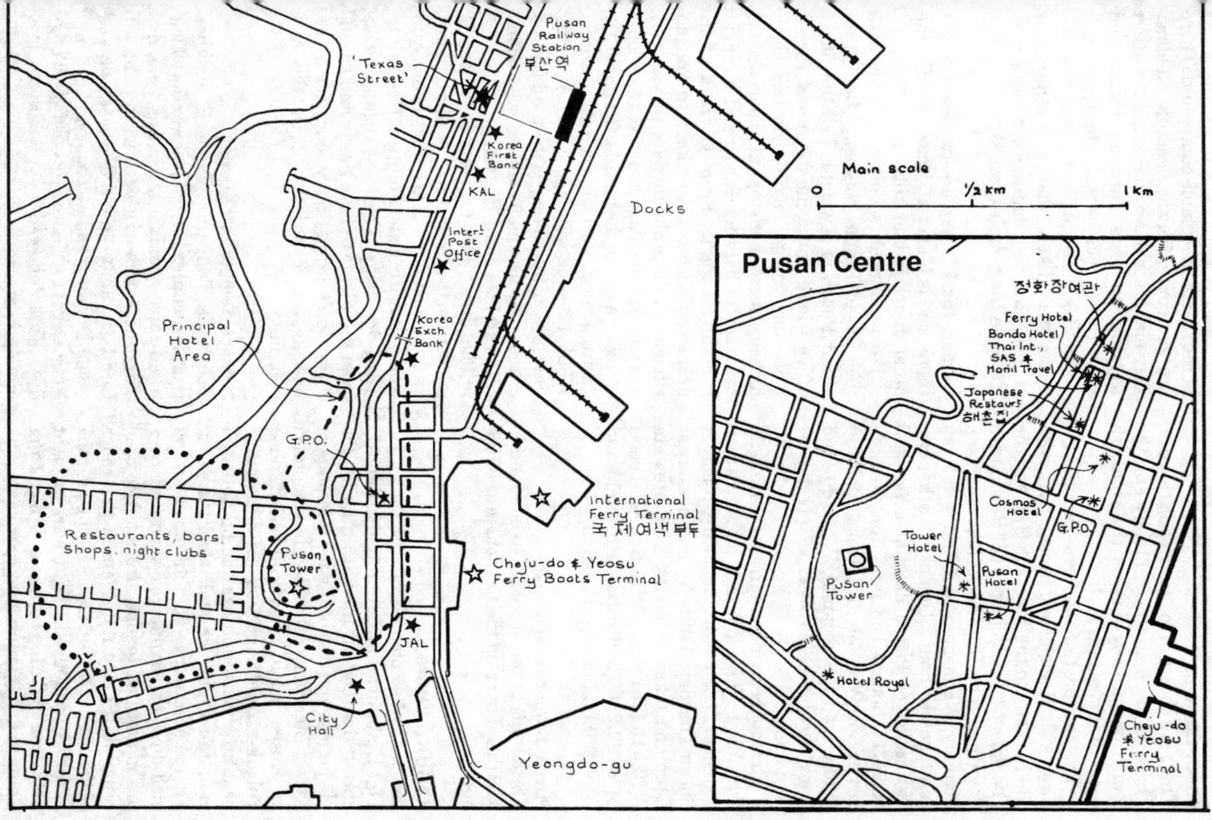
Pusan Railway Station
부산역
'Texas Street'
Korea First Bank
KAL
Inter! Post Office
Korea Exch. Bank
Principal Hotel Area
G.P.O.
Restaurants, bars, Shops, night clubs
Pusan Tower
JAL
City Hall
Docks
International Ferry Terminal
국제여객부두
Cheju-do & Yeosu Ferry Boats Terminal
Yeongdo-gu
Main scale
0
½ km
1 km
Pusan Centre
정화장여관
Ferry Hotel
Bando Hotel
Thai Int.,
SAS &
Hanil Travel
Japanese Restaurt
해촌집
Cosmos Hotel
G.P.O.
Tower Hotel
Pusan Hotel
Pusan Tower
Hotel Royal
Cheju-do & Yeosu Ferry Terminal

Pusan-Cheju-do

There is a choice of four ferries on this run. Three of these go to Cheju City and the fourth one to Sogwipo on the southern coast of the island.

The cheapest of the ferries are the *Do Ra-ji* 도라지 which connects Pusan with Cheju City and the *Yu Song* 유성 and the *Tonghae* 동해 which connect Pusan with Sogwipo. The *Do Ra-ji* leaves Pusan Monday, Wednesday and Friday at 7 pm and takes 13 hours. One of the other two ferries leaves Pusan daily at 6 pm and takes 14 hours. The fares for all three ferries are W6340 (3rd class), W9490 (2nd class without bunk), W14,200 (2nd class with bunk) and W21,270 (1st class with bunk).

The most expensive ferry is the *Hanguk Car Ferry Il-ho* 한국카훼리호 which connects Pusan with Cheju City. It leaves Pusan Tuesday, Thursday and Sunday at 7 pm and takes 10 hours. The fares are W10,340 (3rd class), W13,630 (2nd class B), W20,630 (2nd class with bunk) and W29,420 (1st class with bunk).

Pusan-Shimonoseki (Japan)

The details of this ferry are to be found in 'Getting There' in the first chapter of the book.

AROUND PUSAN

Tongdo-sa Temple 통도사

This Buddhist temple founded in 646 AD during the reign of the 27th Silla king is the largest and one of the most famous in Korea. Like many other Buddhist temples in Korea such as Popju-sa, Kap-sa, Pulguk-sa and Haein-sa it's situated in beautiful surroundings amid forested mountains and crystal clear streams. There are some 65 buildings in all including 13 hermitages scattered over the mountains behind the main temple complex. It's also at this temple that relics of the historical Buddha including his robe or *sarira* are housed. These were brought to Korea by Monk Jajang Yulsa from China in 645 AD and are kept in a pagoda at the rear of the temple compound. There are some exceptionally beautiful buildings here and it's well worth making the effort to stop off here between Pusan and Kyongju or vice versa. There are still about 200 monks in residence here so it's more than likely that a ceremony or chanting will be going on when you arrive. Entry to the temple costs W300.

Getting There There are two ways to get there: one is longer and more scenic, the other direct and no frills.

For the longer, scenic route, you take the Pusan-Taegu chikheng bus from either Pusan or Kyongju. Tell the ticket office where you want to go and they'll make sure you get on the right bus which makes a number of stops at places just off the freeway between Pusan and Kyongju including Tongdo. From where the bus drops you it's less than a km into Tongdo village. You'll probably have to walk this stretch. At the village you have the choice of taking a taxi to the temple. It's about 1½ km from the village) for which the charge is W800-1000 or walking. If you have the time it's worth walking as the road follows a beautiful mountain stream with many rock carvings along the way.

The direct bus to Tong-do village is taken from the Saemyun 삼면 bus terminal in Pusan (W620). This way means you won't have to walk from the freeway to Tong-do village. There are regular buses from the village to both Pusan and Ulsan. If you don't want to carry your pack to the temple you can leave it at the bus station.

Naewon Temple 내원사

South of Tong-do temple is another temple complex, that of Naewon-sa which has a setting similar to that of Tong-do. There is a nunnery here with some 50 Buddhist nuns and the priest, who is called Doryong, will welcome you anytime. You can get to Naewon by bus from Tong-do village followed by a walk along a mountain stream.

KYONGJU (GYEONGJU)

For almost a thousand years, Kyongju was the capital of the Silla Dynasty and for nearly 300 years of that period, following Silla's conquest of the neighbouring kingdoms of Koguryo and Paekje, the capital of the whole peninsula. It had its origins way back in 57 BC at a time when Julius Caesar was laying the foundations of the Roman Empire, and survived until the 10th century AD when it fell victim to division from within and invasion from without. A time span like that is rare for any dynasty anywhere in the world.

Following its conquest by the Koryo Dynasty (918-1392) when the capital of Korea was moved far to the north, Kyongju fell into a prolonged period of obscurity during which time it was pillaged and ransacked by the Mongols in the early 13th century and by the Japanese in the late 16th century. Yet, despite these ravages and the neglect of centuries, the city survived to experience a cultural revival which began early in this century and continues today. A great deal of restoration work has been accomplished, all of it to original specifications, and almost every year archaeologists uncover yet another treasure trove of precious relics which help throw more light on what life was like in this magnificent period of Korean history.

Today, only a small provincial town with friendly, easy-going people, Kyongju is literally an open-air museum. In whatever direction you care to walk you will come across tombs, temples, shrines, the remains of palaces, pleasure gardens, castles, Buddhist statuary and even an observatory. It's an incredible place! But these examples of Silla artistry down in the valley bottom are only the most conspicuous and accessible of the things which Kyongju has to offer. Up in the forested mountains which surround the city are thousands of Buddhist shrines, temples, inscriptions, rock carvings, pagodas and statues. You could spend weeks wandering around these places and never grow tired of it. Needless to say, the views from many of these places high up in the mountains are incomparable. This is definitely one of the most interesting places in the whole of North-East Asia.

Try to arrange to spend as much time as possible here but if you're time is limited then about four days is the minimum time necessary to see the principal sights in and around Kyongju. The only trouble with trying to see the place at this pace is that it will leave you breathless and saturated. The more leisurely pace which a week's stay would allow is far preferable and will give you the opportunity for at least a couple of trips up into the mountains. There is an entry fee to most of the sites (which goes towards maintenance, reconstruction and archaeological digs).

The main sites will be treated according to locality as this way you can avoid too much back-tracking.

Central Area

Right in the heart of Kyongju city is **Tumuli Park** a huge walled area containing the tombs of 20 of the Silla monarchs and members of their families. Many of them have been excavated in recent years to yield fabulous treasures which are not on display at the National Museum. One of the tombs, the Chonmachong (Heavenly Horse Tomb), is now open in cross-section to show the method of construction. This huge tomb, 13 metres high and 47 metres in diameter, built around the end of the 5th century AD, is the only one so far excavated which contained a wooden burial chamber. Facsimiles of the golden crown, bracelets, jade ornaments, weapons and pottery found here are displayed in glass cases around the inside of the tomb. Tumuli Park is open daily from 8.30 am to 6.30 pm (1st April-31st October) and 8.30 am to 5 pm (1st November-31st March). Entry costs W600 but if you're going to visit a lot of other sites then it's worth buying one of the composite tickets for entry to Tumuli Park and the others.

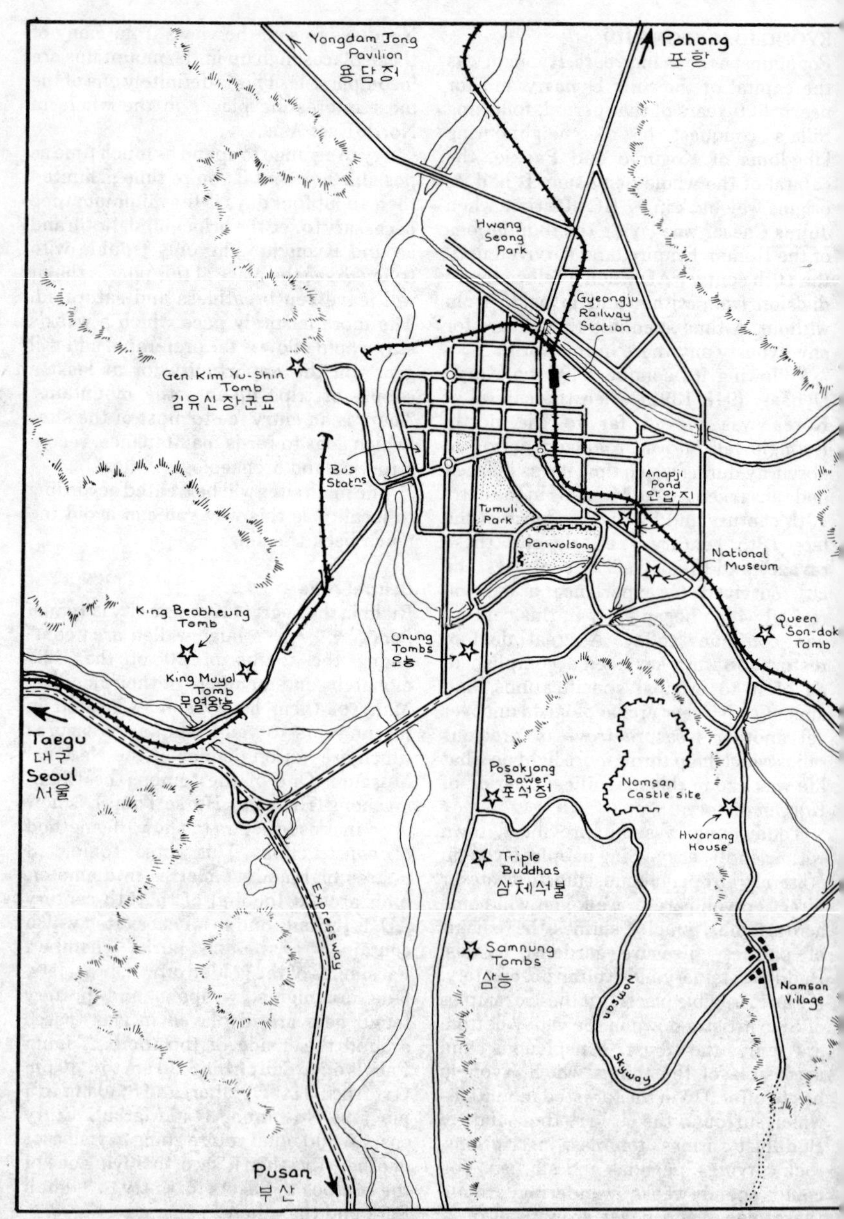

Yongdam Jong Pavilion
용담정
Pohang
포항
Hwang Seong Park
Gyeongju Railway Station
Gen Kim Yu-Shin Tomb
김유신장군묘
Bus Statns
Anapji Pond
안압지
Tumuli Park
Panwolsong
National Museum
King Beobheung Tomb
Onung Tombs
오능
Queen Son-dok Tomb
King Muyol Tomb
무열왕능
Taegu
대구
Seoul
서울
Posokjong Bower
포석정
Nomsan Castle site
Hwarang House
Triple Buddhas
삼체석불
Expressway
Samnung Tombs
삼능
Namsan Skyway
Namsan Village
Pusan
부산

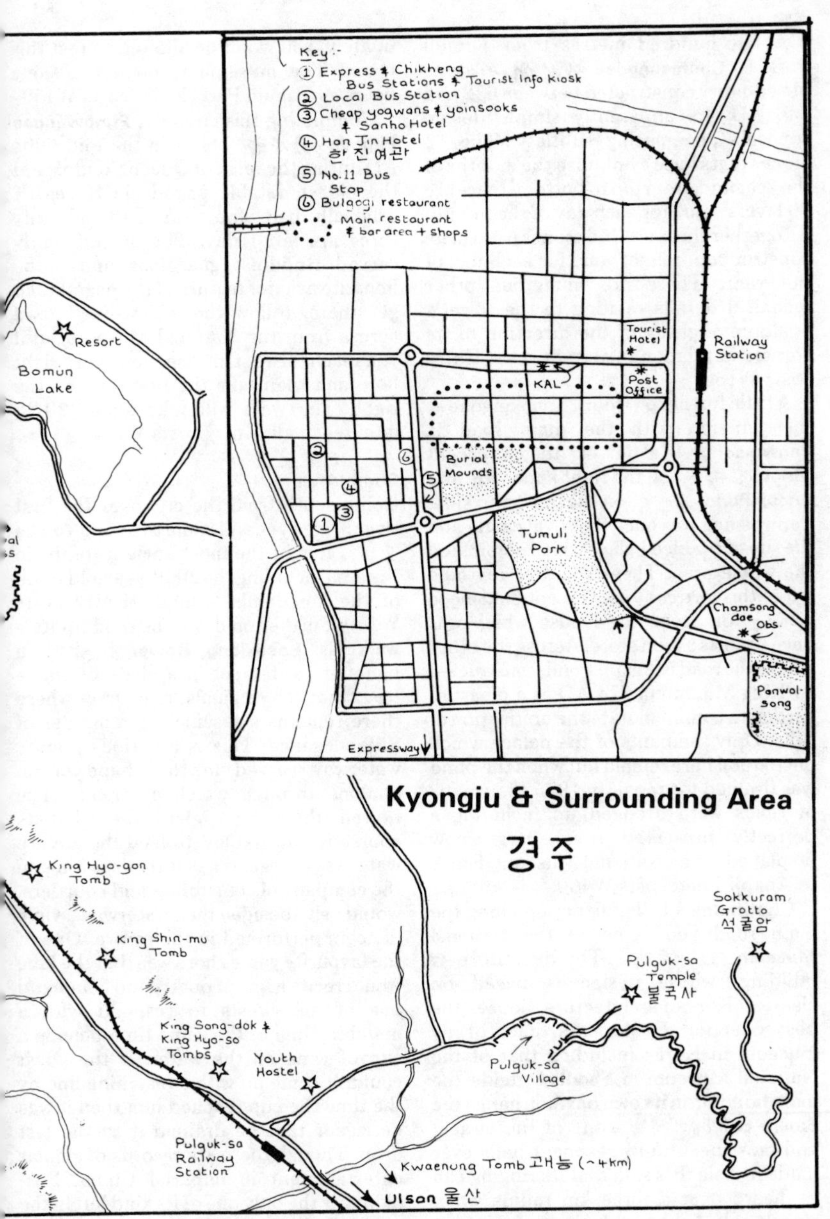
Key:-
① Express & Chikheng Bus Stations & Tourist Info Kiosk
② Local Bus Station
③ Cheap yogwans & yoinsooks & Sanho Hotel
④ Han Jin Hotel
한 진 여관
⑤ No. 11 Bus Stop
⑥ Bulgogi restaurant
Main restaurant & bar area + shops
Resort
Bomun Lake
Tourist Hotel
Railway Station
KAL
Post Office
Burial Mounds
Tumuli Park
Chamsong dae Obs.
Panwol-song
Expressway
Kyongju & Surrounding Area
경주
King Hyo-gon Tomb
King Shin-mu Tomb
King Song-dok & King Hyo-so Tombs
Youth Hostel
Pulguk-sa Railway Station
Sokkuram Grotto
석굴암
Pulguk-sa Temple
불국사
Pulguk-sa Village
Kwaenung Tomb 괘능 (~4km)
Ulsan 울산

A few hundred metres from Tumuli Park is **Chomsongdae** 첨성대 a stone observatory constructed between 632 and 646 AD. Its apparently simple design conceals an amazing subtlety. The 12 stones of its base symbolise the months of the year and, from top to bottom, there are 30 layers – one for each day of the month. Altogether there are 366 stones used in its construction, roughly one for each day of the year. There are numerous other technical details relating to the tower's position, angles and the direction of its corners in relation to certain stars. Entry costs W150.

A little further on from Chomsongdae at the junction with the main road is **Panwolsong** (Castle of the Crescent Moon) 반월성 on the right hand side and **Anapji Pond** 안압지 on the left-hand side. Panwolsong was once the royal castle and the site of a fabled palace which dominated the whole area. There's hardly anything left of this fortress today except **Sokbinggo** 석빙고 or Stone Ice House which was once used as a food store. Across the other side of the road is Anapji Pond, constructed by King Munmu in 674 AD as a pleasure garden to commemorate the unification of Silla. Only remnants of the palace which once stood here remain but when the pond was drained for repair in 1975 thousands of relics were dredged up including a perfectly preserved royal barge now displayed in the National Museum. Entry to Anapji Pond costs W400.

Continuing a little further up along the main road you come to the **National Museum** 경주 박물관 . This beautiful new building, whose design is based on classical Korean architecture, houses the best collection of historical artifacts of any museum in Korea including that of the National Museum in Seoul. Outside the main building in its own pavilion hangs the **Emille Bell** 에밀레종 one of the largest and most beautifully resonant bells ever made in Asia. It's said that its ringing can be heard over a three km radius when struck only lightly with the fist. Unfortunately, you won't be allowed to test this claim! The museum is open the same hours as Tumuli Park. Entry costs W150.

Completing this circuit is **Punhwangsa Pagoda** 분황사탑 built in the mid 600s AD during the reign of Queen Sondok and the oldest datable pagoda in Korea. It originally had nine storeys though only three are left today. The magnificently carved Buddhist guardians and stone lions are a major feature of the pagoda. To get there, follow the willow-lined road across from the National Museum until you reach the first intersection. Turn right here and then take the first lane on the right. The walk will take about 20-25 minutes in all. Entry costs W200.

South Area

Going south from the city over the first river bridge you will come to **Onung Tombs** 오능 , five of the most ancient tombs in the area including the 2000-year-old tomb of the kingdom's founder. Entry costs W150. Further on down the road (quite a walk) is **Posokjong Bower** 포석정 a banquet garden set in a glade of shade trees (not the originals, of course) where there remains a fascinating reminder of Silla elegance. This is a curious granite waterway carved in the shape of an abalone through which a stream once flowed (the stream is still there but its course is now too low to feed the granite waterway). Legend has it that the king, in the company of concubines and courtiers, would sit beside the waterway while dancers performed in the centre. One of the favourite games here was that the king would recite a line of poetry and command one of his guests to respond with a matching line at the same time placing a cup of wine on the water. If the guest couldn't come up with a matching line by the time the cup reached him then it was de rigeur that he drained it to the last drop. Though there are records of similar entertainment in imperial China, Posokjong is the only one of its kind left in the world. Entry costs W200.

Less than a km down the road from the Posokjong on the left-hand side are three mysterious statues known as the **Triple Buddhas** 삼체 석불 Discovered only in 1923, it's not known how they came to arrive here since they are not of Silla origin but display the massive boldness characteristic of the Koguryo style.

Last on this circuit, just a few minutes walk past the Triple Buddhas, are a group of four tombs known as the **Samnung Tombs** 삼능 . The one which stands separate from the rest is the burial place of King Kyongae, the second to the last Silla king, who was killed when a band of robbers raided Posokjong during an elaborate banquet. Nearly 1000 years separates these tombs from those in the Onung compund.

West Area

The two main points of interest west of the city are the **Muyol Tombs** 무열왕능 and the **Tomb of General Kim Yu Shin** 김유신 장군묘 . The main tomb of the Muyol group is that of King Muyol who, in the mid-7th century, paved the way for the unification of Korea by conquering the rival Paekje kingdom. Just as you enter the tomb compound there is an interesting monument to his exploits in the form of a tortoise carrying a capstone finely carved with inter-twined dragons symbolising the power of his position. Entry to the tombs costs W200.

Back towards town and along a branch road which initially follows the river is the tomb of General Kim Yu Shin, one of Korea's greatest military heroes who led the armies of both Muyol and his successor, Munmu, in the 7th-century campaigns which resulted in the unification of the country. Though smaller in scale than the tomb of King Muyol, the tomb of General Kim is much more elaborate and surrounded by finely-carved figures of the zodiac. The tomb stands on a wooded bluff overlooking the city. Entry costs W200.

South-East Area

Built on a series of stone terraces about 16 km from Kyongju is **Pulguk-sa Temple** 불국사 the crowning glory of Silla temple architecture and probably Korea's most famous temple. And it really is magnificent. Korea has never gone in for huge, monolithic (though magnificent) temples like the Potala Palace in Lhasa; instead it concentrates on the excellence of its carpentry, the incredible skill of its painters and the subtlety of its landscapers. Originally built in 528 AD during the reign of King Beobhoung and enlarged in 751, it survived intact until destroyed by the Japanese in 1593. From then until the recent past it languished in ruin and though a few structures were rebuilt it never regained its former glory until, in 1970, the late President, Park Chee Hung, ordered its reconstruction along the original lines. Work was completed in 1972.

Standing on the highest level and looking down you are presented with a rolling sea of tiles formed by one sloping roof after the next. The painting of the internal woodwork and of the eaves of the roofs must be one of the Seven Wonders of the World. Down in the courtyard of the first set of buildings are two pagodas which survived the Japanese vandalism and which stand in complete contrast to each other. The first, Tabotap pagoda, is of plain design and typical of Silla artistry while the other, Sokkatap pagoda, is much more ornate and typical of those constructed in the neighbouring Paekje kingdom. Copies of these two pagodas stand outside the main building of the Kyongju National Museum.

To get to Pulguk-sa from the city take bus No 11. The fare is W110. The bus goes via **Bomun Lake**, a resort area between Kyongju and Pulguk-sa designed for the well-heeled tourist, and ends up at Pulguk village just below the temple. Entry to the temple costs W600.

High up in the mountains above Pulguk-sa, reached by a long, winding sealed road is **Sokkuram Grotto** 석굴암 , the spiritual shoreline guardian of the Silla kingdom. A seated image of the Sakyamuni Buddha looks out over the spectacular landscape towards the distant East Sea. The grotto, dedicated in the 8th century, was constructed out of huge blocks of granite quarried far to the north at a time when the only access was a narrow mountain path. It must have involved a lot of heavy and dedicated work! Entry to the grotto costs W600.

To get to the grotto from Pulguk-sa, take one of the frequent minibuses which leave from the Tourist Information pavilion in the car park below the temple. The return fare is W750. The minibuses terminate at a car park and from there it's a 400 metre walk along a shaded gravel track to the grotto. You get about 45 minutes to visit the grotto before the buses return.

Both Pulguk-sa and Sokkuram Grotto literally crawl with tourists everyday of the week during the summer months and the place can take on the air of a mass picnic so be prepared for this.

Several km further off to the south-east along the main road is **Kwaenung Tomb** 괘능 , worth visiting for its unusual carved figures which line the approach to the tomb – military guards, civil officials, lions and monkeys. The military figures are quite unlike any others in the Kyongju area with their wavy hair, heavy beards and prominent noses. It's said they may represent the Persian mercenaries who are known to have served the court of Silla. The tomb itself is decorated with carved reliefs of the 12 animals of the zodiac. This tomb compound is rarely visited. Entry costs W200.

To get to Kwaenung from Pulguk-sa take bus No 11 which will take you down the road past the *Kyongju Youth Hostel* to the junction with the main road where Pulguk railway station is situated. Change here for a bus going along the main road and tell the driver where you are heading. It's usually four or five stops from here depending on who wants to get off or on. The fare is W110. Where you get off there is a billboard at the side of the road with an illustration of Kwaenung Tomb on it. Take the tarmac road on the left hand side and follow it for about one km. It takes you direct to the tomb. There are frequent buses back into Kyongju from the main road which go via the National Museum and the railway station – Nos 15 and 35 are two which cover this route. The fare is W130.

KYONGJU EXCURSIONS

There are literally thousands of other relics of the Silla kingdom scattered over the mountains all the way from Kyongju to Pohang on the eastern seaboard, to Taegu in the west and to Pusan in the south. An exhaustive description of them is impossible in a book this size so if you're going to spend a lot of time here it's worth getting hold of a copy of *Kyongju Guide – Cultural Spirit of Silla in Korea* by Edward B Adams, published by the Korea National Tourism Corporation (1979). This is a beautifully illustrated guide to all known Silla sites written by a man who lives in Korea and has spent years exploring the mountains and valleys around the city. It also contains many detailed and invaluable maps.

Probably one of the most rewarding areas to explore within easy reach of Kyongju is Namsan Mountain, south of the city. Not only is it worth hiking around this area purely for its scenic beauty but the mountain is strewn with royal tombs, pagodas, rock-cut figures, pavilions and the remains of fortresses, temples and palaces. There are hundreds of paths which you can follow alongside the streams which come tumbling down the mountain as well as the 'Namsan Skyway' – a winding gravel road which starts out close to Posokjong Bower, skirts the ridges of Namsan and ends up at Namsan Village near Unification Hall. The paths and tracks are all well-trodden and you cannot get lost though here and there you will need to scout around for relics which are not immediately visible since few of them are signposted. Whichever point you decide to take off from you're in for an exhilarating experience.

If your time is limited then two suggested day-long trips are:

(1) Take local bus No 23 from the local bus terminal and get off at Posokjong Bower on the west side of Namsan (or at the Samnung Tombs if you've already visited Posokjong). From Posokjong walk to the Samnung Tombs (about one km) via the Sambul-sa triad. From the Samnung Tombs take the track which follows the stream up the side of Namsan to the crest of the mountain. On the way up there you will pass many free-standing and rock-cut images and a small hermitage near the summit where an old bearded monk lives. Follow the trail along the saddle until it joins the Namsan Skyway – the views from the saddle are incredible!

Carry on along the Skyway towards Namsan village for about half a km until the road makes a sharp turn to the left. A detour straight on from this point will bring you to two pagodas. Neither of these are visible from the road and the trail leading to them is somewhat indistinct. Also, the pagoda furthest from the road is not visible until you are just past the first so it's easy to miss. From here, backtrack to the Skyway and continue on down to Namsan village where you should visit the twin pagodas and **Sochul-ji Pavilion and Pond**. The latter is an idyllic little spot described in legends going back to the early days of Silla. If you've had enough for one day at this point you can catch local bus No 11 back to Kyongju from Unification Hall. If not, you could carry on past Namsan village to the seven Buddha reliefs of **Chilbul-am**. From there you would have to return to Namsan village and take a bus back to Kyongju.

(2) Take local bus No 11 and get off as soon as the bus crosses the river about 2½ km past the National Museum. From here you can visit **Pori-sa Temple** in the Miruk valley – a beautifully reconstructed nunnery set amidst old conifer trees with a number of ancient free-standing images. It is possible to make your way over the hill at the back of this temple to **Pagoda Valley** but it's a rough climb. It's perhaps easier if you don't have the right footwear to backtrack down to the bridge over the river and turn left there. Take the track along the west side of the river for several hundred metres until you come to a small village. Turn left here and head up Pagoda Valley. The first place you come to here is **Okryong-sa Temple**. Just beyond it you will find the greatest collection of relief carvings anywhere in Korea as well as a pagoda.

Returning to the river bridge and looking across to the main road to Ulsan you will see two stone pillars standing in a copse of trees in the middle of paddy fields. These pillars are all that remain standing of what was once a huge temple complex during Silla times. If you like fossicking for ancient reliefs then this is the spot to do it. If that doesn't particularly interest you then head off down to Namsan village and take any of the trail which lead up to the mountains.

About one hour from Kyongju by local bus is **Daebon Beach**, a very pleasant spot known to Koreans but almost unheard of by others. Nearby is the underwater mausoleum of the Silla king, Mungmu, who had himself cremated when he died and his ashes buried among a group of rocks in the sea in the hope that he would become a dragon and so be able to protect the eastern seaboard of Korea. There are yogwans and yoinsooks on the beach where you can stay the night (average price around W5000 a single or double) but camping may be prohibited (there are sometimes scares about North Korean spy boats in the area). There's only one restaurant. It's run by a Mr Kim who not only serves excellent fish but other seafood as well. He speaks English too.

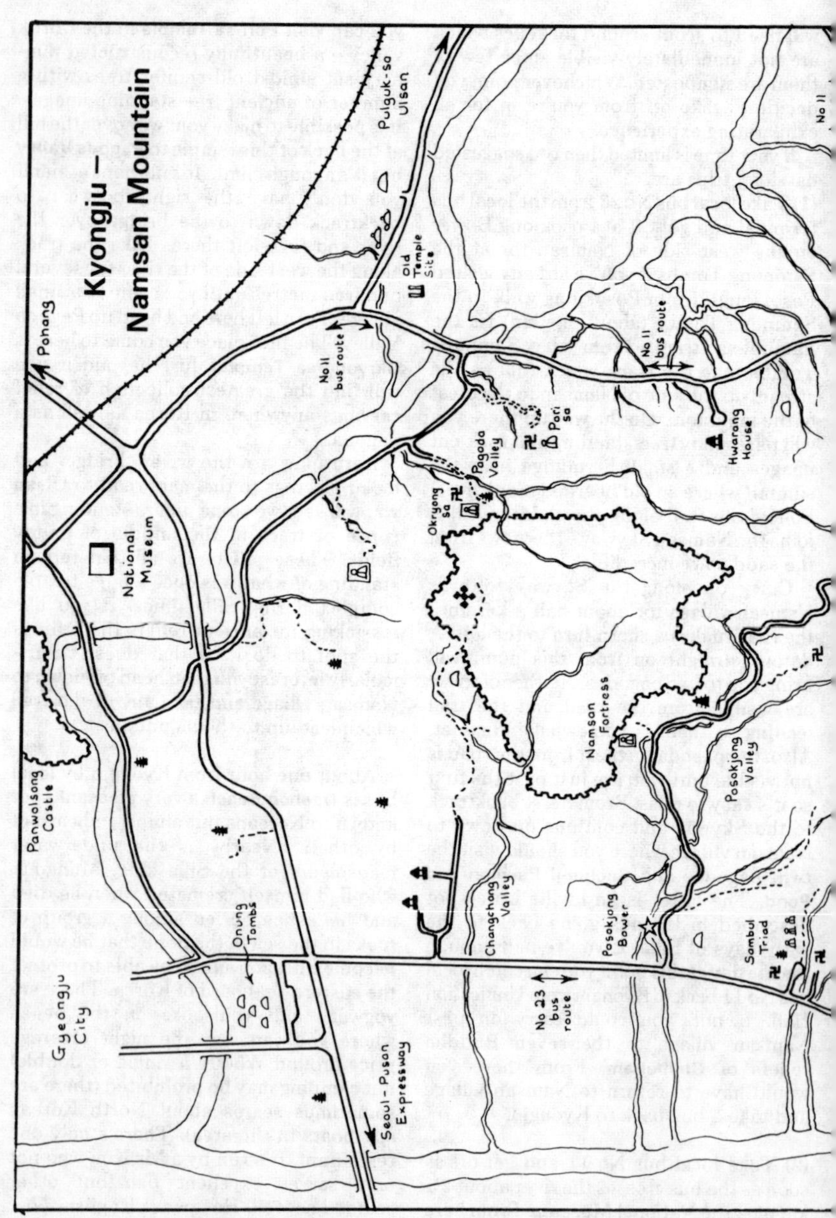
Kyongju – Namsan Mountain
Pohang
Pulguk-sa Ulsan
Old Temple Site
No 11 bus route
No 11 bus route
No 11
Pori sa
Pagoda Valley
Hwarang House
Okryong sa
National Museum
Panwolsong Castle
Namsan Fortress
Posokjong Valley
Changchang Valley
Onung Tombs
Gyeongju City
Seoul-Pusan Expressway
No 23 bus route
Posokjong Bower
Sambul Triad

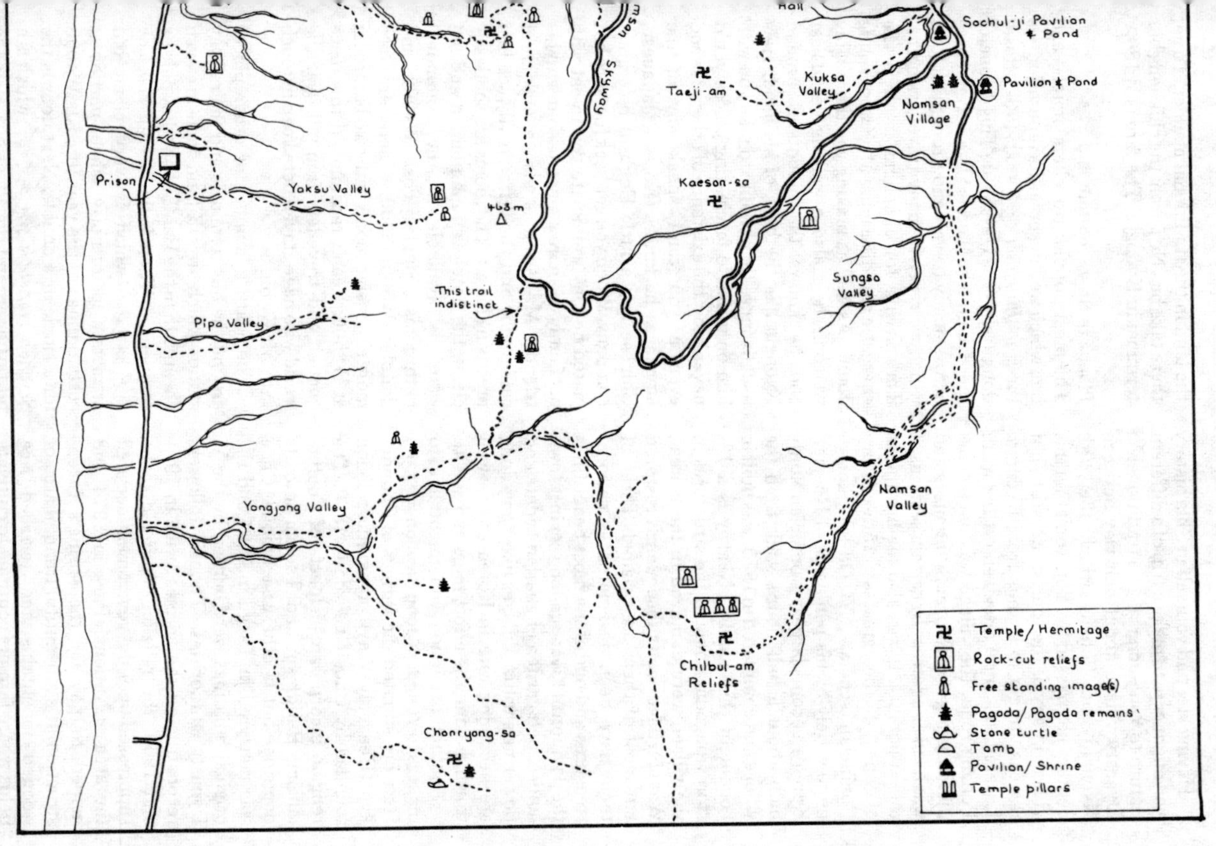
Sochul-ji Pavilion & Pond
Pavilion & Pond
Namsan Village
Kuksa Valley
Taeji-am
Skyway
Kaeson-sa
Sungso Valley
Namsan Valley
Prison
Yaksu Valley
463 m
This trail indistinct
Pipa Valley
Yongjang Valley
Chilbul-am Reliefs
Chonryong-sa
Temple / Hermitage
Rock-cut reliefs
Free standing image(s)
Pagoda / Pagoda remains
Stone turtle
Tomb
Pavilion / Shrine
Temple pillars

Having steeped yourself in Silla history you might care to make a trip of a different nature to **Yang-dong** 양동 a traditional Yi Dynasty village about half way between Kyongju and Pohang which the 20th century has passed by. You won't find this village in any of the tourist literature but it's easy to get to by bus from Kyongju. Located in a rural area well off the main Pohang road, the village was once considerably larger with over 300 houses and was used as a retreat by certain sections of the Yi nobility. It was also the birthplace of one of the greatest 15th-century Confucian scholars, Yi On-jok (known more widely by his pen name of Hoejae). Korea's second largest Confucian study hall, about a half hour's walk from the village and completed in 1575, was built in honour of this scholar. Nearby is a 13-storey pagoda. Some of the structures in the village were damaged in the Korean War and have been subsequently restored but most of them are original. Three of them have been designated as national treasures and one of the most beautiful is the pavilion of **Kwangga-jong** set in its own landscaped garden of gnarled cedars and flowering shrubs. Villages like Yang-dong are becoming rare in Korea so it's well worth making the effort to go and see it.

Another excursion you might like to make is to **Yongdam Jong Pavilion** 용담정 . Here are situated the shrines of Chundo-kyo (Heavenly Way), a unique religion founded by Choe Che-woo in 1860. The religion incorporates aspects of Confucianism, Buddhism and Taoism into its doctrines but is otherwise unique. Choe was martyred in Taegu in 1864 and the original buildings were burned by the Yi Dynasty authorities. Though followers reconstructed the shrines twice in 1914 and 1960, the religion continued to be suppressed until the government declared the area a National Park in 1974 and helped to pay for the shrine's reconstruction. It's a beautiful tranquil area of wooded mountains and terraced rice fields where farmers continue to cultivate the land in the traditional manner. To get there take bus No 5 from the chikheng bus terminal in Kyongju. The fare is W180.

Places to Stay – bottom end

The most popular travellers' hotel – and one which well deserves its reputation – is the *Han Jin Hotel* 한진 여관 173-1 Rose-dong (tel 2-4097/2-9679). This is one of the friendliest hotels I've ever come across on my travels and, from the letters which we receive, many travellers agree. The driving force behind it all is the energetic and disarming Mr Kwon Young Joung. As well as making you thoroughly welcome he's also a walking enthusiast and he knows the mountains around Kyongju like the back of his hand. He's usually more than willing to take you with him on walks to fascinating places you'd never know the existence of otherwise and even if you can't speak any of the languages he knows (Korean, Japanese, Chinese and a little English) he's great company. When you get back footsore but elated he may well invite you to eat with his family or share a ginseng soju with his friends. Mr Kwon is also a master of calligraphy and you'll frequently see him practising his art. The rooms are spotlessly clean, the hotel well-maintained and hot water is available in the communal bathrooms. Singles cost W4000 and doubles W5000-6000. There are also more expensive rooms with own bathroom at W8500. I can't recommend this place enough and travellers from all over the world who have stayed here keep in touch with Mr Kwon.

There are a number of other places around the bus terminals and the railway station which are OK (and some are even cheaper than the Han Jin) but they pale by comparison. There is the *Chon-il Yoinsook* 전일 여인숙 which is very clean but attracts a lot of noisy school parties at certain times of the year. It costs W4000 for a single or a double. Next door is the *So-chon Yoinsook* 서천 여인숙 which is a bit tattier around the edges but costs the same. On the same street you might like to try the *Sanho Hotel* 산호여관 which is really a mid-range hotel and has rooms with their own bathrooms for W10,500. It's just opposite the express bus terminal.

Outside of Kyongju between Pulguk-sa Temple and the main road to Ulsan is the *Kyongju Youth Hostel*, 145-1 Kujong-dong, Kyongju (tel 2-9991/6). This is a huge building with room for 600 guests and although you can get a dormitory bed here for W3050 the double rooms are quite pricey at US$30. The bathrooms have hot and cold running water and there is a restaurant and coffee shop on the premises. They also have money changing facilities. To get there from Kyongju take bus No 11 which goes right past the front entrance.

Places to Eat

There are many cafes and restaurants between the bus stations and the railway station with a choice of Korean, Chinese, Japanese and western food but few of them stand out as being exceptional either for the quality of food or the price except perhaps for the 'bulgogi' restaurant round the corner from the bus stations (marked on the map). Two people can eat here for W3600. It's not cheap but the food is very good. Since Kyongju is a town geared to catering for tourists you may find that many restaurants are on the expensive side so you'll probably find yourself eating at a place which suits your pocket rather than one which fulfils your quest for good food. There's definitely scope for an enterprising person who could cater for budget travellers.

Getting There

There are three bus stations in Kyongju. The first one nearest the expressway link road is the express bus terminal. Next to that is the chikheng bus terminal and after that the local bus terminal. There is, however, some overlap since the stopping bus to Pusan which calls at Tongdo-sa uses the express bus terminal.

There are the following buses from the express bus terminal:

To Kangnung 강릉 Every hour from 5.50 am to 1 pm. The fare is W4350 and the journey takes 5¾ hours.

To Kim Hae Airport (Pusan International Airport) The buses from Kyongju to Kim Hae Airport leave from Bomun Lake where the top end hotels are situated. There are five buses a day between 9.40 am and 2.30 pm.

To Pohang 포항 Every five minutes from 5.50 am to 11 pm. The fare is W480 and the journey takes 40 minutes.

To Pusan 부산 There are buses every 10 minutes from 6.20 am to 9.20 pm. The fare is W1200 and the journey takes about 1¼ hours.

To Seoul 서울 There are 19 buses a day from 7 am to 6.10 pm. The fare is W4840 and the journey takes about 4½ hours.

To Taegu 대구 Every six minutes from 5.50 am to 10.40 pm. The fare is W920 and the journey takes 50 minutes.

From this terminal you can also catch buses which will take you to **Tongdo-sa Temple** half way between Kyongju and Pusan. For this you need the chikheng bus rather than the kosok bus (which doesn't stop). There are some 28 buses daily and the fare to Tongdo-sa is W500.

TAEGU 대구

Taegu, although the third largest city in South Korea, is usually just an overnight stop for travellers. Most travellers use it as a convenient place from which to visit one of the country's most famous temples and one of its largest monasteries – **Haein-sa Temple** 해인사.

The temple is some considerable distance from Taegu high up on the steep, forested slopes of **Mt Gaya National Park** and is the repository of the **Tripitaka Koreana** – more than 80,000 carved wood blocks on which are the complete Buddhist scriptures as well as many illustrations remarkably similar to those you're likely to encounter

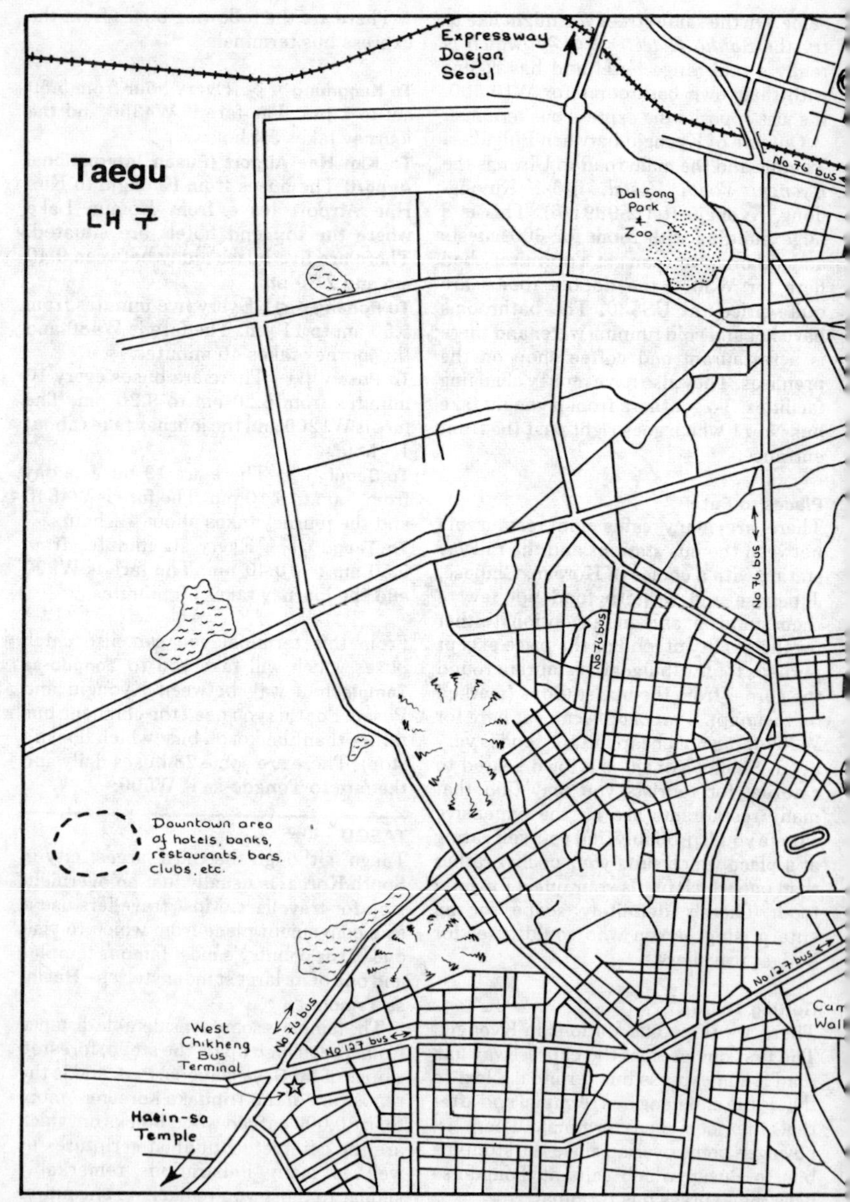

Taegu
CH 7
Expressway
Daejon
Seoul
Dal Song
Park
&
Zoo
No 76 bus
No 76 bus
No 76 bus
No 127 bus
No 127 bus
No 76 bus
Downtown area
of hotels, banks,
restaurants, bars,
clubs, etc.
West
Chikheng
Bus
Terminal
Haein-sa
Temple

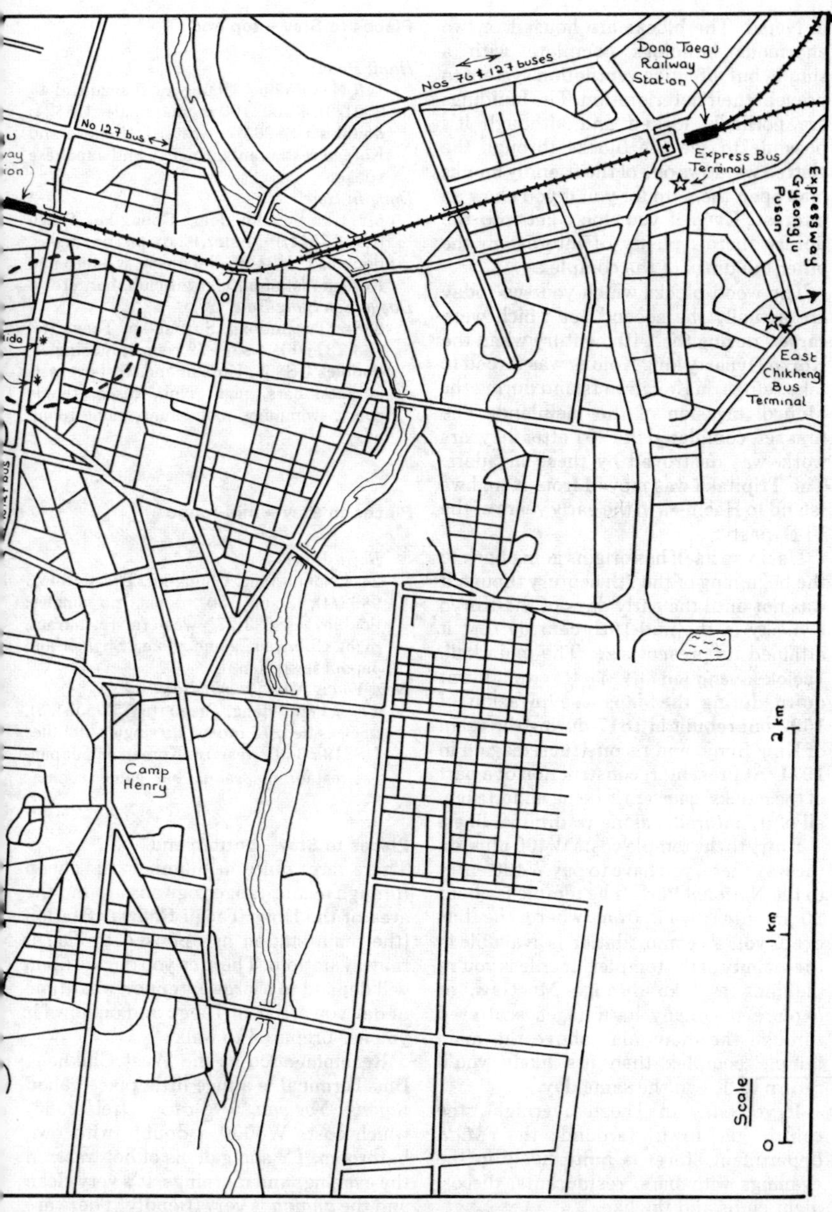
Dong Taegu
Railway
Station
Nos 76 & 127 buses
No 127 bus
Express Bus
Terminal
Expressway
Gyeongju
Pusan
East
Chikheng
Bus
Terminal
Camp
Henry
2 km
1 km
0
Scale

in Nepal. The blocks are housed in two enormous buildings complete with a simple but effective ventilation system to prevent their deterioration. The buildings are normally locked and although it's possible to see the blocks through the slatted windows one of the friendly monks may open them up for you if you show an interest. Even if you don't get into the library there's plenty of interest in the other buildings of the complex.

The wood blocks which you see today are actually the second set which were carved during the 14th century when the Koryo Dynasty king Kojong was forced to take refuge on Kanghwa Island during the Mongol invasion of the mainland. The first set, completed in 1251 after 20 years work, was destroyed by these invaders. The Tripitaka was moved from Kanghwa Island to Haein-sa in the early years of the Yi Dynasty.

Haein-sa itself has origins going back to the beginning of the 9th century though it was not until the early days of the Koryo Dynasty in the mid-10th centruy that it attained its present size. The main hall, **Taejok-kwang-jon** 대적광전 was burnt down during the Japanese invasion of 1592 but rebuilt in 1817 during the reign of King Sunjo and reconstructed again in 1971. At present, reconstruction of a part of the monks' qaurters is being undertaken, all of it, naturally, along traditional lines.

Entry to the temple costs W400 plus, on the way there, you have to pay W400 entry to the National Park. The temple is about 20 minutes' walk from where the bus drops you. Accommodation is available in the vicinity of the temple but unless you're planning to hike through Mt Gaya or explore the many hermitages scattered through the mountains above the main temple complex then it's likely you'll return to Taegu the same day.

If you stay in Taegu overnight, the centre of town (around the *Mida* department store) is quite lively in the evenings with bars, restaurants, discos, night clubs and the like.

Places to Stay – top end

Hanil Hotel
110 Namil-dong, Chung-ku, Taegu (tel 45 2301/9), 4-star, 100 rooms, singles US$24, doubles US$26-37, western, Chinese and Korean restaurants, English and Japanese spoken

Dong In Hotel
5-2 1-ka Samdok-dong, Chung-ku, Taegu (tel 46 7211/9), 4-star, 92 rooms, no singles, doubles US$34-35, Japanese, western and Korean restaurants, night club, bar, etc

Daegu Soo Sung Hotel
888-2 Tusan-dong, Susong-ku, Taegu (tel 763-7311/6), 4-star, 72 rooms, no singles, doubles US$36, Korean and western restaurants, bars, night club, disco, tennis court, swimming pool, sauna, game room, etc

Places to Stay – mid-range

Royal Hotel
24-4 Namil-dong, Chung-ku, Taegu (tel 23 9862/4), 2-star, 50 rooms, no singles, doubles US$23-27, western restaurant, night club, bar, game room. English and Japanese spoken.

New-Young Nam Tourist Hotel
177-7 Pomo-dong, Taegu (tel 752 5551/5), unclassified, 73 rooms, no singles, doubles US$19.50-30, western, Korean and Japanese restaurants, sauna, bar, games room.

Places to Stay – bottom end

There are quite a number of cheap through to mid-range yogwans around the area of the Dong Taegu Railway Station (the main station as opposed to Taegu railway station). The area you decide upon will depend to a large extent on what time of day you arrive in Taegu and on how far you are prepared to walk.

Recommended at the West Chikheng Bus Terminal is a nice little place called *Sujong Yogwan* 수정여관 (tel 2386) which costs W8000 a double with own bathroom, TV and gallons of hot water in the evenings and mornings. It's very clean and the *ajimah* is very friendly. There are cheaper places available if this is too expensive.

There are plenty of cheap restaurants around this bus terminal with a choice of Chinese, Korean and unadulterated seafood restaurants.

Getting There
Taegu station 대구역 in the centre of town is for local trains only and of little interest to travellers. Express trains from other major centres of population stop at Dong Taegu station 동대구역 on the east side of the city close to the Express Bus Terminal and the East Chikheng Bus Terminal.

There are five bus terminals altogether in Taegu – the Express Bus Terminal, the East Chikheng Bus Terminal 동부정류장, the West Chikheng Bus Terminal 서부정류장, the South Chikheng Bus Terminal 남부정류장 and the North Chikheng Bus Terminal 북부정류장. Only the first three will be of interest to travellers. Local buses which connect the East Chikheng Terminal with Dong Taegu station and the West Chikheng Terminal include Nos 126 and 127. Two other buses which you can use between the East and West Chikheng Terminals but which don't go past the railway station are Nos 33 and 120. In addition, No 76 connects Dong Taegu station with Taegu station and the West Chikheng terminal. Should you be anywhere else in the city and want to get to the West Chikheng Bus Terminal then bus Nos 1, 12, 31, 32, 35, 71, 75, 88, 89 and 101 will get you there.

The West Chikheng Bus Terminal is where the buses to Haein-sa Temple leave from. There are buses every 20 minutes from 6.30 am to 7 pm. The fare is W1050 and the journey takes 1½ hours. Buy your ticket at booth No 4. Don't forget that you will also have to pay W400 extra to enter the Mt Gaya National Park.

From the East Chikheng Bus Terminal there are also express buses to Kyongju every eight minutes from 5 am to 10 pm. The fare is W920 and the journey takes 50 minutes.

To Pusan 부산 Every hour from 6.30 am to 9 pm from the Express Bus Terminal. The fare is W1520 and the journey takes one hour and 20 minutes.

POHANG 포항
Pohang is a fairly small city but also an important industrial centre on the east coast about 45 minutes from Kyongju by bus. It's from here that the ferries leave for Ulleung-do, over 260 km north-east of Pohang about half way between Korea and Japan. (During the summer months there are also ferries from Imwon and Tonghae further up the east coast). There isn't much of interest in Pohang itself and for most travellers who come here it's just an overnight stop before taking the Ulleung-do ferry.

If the ferry is cancelled for a day or so and you'd like something to do then it's worth visiting **Po Kyong-sa Temple**, north of Pohang. It's a beautiful mountainous area with peculiarly shaped rocks and behind the temple there are 12 picturesque waterfalls.

Places to Stay – top end
The only western-style hotel in Pohang is the *Pohang Beach Hotel*, 311-2 Songdo-dong, Pohang (tel 3-1401/9) situated, as its name suggests, on the beach east of the city. There are no singles and doubles cost US$25-28. Western and Korean food is available and there is a night club, bar, game room and coffee shop.

Places to Stay – bottom end
There are plenty of yogwans and yoinsooks in the streets going back from the ferry terminal. Most of them cater for the overnight ferry trade and there's not a lot to choose between them. One of the better ones is the *Se Han-il Yogwan* 새한일여관 (tel 2-5877) right in front of the ferry terminal. This costs W7500 a double for the downstairs rooms and W8000 a

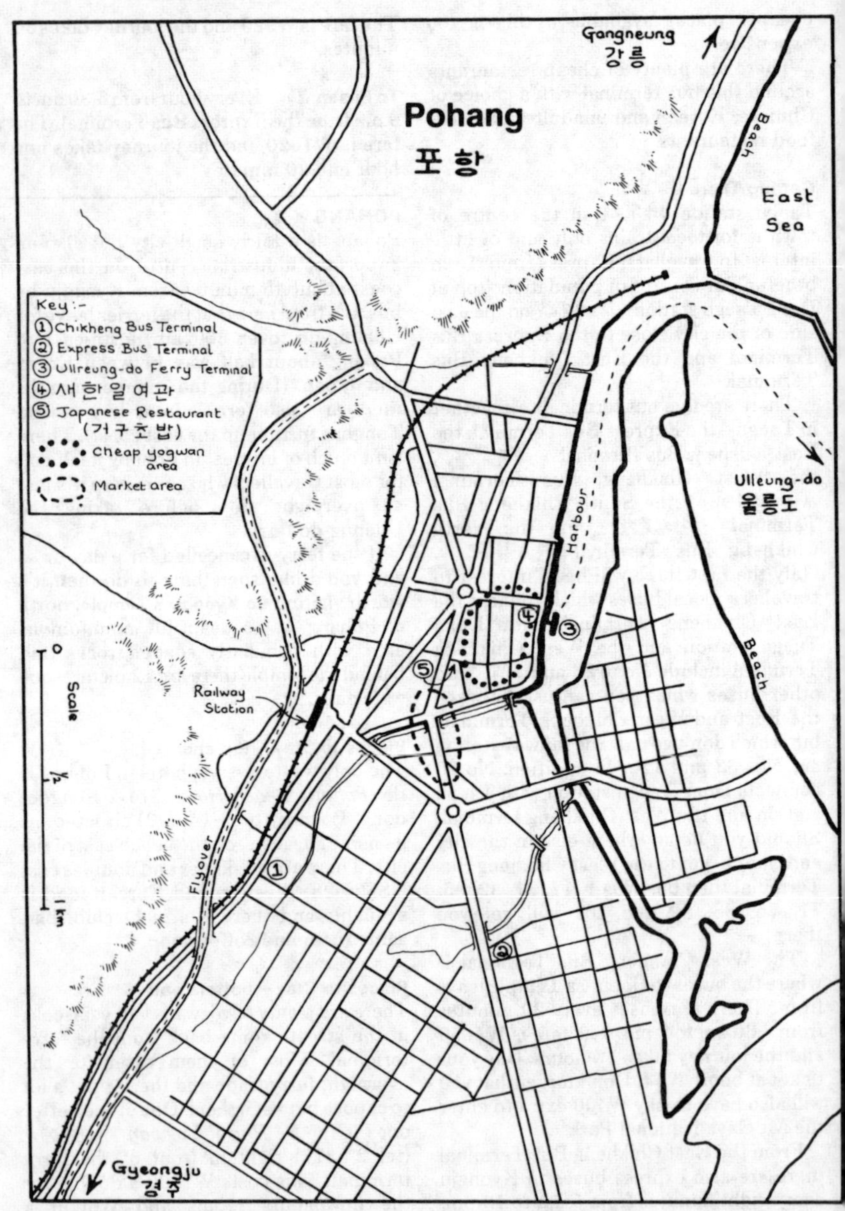
Pohang
포항
Gangneung
강릉
Beach
East
Sea
Key :-
① Chikheng Bus Terminal
② Express Bus Terminal
③ Ullreung-do Ferry Terminal
④ 새한일여관
⑤ Japanese Restaurant
(거구초밥)
Cheap yogwan area
Market area
Ulleung-do
울릉도
Harbour
Beach
Railway Station
Scale
0
½
1 km
Flyover
Gyeongju
경주

double for the upstairs rooms. All the rooms have their own bathrooms with hot water, TV and are very clean and pleasant.

Places to Eat

There are plenty of cheap restaurants in Pohang but the place which deserves a recommendation above all others is the Japanese sea-food restaurant *Gogu Chobap* 거구초밥 . Whatever you order here the food is excellent and it's surprisingly cheap. It's spotlessly clean and the owner is very friendly indeed. Two people can have fried or raw fish, soup, two different 'kimchis', pigeon eggs, dressed coleslaw, cockles, seaweed and rice for around W2000. If you prefer 'kimpa' the cost is the same.

Getting There

Ulleung-do Ferries

The *Hanil 3-ho* 한일호 leaves Pohang daily at 2.30 pm between May and August and every other day at 10 am between September and April. The fares are W11,240 (2nd class) and W12,700 (1st class) and the journey takes about 4½ hours. Second class is fine and the best one to travel in if you'd like an enjoyable time with local people.

Both this ferry and the ones which operate from Imwon and Tonghae during the summer months are often cancelled due to rough weather. If you want to check this out before you go to Pohang then ring 3-1808 which will put you through to the ferry terminal but you need to speak good Korean (or get a Korean friend to ring them) as no English is spoken there.

Buses

There are two bus terminals in Pohang, the Express Bus Terminal and the Chikheng Bus Terminal. The following buses go from the Express terminal:

To Pusan 부산 Every 15 minutes from 5.30 am to 8.30 pm. The fare is W1680 and the journey takes two hours.

To Kyongju 경주 There are several buses per hour from 5.30 am to 10 pm. The fare is W500 and the journey takes 40 minutes.

To Taegu 대구 Every 10 minutes from 5.30 am to 10 pm. The fare is W1400 and the journey takes one hour 50 minutes.

ULLEUNG-DO 울릉도

If you have a yen for remote, mysterious islands where you won't see another traveller (let alone a tourist) from one month to the next then this is it. Isolated out in the storm-ravaged East Sea between Korea and Japan, this beautiful island is difficult to get to at the best of times (the ferries are frequently cancelled due to gales) but well worth the effort.

It was captured from pirates as the result of an order from King Yeji, the 22nd king of the Silla Dynasty, in order to secure the east coast of the peninsula. From then until 1884 this small volcanic island remained just a military outpost but from that year migration to the island for settlement was sanctioned by the government. From the large number of small churches you might well be forgiven for thinking that a large part of the population are not only Christian but came here for some religious purpose.

Because of the rugged forested mountains and spectacular cliffs which rise steeply out of the sea, the island is only sparsely populated and farms are small. Out of a population of 20,000, 10,000 live in Dodong and another 5,000 in Jeodong. The majority of the people live in small villages along the coast making their living from the sea evidenced by the racks of drying squid, seaweed and octopus everywhere. There are virtually no roads, and transportation, except for two buses, is limited to fishing boats and walking.

There are no banks in Ulleung-do, so take enough local currency with you (including enough to see you through a cyclone). It's also a good idea to get a good map of Ulleung-do in Seoul before you set off if you plan to hike extensively, otherwise you'll have to make do with the W500 *Guide Map of Ulleung-do* available from the the first souvenir shop in Dodong, about five stores up the main street on the right.

Where to Stay & What to See

If you take the ferry from Pohang you will arrive at **Dodong harbour**, narrow with steep cliffs rising from either side. The summer-season ferries from both Imwon and Mukho, however, dock at Jaedong. If you travelled 2nd class, you may already have been offered accommodation with a family which lives on the island, but if you haven't it's no problem. Every ferry is met by a gaggle of *ajimahs*, all of them extolling the virtues of their *yogwans*, and there are quite a few of them. Recommended in Dodong is the *Young-Il Yogwan* 영일여관 , Kung Bug, Dong 41-5 (tel 0566-2663), which is a small family-run yogwan with common bathrooms but no hot water. The rooms cost W5000 a double or single and W6500 for a small three-person room. You may cook in your own room. The proprietor is Jang Chang Soo. If you want something more comfortable then try the *San Hai Hotel*, right opposite the ferry landing which costs W10,000 a double with own bathroom (cold water), a colour TV, a wonderful view of the harbour and a witch of an *ajimah*.

In Jaedong the yogwan (no name) by the big tree on the way to the Pok-lae waterfall. A double room with TV, private bath and boiling hot water costs W10,000.

Yogwan prices in Ulleung-do rise steeply in the summer season (20 July – 20 August) when the island is thronged with Korean vacationers, so if possible avoid this time of year.

You'll probably also meet the chief of police who will want to see your passport (he's very civil and will return it to you as soon as he's checked it out).

Along the main uphill/downhill road through Dodong are various food shops, yogwans, restaurants and even an OB bar where you can have your brew fresh-poured from a tea kettle. Be careful of the seafood snacks here as their prices vary.

Although there are just two public bus services – Dodong to Jeodong (two km) and Dodong to Tonggumi (seven km) – this island is made for walking. The main 'sights' and walks are:

Pokpo Falls A half-day hike there and back will get you to this beautiful double-tiered waterfall. Either take the bus or walk over the low pass (very scenic) to Jeodong, the largest harbour on the island. In town, continue along the shore/harbour front until you cross a small turbulent stream. Turn left and follow this upstream until the paved street turns into a path. The falls are just a short hike upstream. The upper tier can be reached by rock-hopping through the stream past the end of the trail and scrambling up the right wall (only recommended for sure-footed people).

Songingpung Mt This is the highest peak on the island and is the tip of a now-dormant volcano. Various pathways lead to the summit. One suggested route is to take the road to Sadong (where there's a military barracks), turn right and just keep going up through the houses and fields. You'll eventually find a trail at the end of the fields. There are occasional signs where you can get your bearings. Even if you get lost (unlikely) it doesn't matter since the island is so small. From the summit there are incredible views over the whole island.

Another suggested route is to follow the main street uphill in Dodong until you reach the stream. Follow the stream course for 100 metres past the last house where you will see a trail branch off to the right. Follow this straight up. The path to the summit is marked at regular intervals. After about an hour's climb you reach an area with wooden benches and tables that serve as a tea house during the peak season. It's a 1½-hour climb from here to the summit. Coming down, return to the tea house and take the path leading to the waterfall 폭포 . After half an hour you reach the first barn. Continue around it (avoiding the path forking off to the right) and down to the second barn and then

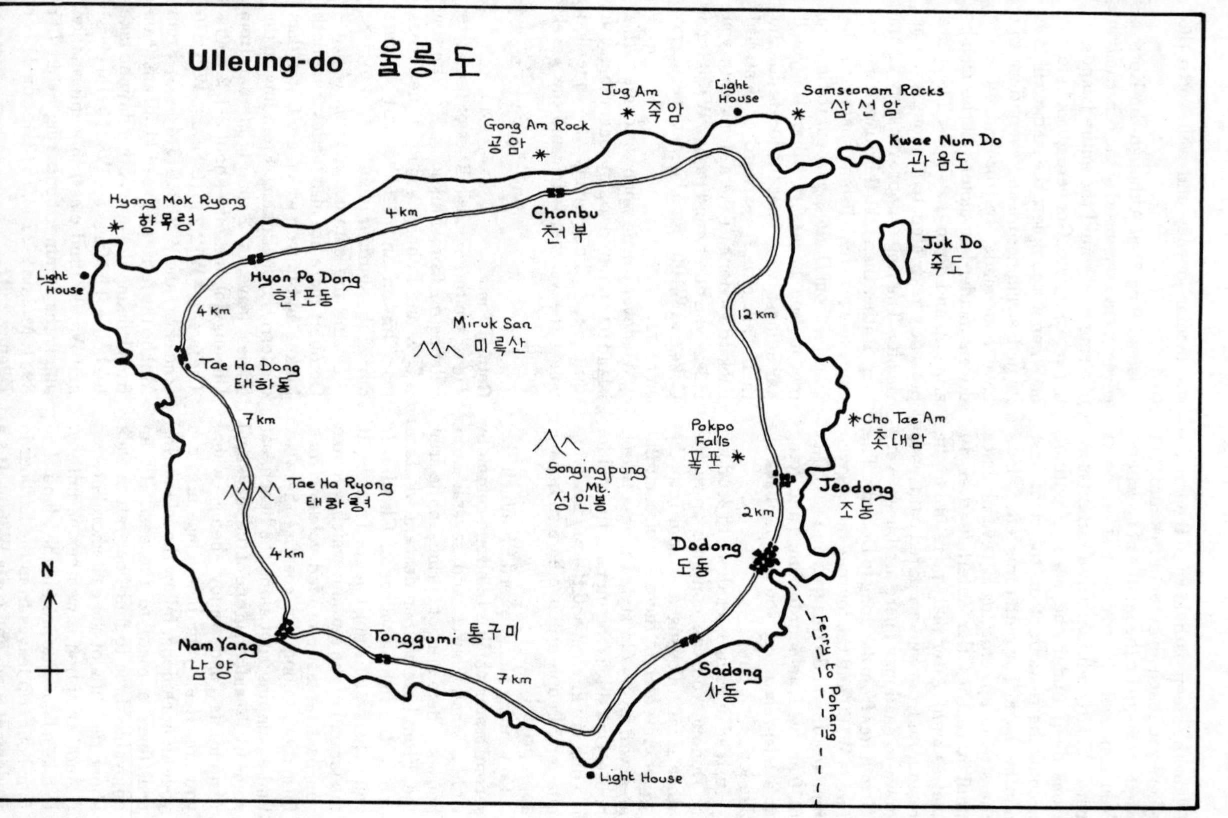
Ulleung-do 울릉도
Jug Am 죽암
Light House
Samseonam Rocks 삼선암
Gong Am Rock 공암
Kwae Num Do 관음도
Hyang Mok Ryong 향목령
4 km
Chonbu 천부
Juk Do 죽도
Light House
Hyon Po Dong 현포동
4 Km
12 Km
Miruk San 미륵산
Tae Ha Dong 태하동
7 km
Cho Tae Am 촛대암
Pokpo Falls 폭포
Songingpung Mt. 성인봉
Tae Ha Ryong 태하령
Jeodong 조동
2 km
Dodong 도동
4 km
N
Tonggumi 통구미
Nam Yang 남양
7 km
Sadong 사동
Ferry to Pohang
Light House

follow the steep path down to the stream where you reach an outdoor restaurant in what seems to be the middle of no-where. You can cool off here in a stone room naturally airconditioned by a current of air from deep under the earth. Continue around the restaurant on the right past another barn. The path turns left, follows the stream up, crossing it several times until it reaches the waterfall (over 40 metres high). After that you return to the restaurant from where a paved path leads down to Jaedong. There are buses every 40 minutes from Jaedong to Dodong. The fare is W160 and the journey takes seven minutes. If you do this trek and set off at 6.30 am, with an hour for lunch and going at a leisurely pace, you can be back in Jaedong by 3 pm.

Instead of going back down to Jeodong or Dodong you can continue down the other side, following a stream into the upper crater. Here there is a circular flat area with a very old-style Chinese thatch house. One side is for animals, the middle is a dug-out kitchen and the third is living quarters. People still live here so behave appropriately.

Continuing along toward Chonbu is the second crater which is tilled and complete with a small church and several farm houses. There are hot springs in the area too. From here a steep descent will take you to the fishing village of Chonbu. If you're lucky, a fishing boat taxi may be at the far end of the harbour which will take you past fantastic eroded volcanic rock formations along the coast. Otherwise, find a camping spot along the beach, eat some fresh seafood in one of the very small restaurants and enjoy being where you are. If all your belongings are in a yogwan in Dodong, follow the island ring trail (here a road) to the east. It's an enjoyable three to four-hour-return walk above the cliffs of the east shoreline.

Another option is,weather permitting, to take a boat-ride around the island. The four-hour trip leaves from the harbour in Dodong at 9 am and costs W3600. It's a spectacular journey and well worth the cost.

Island Ring Trail Although the Korean government is sponsoring the construction of a ring road round the entire island it's not yet complete. Get here quick before it is. When it's complete the island will lose its pedestrian nature and every town will have homemade, tractor-engined, belt-driven, muffler-less motor vehicles clambering up and down the slopes. These are presently restricted to Dodong and the vicinity. The ring is approximately 40 km long. Rather than take this road, it's more enjoyable to catch a fishing boat taxi in the morning from Dodong harbour to Chonbu (negotiation necessary otherwise you'll pay at least twice what the locals do) and then walk either westward or eastward back to Dodong. Take a drink with you unless you don't mind paying W700 for a Coke and W1000 for a beer at the villages en route.

Whatever you do when you come to this island be prepared to stay longer than you anticipated. The ferries are cancelled unless the weather is fair and the waves small.

Getting There

There are three possibilities of ferries to Ulleung-do from Mukho 묵호 , Imwon 임원X and Pohang 포항 but the ferries from Imwon and Mukho only operate during the summer months.

During the summer months (April – October) there are also ferries from both Mukho and Imwon which are faster than the ferries from Pohang. From Imwon the ferries leave at 2 pm (7.30 am from Ulleung-do) and take about 3-1/2 hours. The fares are W12,230 (1st class), W11,570 (2nd class) and W10,910 (3rd class). From Mukho the ferries leave at 11.30 am (9 am from Ulleung-do) every other day and take 6½ hours. The fares are W8210 (1st class) and W5480 (2nd class). For information about the summer boats ring Seoul 725 8931, Mukho 2-2703/7813, Inwon 313 or Ulleung 2897.

From Tonghae the *Commodore* leaves Tonghae daily during the summer months at 12.30 pm or 2 pm. The journey takes 3¾ hours. For the fares on this ferry and the details of the ferries from Imwon you must make enquiries at the tourist office in Seoul or Pusan.

All the above ferries are subject to cancellation if there is rough weather – which there often is. If that's the case you could be hanging around for days at either end. Don't go to Ulleung-do if time is critical to you.

(Many thanks to Jackie Feldman, and to Todd Stradford who provided the information and the map for Ulleung-do despite the facts that he 'procrastinated on writing in an attempt to keep the place out of our guidebook'.

OTHER PLACES

In a book of this size we can naturally only include a selection of the places which are worth visiting in Korea. There are, of course, many more and as time goes on we will attempt to include some of them. For the present, we'd like to include some readers' suggestions for the area east of the Seoul-Pusan expressway.

Andong 안동

This is a country town in the centre of an area strong in Confucian traditions. It's located west of Yongdok between Kangnung and Taegu. An interesting side trip you can make from this town is to **Tosansowen**, a restored Confucian Academy. You can get there by local bus from Andong. Access to Andong itself is best by bus from either Taegu (Northern Bus Terminal) or from Yongdok.

Hwaom-sa 하 원 사

This is one of several temples in the Chirisan National Park north of Suncheon though Hwaom-sa is probably the most beautiful. There is a 'resort village' nearby where you can find accommodation but it's not as large as the complex at Sorak-dong. There's also the possibility of staying in a yogwan or yoinsook in the nearby town of Kurye, 15 minutes' distant by bus.

At Kurye itself there is a lively market once and sometimes twice a week but for the rest of the time it's a sleepy, pleasant little town where ox-carts are more common than tractors and many older people still wear traditional dress. You can get here by bus from Kwangju or Suncheon though the latter route is mostly over dirt tracks. From either place the journey time will be about 1½ hours.

If you're coming from Kwanju there is the Zen Buddhist temple of **Songkwang-sa** between Kwangju and Suncheon. There are a few yogwans near where the bus stops.

Taiwan

Taiwan – Introduction

The label 'Made in Taiwan', seen increasingly on manufactured goods for sale in the west, bears testimony to the island republic's phenomenal transition over the last 30 years from an undeveloped agricultural country into a highly industrialised nation with the second highest per capita income in Asia. It's easy to get the impression that this 'economic miracle', as it's often labelled, with its attendant problems of over crowed cities, urban sprawl and pollution has transformed Taiwan out of all recognition and destroyed those unique and intriguing qualities which make Asian countries so popular with travellers. Yet this is only one side of Taiwan.

The other side is one of superb mountain landscapes, fantastic gorges, endless tropical and temperate forests and a fascinating culture with roots going back to the dawn of civilisation. It's these things which will continue to make the name 'Ilha Formosa' (Beautiful Island), given to it by the early Portuguese mariners, appropriate for a long time to come.

Facts about Taiwan

HISTORY

Taiwan may have been visited by people from the mainland as early as the Sui Dynasty (9581-618AD) but the first wave of settlers arrived four centuries later after the island had been made a protectorate of the Chinese empire in 1206. The next wave of settlers arrived with the armies of Cheng Ching-kung (Koxinga) in 1661 in the wave of the invasion of the mainland by the Ching (Manchu) forces at the end of the Ming Dynasty. It was during this period of turmoil that attempts were made by the Spanish and Dutch to colonise the island. The Dutch eventually gained the upper hand and established their trading capital at Tainan where the remains of the two forts which they constructed can still be seen. Their occupation of the island, however, lasted a mere 37 years and they were forced to surrender to the overwhelmingly superior forces of Cheng Ching-kung, the most famous of the Ming Dynasty generals and the island's national hero.

The next major event in the island's history came with the Japanese occupation which lasted from 1895 until the end of World War II. Though hated as colonialists, the Japanese did provide Taiwan with its first major roads, railways and factories thus helping to pave the way towards modernisation. They were also responsible for construction of the narrow gauge Alishan Forest Railway up to Alishan at 2333 metres (7465 feet) which is one of the principal highlights of a visit to Taiwan. The last wave of settlers were to arrive only a few years after the end of World War II with the evacuation of the Kuomintang (National Government of China) forces from the mainland following their defeat at the hands of the Communists under the command of Mao Zedong. Since the Nationalist Government was moved here in 1949 there has continued to be intense military and diplomatic rivalry between the two Chinas though neither has had the capacity or would be willing to risk the consequences of an outright invasion of the other. For many years Taiwan was supported by the United States and it was from this country that it recieved the bulk of its development aid but with the visit to Peking by Nixon in the early '70s, Communist China's admittance to membership of the UN and its official diplomatic recognition by the US under the Carter administration (together with derecognition of the Nationalist Government of Taiwan), the tide seems to be turning in favour of the mainland. Nevertheless, Taiwan's economic success with its US$31 billion worth of foreign trade annually has forced most countries, including the US, which now officially recognise mainland China to tread very warily. Most walk a diplomatic tight-rope between recognition of China and business as usual with Taiwan. A solution to the reunification of the two Chinas is probably as far off as it ever was.

GEOGRAPHY

Taiwan lies about 160km off the coast of south-eastern China between Japan and the Philippines with the Tropic of Cancer passing through the southern part of the island. Apart from the main island it includes the 64 wind-swept island of the Penghu (Pescadores) group, 13 other scattered islands, the main ones of which are Lanyu and Lutao off the east coast, and the Kinmen (Quemoy) and Matsu group right up against the Chinese mainland. The latter two were the target of frequent shelling from the mainland during the early years following the Communist victory over the Kuomintang. The central mountain range of Taiwan proper slopes gently to the sea in the west, eventually becoming a broad agricultural plain. In the east, however, the mountains drop precipitously into the ocean providing some of Taiwan's most spectacular geographical features. The island's uplands and forests are so extensive that only about a fourth of Taiwan is arable. These uplands include several of the highest mountains in South-East Asia including its highest – Yushan (Mt Morrison) with a height of 3998 metres (13,114 feet).

PEOPLE

Except for some 300,000 aborigines, the most well known of which are the Ami tribe of the east coast and the Yami of Lanyu (Orchid Island), the population of Taiwan is made up almost entirely of ethnic Chinese largely from Fukien and Kwangtung provinces on the mainland. With a total of more than 18 million at around 490 people per square km Taiwan is the world's most densely populated country. There is, naturally, rivalry and, in some cases, resentment between the islanders and the mainlanders who arrived with Chiang Kai-shek's forces in 1949 but it's unlikely you'll come across this as a traveller. There's also the mellowing factor that the government, however vehement it might be publicly in its commitment to 'liberate' the mainland, has been forced to accept that the likelihood of this happening is very remote and so has been gradually increasing the powers of the provincial assembly.

RELIGION

Like mainland China before the communist takeover, the religion here is a patchwork of Taoism, Buddhism and Confuciansim but with the difference that there is a very sizeable minority of Christians – about one million in total, equally divided between the Catholic and Protestant branches. There's a considerable amount of overlap between Taoism with its 2000 or so temples and Buddhism with its eight million followers and over 2500 temples. The faithful pray in each others temples and the deites of both are venerated. Both religions have taken under their wing many of the popular deities central to Taiwanese folk religion so you'll find that most temples have many side alters. Lungshan Temple in Taipei, for example, thought dedicated to Kuan Yin, the Goddess of Mercy (Avalokitesvara Bodhisattva in the Buddhist pantheon), also has some 30 other gods and goddesses enshrined there including Ma Tsu (Goddess of the Sea), Kuantai (the famous red-faced hero of the Three Kingdoms period) and Sungsheng Nian-niang (the goddess prayed to by women who want children). Confucianism is not strictly a religion, more a philosophy which has given China an ethical system that has endured for nearly 2500 years. Its temples are not places of worship and they contain no images. Generally speaking, most Chinese, regardless of religious affiliation or lack of it, may be considered Confucianistic.

CLIMATE

The climate is subtropical with an average annual temperature of 22°C in the north and 24°C in the south. Summers last from May until October and are usually hot and dry. Winters are short and last only two months from January to February but it can get chilly at this time of year and it sometimes rains for weeks on end. Typhoons occur from time to time in summer.

LANGUAGE

Mandarin is the official dialect and is the one which is taught in schools though there are still a substantial number of speakers of other regional dialects particularly the one which is spoken by the aboriginal people of the mountain areas. Many older people can speak fluent Japanese as this was the language taught in schools during the Japanese occupation from 1895 to 1945.

One of your first impressions of Taiwan is going to be the almost complete absence of signs in any language other than

Chinese. Unfortunately, you're not going to be able to pick up a great deal in the time that you're there – the number of words needed for everyday living is about 3000 and a working vocabulary sufficient for reading newspapers is about 700 characters. A little time spent learning to recognise the characters for the major cities and towns, however, will repay itself over and over again. Very few people – even in tourist bureaux and transport terminals – understand sufficient English to be able to do more than point you to a ticket booth. Taxi drivers certainly don't understand English and very few hotel owners do either – especially at the cheap end of the market. This demands that you have your destination written down in Chinese characters. The difference this makes to finding your way around is quite remarkable. They're very friendly people here and if they understand where it is you want to go they'll often make a lot of effort to ensure that you get there. There were many times when I was escorted half way across cities by people anxious to see that I got to the right place. If you're really stuck and haven't it written in Chinese, try approaching young people as they can often speak some English.

The big saving grace is that Arabic numerals are used on buses and for telephone numbers, times and dates so if you can write down your destination in Chinese characters plus the time and date you want to go then you'll never find yourself on the wrong train or bus. Note, however, that the dating system is different from that in the west. For instance, 21 August 1982 on the western calender would be 71/8/21 on the Chinese and 21 July 1983 would be 72/7/21.

Some useful Chinese words and phrases are as follows:

Hello	*Ni hao*
Good morning	*Tsao an*
Good evening	*Wan an*
Welcome	*Huan ying*
Friend	*Peng yu*
Who is it?	*Shui ya?*
How do you do?	*Ni hao ma?*
Fine, thanks	*Hao, hsieh-hsieh ni*
Goodbye	*Tsai chien*
How much?	*To shao chien?*
How many?	*To shao ke?*
Cheap	*Pien yi*
Expensive	*Hen kuei*
Go straight	*Yi chih tso*
Turn right	*Yupien chuan*
Turn left	*Tsopien chuan*
Stop	*Ting-yi-ting*
Go	*Tso*
Good	*Hao*
Bad	*Pu hao*
Mr	*Hsien-sheng*
Mrs	*Tai-tai*
Miss	*Hsiao-chieh*
I	*Wo*
You	*Ni*
He/she	*Ta*
We	*Wo men*
You (plural)	*Ni men*
They	*Ta men*
Mine	*Wo te*
Yours	*Ni te*
His/hers	*Ta te*

Numerals

1	*Yi*
2	*Er*
3	*San*
4	*Sze*
5	*Wu*
6	*Liu*
7	*Chi*
8	*Pa*
9	*Chiu*
10	*Shih*
11	*Shih yi*
20	*Er shih*
25	*Er shih wu*
100	*Yi pai*
900	*Chiu pai*
1000	*Chien*
6000	*Liu chien*
10,000	*Yi wan*

Taiwan – Facts for the Visitor

INFORMATION

Taiwan produces a prodigious amount of booklets and leaflets about the island, some of it, particularly the lists of addresses, contacts and street maps, is excellent. Two things you should make sure you pickup on arrival at Chiang Kai-Shek International Airport are the booklet, *This Month in Taiwan*, and a street map of Taipei. Both are free. Unfortunately, much of the information is orientated towards businessmen and well monied tourists who will spend most of their time in Taipei and take a few organised one and two-day trips to other places around the island. The main thing you should beware of in this literature, however, is the tendency to be carried away with its own rhetoric. Reading alot of this stuff you could be forgiven for imagining that you're about to visit an island stacked full of contenders for the 8th Wonder of the World. It will tell you, for instance, that Wulai, wouth of Taipei, is the nearest aboriginal village to the capital. The Taiwanese equivalent of Disneyland for day-trippers from Taipei would be more accurate. It will encourage you to go to Kaohsiung, Taiwan's second city and largest port, to see the bigest ship breaking yard in the world, take a fascinating ferry ride across the harbour and visit the popular beach. Which is all very well if you have an interest in ship breaking yards. The ferry ride across the harbour takes all of 10 minutes and the 'beach' is just a bad joke. With breathless enthusiasm it will have you on a bus to Keelung to see the 23-metre-high statue of Kuan Yin, the Goddess of Mercy, but having seen it there's absolutely nothing else to do in Keelung.

The intention of the above is not to discourage you going to Taiwan but to take what the tourist literatures raves about with a large pinch of salt. There are quite a few places to visit whose beauty, interest or whatever justifies the enthusiasm bestowed on them. At the risk of being contradicted I would say they include, Taroko Gorge, Lanyu Island (Orchid Island), Kenting, Alishan, Tainan, the Lion's Head Mountain and Taipei itself. The mountains of central and eastern Taiwan are particularly spectactular.

VISAS & PERMITS

All intending visitors to Taiwan must be in possession of a visa. Most travellers apply for the Tourist 'A' visa which is valid for six months from the date of issue, good for a stay of one month and can be extended free of charge for one more month. The two other types of visa are the Transit visa (valid for three months from the date of issue, good for a two-week stay and not extendable) and the Tourist 'B' visa (good for a stay of two months and can be extended twice for a total stay of six months).

Unlike obtaining a visa for most countries which require them where you apply at the nearest embassy or consulate, very few countries maintain official diplomatic relations with Taiwan so their embassies are very few and far between. One principal exception in the area is South Korea so if you're coming through there you can get your visa in Seoul. On the other hand, few countries can afford to ignore Taiwan's economic juggernaut so most maintain unofficial relations which are embassies in all but name. The Taiwanese equivalent of these abroad are known as 'Taiwan Visitors Associations' or Travel Services' and it's here you apply for a visa. After completing a form and paying the fee (the fee varies depending where you apply – in Australia it's free but you pay about A$6 on arrival in Taiwan; in Hong Kong it's HK$40) you'll be issued

Top: Posokjong Bower – once a pleasure garden for the Silla aristocracy
Bottom: Kap-sa Temple, Mt Geryeong-san National Park

Top: Central Taipei, old city gate & flyover
Left: Lungshar Temple, the oldest in Taipei
Right: Pagoda at Mutsu Temple Taitung

with a 'Visa Recommendation' slip which is exchanged on arrival in Taiwan for a visa proper. If you apply for this recommendation slip by post there's no need to send in your passport with the completed form since nothing will be stamped in it. If you're applying personally you may be required to show an onward ticket.

'Visa recommendation' slips are available from:

Argentina
Oficina comercial de Taiwan, Parana 597, 10 Piso, 1017 Buenos Aires, Capital Federal (tel 409806-7)

Australia
Far East Trading Co., 7th Floor, 71 Queens Rd, Melbourne. (tel 519793)

Belgium
Centre Cultural Sun Yat-Sen, Rue de la Loi, 24, 1000-Bruxelles. (tel 5110887, 5111528)

England
Free Chinese Centre, 4th Floor, Dorland House, 14-16 Regent Street, London. (tel 01-9309553)

Fiji
East Asia Trade Centre Ltd., 4th Floor, AIR Pacific House, Corner MacArthur and Butt Sts., Suva. (tel 23922, 311738)

Germany (West)
Fernost Informationen, 5300 Bonn Bad Godesberg, Burgstrasse. (tel 0228 356097)
Fernost Informationen Hamburg, Mittelweg 149, 2000 Hamburg 13, (tel 040 447788)
Fermost Informationen Berlin, Dahlmannstr 23, 1000 Berlin 12, (tel 3232752)
Asia Trade Center, Dreieichstrasse 59, 6000 Fankfurt/Main 70, (tel 0611 610743)

Holland
Far East Trade Office, Javastraat 58, 2585 AR, The Hague, (tel 070 469438)

Hong Kong
Chung Hwa Travel Service, Room 1009, Takshing House, 20 Des Veoux Rd., (tel H-258315-8)

Japan
Association of East Asian Relations (Toyko Office), 3F., 39th Mori Bldg., 4-5 Azabudai, 2-Chome, Minato-Ku, (tel 434-1181)

New Zealand
East Asia Trade Center, 7th Floor, IBM House, 155-161 The Terrace, Wellington. (tel 736474-5)

Norway
Taipei, Trade Center, Ivar Aasensvei 19, Oslo 3, (tel 143219)

Philippines
Pacific Economic and Cultural Center, 8th Floor, BF. Homes Condominium Building, Aduana St., Intramuros, Manila, (tel 472261-65)

Singapore
Trade Mission of the Republic of China, Suite 1301, UIC Building, 5 Shenton Way, (tel 2224951-53)

Sweden
Taipei Trade Tourism & Information Office, Birger Jarlsgatan 13/1V, S-111 45 Stockholm, (tel 08-205011)

Switzerland
Centre Sun Yat-Sen, 54, Avenue de Bethusy, 1012, Lausanne, (tel 021 335005-6)

Thailand
The Far East Trade Office, 10th Floor, Kian Gwan Building, 140 Wit Thayu Rd., Bangkok, (tel 2519274-6)

USA
CCNAA, Bethesda, 5161 River Rd, Bethesda, MD 20815
CCNAA, Atlanta, Suite 2412, Peachtree Center, Cain Tower, 229 Peachtree St, N.E.
CCNAA, Chicago, 20, N, Clark St, 19th Floor.
CCNAA, Houston, 11 Green Way Plaza, Suite 2006.
CCNAA, Los Angeles, 3660 Wilshire Boulevard, Suite 1050.
CCNAA, New York, 801, Second Avenue, 9th Floor.
CCNAA, Seattle, 24th Floor, Westin Bldg, 2001 Sixth Avenue, Suite 2410.
CCNAA, Honolulu, 2746 Pali Highway.

Note that the Hong Kong agency is sometimes spelt 'Chung Hua' but not in the phone directory. This agency definitely required onward tickets.

Visas can be renewed at the Foreigners Service Centre, Taipei Police Headquarters (tel 361-0159) which is located between the GPO and City Hall on Chung Hua Rd.

Mountain Trail Permits

If you're planning on hiking to Taiping Mountain near Ilan, from Wushe/Lushan to Tayuling on the East-West Cross Island Highway, from Lushan to Hualien along the Powerline Patrol Road, or along the Southern Cross Island Highway then you need special permits. Permits are not required to travel from Taroko Gorge to Taichung via Tienhsiang and Lishan. The permits for Wushe/Lushan to Tayuling and the Southern Cross Island Highway are simply a formality, costs NT$5, two photographs and are issued while you wait. Permits for the other two trails are more difficult to obtain and are likely to be refused unless you have a letter on headed notepaper from a university or college saying you're studying something like anthropology or botany or you have a letter requesting assistance from the American Institute in Taiwan, 7, Lane 134, Hsin Yi Rd., Section 3, Taipei (tel 708 4150). This latter place which is the unofficial American embassy is open Monday through Friday from 8.15 to 11.45 am and 3 to 4.30 pm. It will provide these letters to USA and British passport holders only. If you're not travelling on one of these passports then forget about it.

For all the above permits you must apply at the Foreigners Affairs Office, Taiwan Provincial Police Administration, 7 Chunghsiao E Rd, Section 1, Taipei (tel 321 2374/5). The office is open Monday through Friday from 8 to 11.45 am and 1.30 to 4.30 pm and on Saturdays from 8 to 11.30 am.

Embassies, Consulates & Cultural/Trade Associations

Apart from the South Korean embassy all the 'consular' offices listed below are unofficial. Taiwan's lack of diplomatic recognition can create lots of problems for you if you ever lose your passport in Taiwan. The Australian, French, German and UK offices do not offer passport or visa services.

Australia
: Australia-Free China Society, 10th Floor, 34 Jenai Rd, Section 2 (tel 393 8800/351 8844)

France
: France Asia Trade Promotion Association, Room 1008, Chia Hsin Building, 10th floor, 96 Chung Shan North Rd., Section 2 (tel 551 5211)

Germany (West)
: German Cultural Centre, 5th Floor, 33 Chung Hsiao West Rd., Section 1 (tel 331 3741)

Japan
: Interchange Association, 43 Chi Nan Rd., Section 2 (tel 351 7250/4)

Korea (South)
: Embassy of South Korea, 345 Chung Hsiao East Rd., Section 4, (opposite the Sun Yat Sen Memorial Hall) (tel 761 9361/5)

Philippines

Asian Exchange Centre Inc., Suite 305, 3rd Floor, Hua-Teh Building, 575 Lin Shen North Rd., (tel 592 8110)

Singapore
: Singapore Trade Representative, 5th Floor, 121 Chungshan North Rd, Section 2 (tel 562 8235)

Thailand
: Thai Airways Administration International Ltd, Room A, 4th Floor, 124 Nanking East Rd, Section 2 (tel 531 0364/5)

UK
: Anglo-Taiwan Trade Committee, 11th Floor, China Building, 36 Nanking East Rd, Section 2 (tel 521 4116/8)

USA
: American Institute in Taiwan, 7 Lane 134, Hsin Yi Rd., Section 3 (tel 708 4151/8 or 752 6040 for visas)

MONEY

A$1 = NT$31
US$1 = NT$39
£1 = NT$44

The unit of currency is the New Taiwan Dollar (NT$) = 100 cents. Three coins are in circulation NT$0.50 (bronze colour), NT$1 (silver colour) and NT$5 (silver colour). Bank notes are in denominations os NT$10, NT$50, NT$100, NT$500 and NT$1000. There's no restriction on the import of local currency but export is limited to NT$8000.

Travellers' cheques can only be cashed at the Bank of Taiwan and its branches and changing money there can sometime take up to half an hour. Banking hours are Monday through Friday from 9 am to 3.30 pm and Saturday from 9 am to 12 noon. There is a bank at Taipei International Airport open from 7.30 am to 7.30 pm daily. Keep the exchange receipt slips which the banks give you in case you need to reconvert any unspent Taiwanese Dollars when you leave. There's no limit on reconversion but you must have the bank receipt slips. The airport departure tax for international flights is NT$150.

If you'd like to keep the cost of your trip down somewhat then take advantage of the duty-free allowances – two bottles of spirits, 400 cigarettes, 1 lb of tobacco and 50 cigars – as these can be sold fairly easily for a handsome profit (tobacco and alcohol is a government monopoly). Western cigarettes such as 555s sell on the streets for NT$55 per pack of 20 (about US$1.50)! Cognac fetches the best price though the profit on whisky is also good. If you're into selling blood the price is around US$70 per session.

MAIL

The postal system here is very good and all offices have a post restante service. Regular post offices are open from 8.30 am to 5 pm Monday through Saturday. The GPO in Taipei is the North Gate Post Office 北門郵局 which provides a 24 hours service except on holidays. When you're posting mail remember that the red mailboxes are for air mail and special delivery and the green mailboxes for local letters only. Don't worry if you put a letter in the wrong box – it will still get there.

Many post offices offer an excellent and inexpensive packing service for parcels going abroad as well as customs inspections which makes re-opening the parcel before despatch unnecessary. There is one difficulty you may come across, however, if you want to send books back from Taiwan from any post office other than Taipei GPO. Even if your parcel is wrapped so that it's obvious it contains books the postal clerk may refuse to accept it unless you first unwrap it and allow the customs to inspect it. The reason for this strange state of affairs is that Taiwan is not a signatory to the International Copyright Convention and the island is a major centre for pirated editions of best-sellers and the like (records and tapes fall into this category too). In order to minimise the effects of this abroad the authorities have made a number of agreements with foreign governments whereby they won't allow books, records and tapes to be posted abroad unless they've been inspected and certified genuine. You may also come across this on leaving Taiwan if you're carrying with you books, records and tapes bought on the island though it's unlikely they'll be confiscated even if not genuine (assuming you haven't got a suitcase full of them!)

ACCOMMODATION

Cheap Hotels Budget accommodation is not all that easy to find if you prefer your own room and access to reasonable bathroom facilities. Most of the travellers I met agreed that 'developed' nation would be a more appropriate description of Taiwan than 'developing'. The prices for accommodation at the bottom end of the scale are therefore correspondingly higher and you should be prepared to spend between US$5-10 for a room.

There are two exceptions to this general story. Most cheap hotels – and even some more expensive ones – often have a number of 'Tatami' rooms which essentially are shared dormitory rooms provided with mats and sometimes pillows (and, in cold mountain areas where it gets cold at night, a quilt). Bathroom facilities are communal. They vary considerably in quality but usually don't cost more than US$2-4 per night. The big advantage if you're a

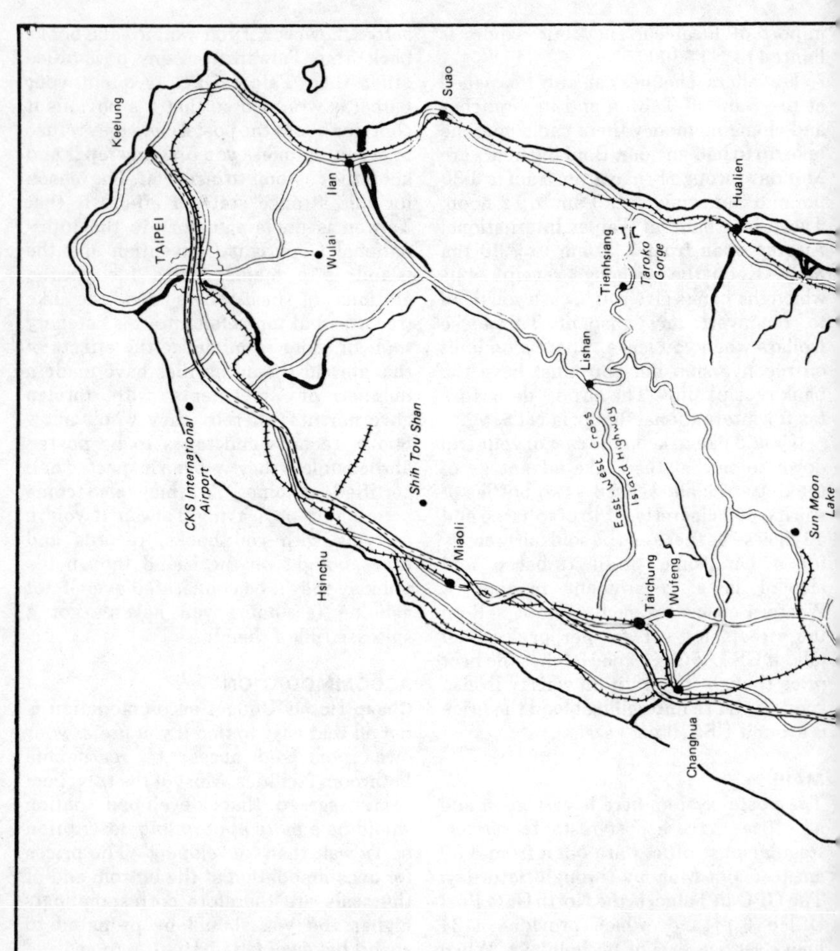
Keelung
TAIPEI
Wulai
Ilan
Suao
Hualien
Tienhsiang
Taroko Gorge
Lishan
East West Cross Island Highway
CKS International Airport
Shih Tou Shan
Hsinchu
Miaoli
Taichung
Wufeng
Sun Moon Lake
Changhua

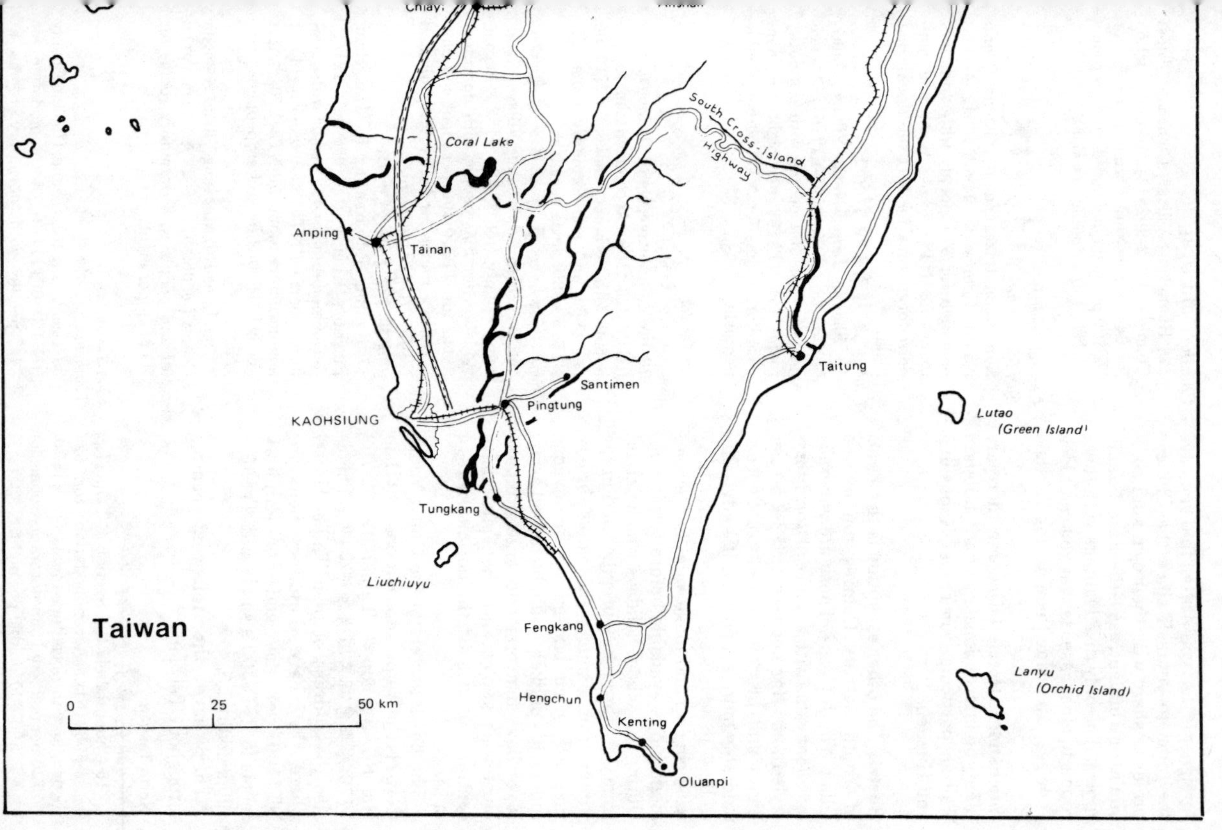
Coral Lake
South Cross-Island
Highway
Anping
Tainan
Taitung
Santimen
Pingtung
KAOHSIUNG
Lutao
(Green Island')
Tungkang
Liuchiuyu
Taiwan
Fengkang
Lanyu
(Orchid Island)
Hengchun
0
25
50 km
Kenting
Oluanpi

foreigner is that you'll often find you have the room to yourself since the Chinese prefer to share with their own kind so, if you're on a budget, ask if there are 'tatami' rooms. The only disadvantage with these rooms in most cases is that you can't lock your gear up inside them during the day.

International Hotels Of course there are plenty of 'international standard' hotels in Taiwan, particularly in Taipei, Kaohsiung and Hualien.

Hostels The other exception is the series of Youth Activity Centres run by the China Youth Corps. These are generally excellent value with a choice of dormitory-style rooms (for between US$2-2.50 per night) and private rooms (usually considerably more expensive). It's advisable to book in advance at these centres or at least ring up and make sure that accommodation is available before turning up. During the school holidays which extend from July through September and in the winter from January through February they are often booked up in advance though it's unlikely you'll be turned away. If you have an aversion to large groups of boisterous adolescents then give these centres – or at least the dormitories – a miss.

The headquarters of the China Youth Corps is the Taipei International, 30 Hsin Hai Rd. Section 3, Taipei (tel 02-709 1770) 台北國際青年活動中心. This is also the address of their Taipei Hostel where they have dormitory beds for NT$100 per day and non-dormitory rooms for NT$300 a single and NT$300-400 a double.

They have the following centres throughout Taiwan:

North Taiwan

Chientan 劍潭青年活動中心
16 Chungshan N Rd, Section 4, Taipei (tel 02-5962151). Accommodation for 627 people with dormitory rooms for NT$70-120 per night and non-dormitory rooms for NT$500-600/double per night.

Chinshan 青山山莊
228 Huangkang Village, Chinshan, Taipei County (tel 032-982511). Accommodation for 644 people with dormitory rooms for NT$90 per night and non-dormitory rooms for NT$400 a double per night.

Central Taiwan

Sun Moon Lake 日月潭青年活動中心
Sun Moon Lake, Yutsu (Fishing Pond), Nantou County (tel 049-855331). Accommodation for 374 people with dormitory rooms for NT$100 per night and non-dormitory rooms for NT$800/double per night.

Chitou 溪頭青年活動中心
15 Shenlin Lane, Neifu Village, Luku, Nantou County (tel 049-612161). Accommodation for 380 people with dormitory rooms for NT$100 per night and non-dormitory rooms for NT$500-600/double per night.

South Taiwan

Tsengwen 曾文青年活動中心
70-1 Michih Village, Nanci, Tainan County (tel 06-223 4189). Accommodation for 346 people with dormitory rooms for NT$100 per night and non-dormitory rooms for NT$250-360/single per night.

Cheng Ching Lake 澄清湖青年活動中心
140 Wenchien Rd, Wusung Village, Kaohsiung County (tel 07-371 7182). Accommodation for 500 people with dormitory rooms for NT$70-100 per night and non-dormitory rooms for NT$400/double and NT$500/triple per night.

Kenting 墾丁青年活動中心
17 Kenting Rd, Kenting Li, Hengchun, Pingtung County (tel 088-861 221/4). Accommodation for 412 people with dormitory rooms for NT$180-600 per night and non-dormitory rooms for NT$1200/double and NT$1000/three to four people.

Penghu
7 Chin Lung Rd, Ma Kung Village, Penghu County (tel 069-371 7182). Accommodation for 256 people with dormitory rooms for NT$120 per night.

East Taiwan

Tienhsiang 天祥山莊
30 Tsienhsiang Rd, Hsiulin, Hualien County (tel 038-691111/3). Accommodation for 344 people with dormitory rooms at

NT$70-120 per night and non-dormitory rooms for NT$360-1200/double per night.

North Cross Island Highway

Fuhsing 復興山莊
(tel 033-332153). Accommodation for 380 people with dormitory rooms at NT$60-120 per night and non-dormitory rooms at NT$360/single and NT$600/double per night.

Paling 巴陵山莊
(tel 033-332153). Accommodation for 120 people with dormitory rooms only at NT$60 per night.

East-West Cross Island Highway

Wushe 霧社山莊
(tel 049-855331). Accommodation for 100 people with dormitory rooms only at NT$60 per night.

Chinshan 青山山莊
(tel 045-244103). Accommodation for 122 people with dormitory rooms at NT$70 per night and non-dormitory rooms at NT$500/triple per night.

Tehchi 德基山莊
(tel 045-244103). Accommodation for 204 people with dormitory rooms at NT$100 per night and non-dormitory rooms at NT$500/double per night.

Tzu-en 慈恩山莊
(tel 038-691111/3). Accommodation for 100 people with dormitory rooms at NT$60 per night.

Tayuling 大禹嶺山莊
(tel 038-691111/3). Accommodation for 200 people with dormitory rooms at NT$60 per night.

Lashao 洛韶山莊
(tel 038-691111/3). Accommodation for 134 people with dormitory rooms at NT$70 per night and non-dormitory rooms at NT$360/double per night.

South Cross Island Highway

Meishan 梅山山莊
(tel 07-747 0134). Accommodation for 120 people with dormitory rooms at NT$60 per night.

Litao 利稻山莊
(tel 089-329891). Accommodation for 150 people with dormitory rooms at NT$60 per night.

Yakou 埡口山莊
(tel 089-329891). Accommodation for 150 people with dormitory rooms at NT$60 per night.

Alishan 阿里山莊
(tel 052-240132). Accommodation for 164 people with dormitory rooms at NT$80 per night.

There are also hostels at Kaohsiung, Taichung and Tainan which are dealt with under the respective city heading.

FOOD

Taiwan doesn't have a great Chinese cuisine of its own but you'll find the whole range of regional Chinese cooking in the country.

Cantonese When people in the west speak of Chinese food they probably mean Cantonese food. It's the best known and most popular variety of Chinese cooking. Cantonese food is noted for the variety and freshness of its ingredients. The food is usually stir fried with just a touch of oil to ensure that the result is crisp and fresh. All those best known 'western Chinese' dishes for into this category – sweet & sour dishes, won ton soup, chow mein, spring rolls.

With Cantonese food the more people you can muster for the meal the better because dishes are traditionally shared so that everyone manages to sample the greatest variety. A corollary of this is that Cantonese food should be balanced – all foods are said to ying or 'cooling' (like vegetables, most fruits, clear soups) or yang or 'heaty' (starchy foods and meat). A cooling dish should be balanced by a hearty dish, too much of one or the other is not good for you.

Another Cantonese speciality is dim sum or 'little heart'. Dim sum is usually eaten at lunchtime or as a Sunday brunch. Dim sum restaurants are usually large, noisy affairs and the dim sum, little snacks, fried, steamed, dumplings, buns, small bowls or whatever, are whisked around the tables on individual trolleys or carts. As they come by you simply ask for a plate of this or a bowl of that. At the end of the meal your bill is toted up from the number of empty containers on your table. Eating dim sum is generally fun as well as tasty.

Cantonese cuisine can also offer real extremes – shark's fin soup or bird's nest soup are expensive delicacies from one end of the scale; mee (noodles) or congee (rice porridge) are cheap basics from the other end.

North & West China Far less familiar than the dishes of Canton are the cuisines from the north and the west of China – Szechuan, Shanghainese and Peking cooking. Szechuan food is the fiery food of China, the food where the peppers really get into the act. Whereas the tastes of Cantonese food are delicate and understated, in Szechuan food the flavours are strong and dramatic – garlic and chillis play their part in dishes like diced chicken or sour & hot soup.

Peking food is, of course, best known for the famous Peking duck where the specially fattened ducks are basted in syrup and roasted on a revolving spit. The duck skin is served as a separate first course. Like the other northern cuisines, Peking food is less subtle, more direct than Cantonese food.

Food from Shangai is to some extent a cross between northern and Cantonese cuisines – combining the strong flavours of the north with the ingredients of Canton.

South China Cantonese is, of course, the best known southern Chinese cuisine but there are a number of other regional styles including Hoddien, Hainanese and Teochew food. Taiwanese food also falls into this category – the best known Taiwenese specialities include rice porridge, a healthy and economical meal, often with small side dishes of oysters, mussels or pork stewed in a rich sauce.

NATIONAL HOLIDAYS

You should avoid travelling in Taiwan on national and public holidays especially between 10th-16th October and the first three weeks in February (Chinese Lunar New Year). At these times you may well find that buses and trains are fully booked out and popular resort areas like Alishan and Kenting very crowded. Most businesses and independent restaurants also close during these periods. The following is a list of the holidays:

January 1
National Holiday (2 days)
March 29
National Holiday (Youth Day)
April 5
National Holiday (Tomb Sweeping Day)
April 29
Landing of Cheng Cheng Kung (Koxinga) on Taiwan 1661
September 28
National Holiday (Confucius' Birthday)
October 10
National Holiday (Double Tenth)
October 21
Overseas Chinese Day
October 25
National Holiday (Taiwan Retrocession Day)
October 31
National Holiday (Chiang Kai-shek's Birthday)
November 12
National Holiday (Dr Sun Yat-sen's Birthday)
December 25
National Holiday (Christmas)

There are also several public holidays which are governed by the lunar calendar so the dates change each year. They are: Chinese Lunar New Year's Eve; Chinese Lunar New Year (1st day, 1st moon); Lantern Festival (5th day, 1st moon); Birthday of Kuan Yin, Goddess of Mercy (19th day, 2nd moon); Birthday of Matsu, Goddess of the Sea (23rd day, 3rd moon); Dragon Boat Festival (5th day, 5th moon); Birthday of Cheng Huang, City God of Taipei (13th day, 7th moon); Mid-Autumn

Moon Festival (15th day, 8th moon); Chung Yuan Festival (15th day, 7th moon).

If you're not familiar with the moon calendar it's going to be difficult for you to work out the corresponding dates on the Gregorian calendar so we've done this for you. Lunar New Year (Feb 10, 1985; Feb 9, 1986; Jan 29, 1987; Feb 17, 1988); Lantern Festival (March 6, 1985; Feb 23, 1986; Feb 12, 1987; March 2, 1988); Birthday of Kuan Yin (April 8, 1985; March 28, 1986; March 18, 1987; April 2, 1988); Birthday of Matsu (May 12, 1985; May 1, 1986; April 20, 1987; May 8, 1988); Dragon Boat Festival (June 22, 1985; June 11, 1986; May 31, 1987; June 18, 1988); Birthday of Cheng Huang (June 30, 1985; June 19, 1986; June 8, 1987; June 26, 1988); Mid-Autumn Moon Festival (Sept 29, 1985; Sept 18, 1986; Oct 25, 1987; Sept 25, 1988).

Taiwan – Getting Around

Transport in Taiwan is a dream come true. It's fast, efficient, runs on time and is relatively cheap. In addition, there's a choice on the trains and buses between air-con luxury, luxury or ordinary express. Services between most major population centres are so frequent and so easy to get on that if it weren't for the different categories of comfort there would be hardly any need to include schedules. The one thing you do need at most railway and bus terminals, however, is the ability to recognise the name of the place you want to get to in Chinese characters otherwise you might well find yourself in the wrong ticket queue.

AIR

There are several domestic airlines which service the island, the main ones being China Air Lines (CAL), which also flies to Hong Kong, and Far Eastern Air Transport (FAT). Two more you're likely to come across if you visit Lanyu (Orchid Island), Lutao (Green Island) or Penghu (Pescadores Island) are Taiwan Airlines and Yong Hsin Airlines. On a limited budget the only ones you're likely to be interested in are the flights from Hualin and Taitung to Lutao and Lanyu and the flights from Kaogsiung, Tainan, Chiayi and Taichung to Makung in the Pescadores.

To Lanyu (Orchid Island) and Lutao (Green Island) You can fly to Lanyu from either Kaohsiung or Taitung but you can only fly to Lutao from Taitung. The flights from Taitung to Lanyu are considerably cheaper (NT$907) than the corresponding ones from Kaohsiung (NT$1406). *FAL* and *TAC* are the two airlines which cover the Taitung-Lanyu and Taitung-Lutao sectors, their planes being either 16-seat or 8-seat Cessnas. Both companies operate five flights per day in either direction to both Lanyu and Lutao. From Taitung the first flight is at 7.30 am and the last at 3.20 pm. From both Lanyu and Lutao the first flight is at 7.55 am and the last at 3.45 pm. The flights take about 15 minutes. The fares are the same on both airlines – NT$907 one-way to Lanyu and NT$454 one-way to Lutao.

In Taitung buy your tickets at the Lan Yu Travel Agency on the main square directly opposite the railway station. They're very friendly people and speak good English. In Lanyu you must buy your ticket either at the airport or at the Lanyu Hotel. Booking more than a day in advance isn't really necessary. Be prepared for a passport and baggage search before boarding the planes. If you want to contact either of these airlines before heading south down the island they both have offices in Taipei: FAL (tel 5817266/7121503) and TAC (tel 5914156).

The alternative to flying is to take the boat from Taitung which costs NT$326 (plus the cost of getting to the harbour which is a long way from Taitung) and takes 8½-9 hours. For details of this see under 'Taitung'.

To Penghu (Pescadores) You can fly to Makung in the Pescadores from Taipei, Taichung, Chiayi, Tainan or Kaohsiung. The latter four offer the cheaper routes (Taipei-Makung costs NT$1001 one-way; Taichung-Makung costs NT$919; Chiayi-Makung costs NT$577; Tainan-Makung costs NT$561 and Kaohsiung-Makung costs NT$589 one-way). China Airlines (CAL), Far Eastern Air Transport (FAT) and FAL all fly to Makung. Between Kaohsiung and Makung there are eight flights per day in either direction, the first at 7.30 am and the last at 5.20 pm. Between Tainan and Makung there is one flight per day at 4.20 pm from Tainan and 3.30 pm from Makung and between Chiayi and Makung there is also one flight per day at 12.55 pm from Chiayi and 12.05 pm from Makung.

To find out about the state of the booking on CAL ring the following: (07) 231-5181/5 (Kaohsiung) (06) 226-2181/4 (Tainan); (05) 223-0118/9 (Chiayi); (04) 229-3961/3 (Taichung). For FAT ring the following: (07) 241-1181/8 (Kaohsiung); (06) 225-8111 (Tainan). For FAL ring the following: (07) 801-3369 (Kaohsiung); (04) 291-4236 (Taichung). The alternative to flying is to take the daily car ferry from Kaohsiung to Makung which costs NT$156 in the cheapest class and takes about 4½ hours as opposed to about – ½ hour by plane – for details see under 'Kaohsiung'.

TRAINS

The train services are excellent in Taiwan and, in express class, only marginally more expensive than the buses. Free tea is served, usually at hourly intervals or after stops at main stations, and hot, packed meals (good value) are sold at lunch and dinner time. Other than local stopping trains on which you cannot reserve a seat, there are several classes which, in order of speed and luxury, are: Chu Kuang 莒光號 which is an air-con, 1st class only express train; Tzu Chiang 自強號 which is an electrified, air-con express; Chu Hsin 莒光號 sometimes called Fu Hsin which is an air-con limited express having 1st and 2nd classes, and the Express 復興號 which is a non-air-con express.

You should reserve your seat in advance wherever possible if you intend to travel by ordinary express since there's considerable demand for seats. The more luxurious trains are very rarely booked up. Booking in advance not only gives you the advantage of knowing you have a seat on the train of your choice but saves a considerable amount of time at the ticket office. All the main stations have different ticket windows for morning and afternoon trains – make sure you get in the right queue! Naturally the queues at current booking ticket windows tend to be long and you can often be in for a half hour wait with no guarantee that you'll get on the train of your choice if it's an ordinary express. If this turns out to be the case then you have a choice of going on a more expensive train (or taking a bus) or travelling later in the day on a different ordinary express. The queues at advance booking windows are usually very short and buying a ticket takes only a few minutes. The carriage number and seat number are written on the back of the ticket. The ticket will be collected at the end of the journey. Ticket clerks, as a rule, speak no English so to avoid mistakes and misunderstandings write down the number of the train, its departure time, the date you want to travel and your destination in Chinese characters on a piece of paper and give this to the clerk. Before I started to do this I was often given a ticket for the wrong train, the wrong date and even, on one occasion, the wrong place (I asked for a Taitung and was given a ticket for Taichung). Remember the different dating system in Taiwan – 21st August 1982 would be 71/8/21 and the same date in 1983 would be 72/8/21.

One train journey you should not miss since it's one of the most spectacular anywhere in the world is the one to Chiayi to Alishan on the Alishan Forest Railway. This 72km long narrow guage railway was built by the Japanese during their occupation of Taiwan and opened in 1912 to serve the logging camps in the area. From sea level at Chiayi it climbs up to 2333 metres (7465 feet) at Alishan over more than 80 bridges, through 50 tunnels and three switchbacks, the last of these being just below Alishan town where an enourmous tree is situated. The ascent takes you from the steamy tropical forests of the lowlands through the mixed subtropical forests and lychee orchards on the slopes to the temperate zone around Alishan which is covered in pine forest. The views all the way up are incredible. You won't find anything like this outside of India where similar narrow guage railways climb the slopes of the Himalaya.

These days the carriages are pulled by diesel engines but up at Alishan you may well catch sight of one of the old miniature steam engines which are still in use – beautiful machines and well looked after. During holidays and at weekends the trains to Alishan are very popular so unless you book in advance you may well find that all but the ordinary train is full – the ordinary stopping train takes all comers and is used by local people to take their produce down to the lowlands and bring supplies back up. It's often very crowded but space will be found for you one way or another. Make sure you book a ticket for the return journey in Chiayi as you cannot book in advance at Alishan and will have to take a chance as soon as the booking office opens there at 7 am on the day you want to leave. Don't miss this journey. It's one of the highlights of Taiwan!

BUSES

The bus network, like the railways, is excellent and only in the more remote areas do you need to think about booking in advance. From any large city or town there are departures every 5-10 minutes to other major centres of population. There's usually only one bus terminal – often located close to if not actually next to the railway station – which caters for all long distance buses. Timetables and signs above ticket windows are usually entirely in Chinese so make sure you get in the right queue especially when there's a choice of air-con and non air-con buses (it's obvious which are which since the air-con fares will be higher). Seats are not numbered so it's first come first served. Most bus terminals have an enquiry desk but don't expect too much in the way of English. Familiarity with the Chinese characters of the places you want to go to will give you access to much more information than you'll ever find out from an enquiry desk.

Buses down the west coast between Taipei and Kaohsiung are of a standard you'd expect to find in Europe and North America and, since the completion of the freeway, faster and cheaper than the trains. Don't worry about having to get off at an obscure place on a local bus. Just write down your destination in Chinese and show it to a few people. When you get there the conductor and everyone else on the bus will be gesticulating wildly and pointing you in the direction you must go.

Bus schedules are included under the city and town sections.

BOATS

Keelung (Taiwan)-Okinawa-Osaka (Japan)

If you'd like to spend a few days in the Okinawa Islands a ferry leaves Keelung every week, usually on Sundays and returns from Okinawa on Fridays. Fares are US$65 (economy group cabin), US$77.50 (1st class – 4-berth cabin) and US$95.50 (1st class – 2-berth cabin). The ferry is operated by Yeong An Maritime Co, 11 Jenai Rd, Section 3 (tel 771-5911/8).

Keelung-Hualien Car Ferry This ferry departs Keelung daily at 9 am and arrives at Hualien at 2.30-3 pm. The return ferry departs Hualien at 10.30 pm and reaches Keelung at 6 am the next day. One-way fares are NT$300 (deck class), NT$420 (4-berth cabin) and NT$540 (1st class – 2-berth cabin). Tickets are sold at 108 Chungshan N Rd, Section 2, Taipei and at Pier No. 2, 16 Kangshi St, Keelung. For information call Mr Wong at 522-1215-7.

Taitung-Lanyu (Orchid Island) If you can't afford to fly to Lanyu of prefer to go by boat anyway there is generally one going there twice a week on Tuesdays and Saturdays from Taitung at 6 am. You need to go to the shipping office personally to book a passage as they tend not to know whether they're sailing until the afternoon before intended departure (probably to make sure there are enough passengers).

The boats go via Lutao (Green Island) where they unload cargo and set down passengers. Unloading cargo can take some time so you shouldn't expect to arrive at Lanyu before 2.30-3 pm. There's usually plenty of room on the boat to stretch out and snacks are available (biscuits and soft drinks). Passports and tickets are checked before you board the boat in Taitung, again when reboarding takes place at Lutao and yet again when you arrive in Lanyu! This isn't something invented especially for foreigners: the locals get it too.

Fares for the boats from Taitung are:

Lutao (Green Island)	NT$260 one-way
Lanyu (Orchid Island)	NT$326 one-way
Lutao-Lanyu	NT$481 one-way*
Lanyu	NT$652 return
Lutao-Lanyu	NT$807 return*

*including Lutao stop-over

In Taitung the boats depart from Fou Kang which is some way up the coast from Taitung. There is supposed to be a 'Golden Dragon' Kaohsiung-Tung Kun bus which goes via Fou Kang and can be caught at the bus station in Taitung at 5.16 am everyday (the enquiry desk confirmed this) but when I got there the ticket clerk told me it wouldn't be in until 6.30 am so I was forced to take a taxi which costs NT$160 by meter and took 15-20 minutes. You can avoid this expense by staying overnight at the hotel in Fou Kang. For further information ring Taitung 322210 and ask for Miss Lai who speaks sufficient English to tell you the score.

Kaohsiung-Makung (Penghu or Pescadores Islands) There is a daily car ferry in either direction between Kaohsiung and Makung in the Pescadores Islands. It's considerably cheaper than the flights. The ferry departs Kaohsiung at 8 am and arrives Makung at 12.30 pm. The return trip departs Makung at 3 pm and arrives Kaohsiung at 7.30 pm. Fares range from NT$156 to NT$372. The ferries are operated by Tai Pong Luan Shipping Co (tel 551-5823). They have a new office in Kaohsiung but, when I was there, not even the travel agents knew where it was so it's best to go down to the ferry terminal and buy your ticket there.

Boats to Liuchiuyu

This small fishing-village island just off the coast of Taiwan and south of Kaohsiung can be reached by boat from Tungkang. There's no regular schedule and you'll have to ask around for a lift on a fishing boat. To get to Tungkung take a bus from the central bus terminal in Kaohsiung.

RAILWAY TIMETABLES

1 WEST COAST – DOWN

	Express (101)	Chua Kuang (1)	Chu Hsin (51)	Tzu Chiang (1001)	Chu Kuang (3)	Express (103)	Tzu Chiang (1003)	Chu Hsin (73)
Keelung 基隆					0740			
Taipei 台北	0630	0700	0730	0800	0820	0840	0900	0920
Hsinchu 新竹	0739	0806	0837	0855	0927	0951	0958	1031
Miaoli 苗栗	0808	0833	0908				1022	1107
Taichung 台中	0903	0934	1011	1008	1047		1113	1210
Chunghua 彰化	0920		1027	1022	1103	1133		
Chiayi 嘉義	1028	1042	1122	1110	1159	1239	1213	
Tainan 台南	1115	1126	1206	1148	1243	1329	1251	
Kaohsiung 高雄	1152	1200	1240	1217	1317	1418	1320	
Pingtung 屏東							1444	

	Express (105)	Chu Kuang (5)	Chu Hsin (53)	Chu Kuang (7)	Express (107)	Chu Hsin (55)	Express (109)
Keelung 基隆	0900						
Taipei 台北	0940	1000	1030	1100	1130	1200	1230
Hsinchu 新竹	1053	1108		1211	1241	1307	1344
Miaoli 苗栗		1134	1157	1239	1314	1335	
Taichung 台中		1232	1251	1333	1410	1322	
Changhua 彰化	1228	1248	1307	1348	1427	1450	1522
Chiayi 嘉義	1332	1344	1413	1444	1529	1549	1627
Tainan 台南	1421	1428	1500	1528	1619	1634	1715
Kaohsiung 高雄	1455	1502	1537	1602	1655	1710	1819
Pingtung 屏東							1845

	Chu Kuang (9)	Chu Hsin (57)	Tzu Chiang (1005)	Chu Hsin (75)	Chu Kuang (11)	Chu Hsin (59)	Express (111)	Chu Kuang (13)
Keelung 基隆			1325				1441	
Taipei 台北	1300	1330	1400	1420	1440	1550	1520	1540
Hsinchu 新竹		1438	1445	1530	1547		1631	1643
Miaoli 苗栗	1427	1509				1630		
Taichung 台中	1523	1602				1727		1810
Changhua 彰化	1539	1618	1607	1715	1719	1747	1807	
Chiayi 嘉義	1639	1717	1657		1820	1849	1911	1922
Tainan 台南	1726	1804	1738		1906	1936	1958	2006
Kaohsiung 高雄	1800	1840	1807		1940	2010	2057	2040
Pingtung 屏東							2131	

	Chu Hsin (61)	Tzu Chiang (1007)	Express (113)	Chu Hsin (63)	Chu Kuang (15)	Tzu Chiang (1009)	Express (3005)
Keelung 基隆				1645			
Taipei 台北	1600	1640	1700	1730	1800	1900	1915
Hsinchu 新竹	1710	1733	1814	1834	1907	1955	2034
Miaoli 苗栗			1844				
Taichung 台中		1841	1945	2000		2103	2231
Changhua 彰化	1839	1855	2002	2021	2036		
Chiayi 嘉義	1948	1942	2101	2119	2137	2202	
Tainan 台南	2036	2021	2149	2204	2224	2240	
Kaohsiung 高雄	2110	2050	2225	2240	2300	2310	
Pingtung 屏東							

	Chu Hsin (77)	Chu Kuang (25)	Express (115)	Chu Hsin (65)	Express (117)	Chu Kuang (17)
Keelung 基隆						
Taipei 台北	1940	2030	2200	2230	2300	2330
Hsinchu 新竹	2048	2145	2326	2354	0025	0053
Miaoli 苗栗	2115	2215	0001			0127
Taichung 台中	2212	2309	0115			0244
Changhua 彰化	2228	2325	0141	0154	0228	0304
Chiayi 嘉義	2338		0307	0320	0352	0426
Tainan 台南	0023		0410	0424	0454	0528
Kaohsiung 高雄			0459	0514	0542	0613
Pingtung 屏東						

2 WEST COAST – UP

	Express (3002)	Chu Kuang (22)	Chu Hsin (72)	Express (102)	Chu Kuang (2)	Chu Hsin (52)	Tzu Chiang (1002)	Express (104)
Pintung								
Kaohsiung				0615	0700	0715	0800	0830
Tainan			0600	0653	0736	0756	0831	0908
Chiayi			0648	0740	0820	0843	0908	0958
Changhua		0650	0755	0843	0920	0949	0955	1109
Taichung	0610	0706	0812	0901	0937		1010	
Miaoli		0758	0909	1003	1034			
Hsinchu	0804	0831	0943	1036	1101	1121	1116	1248
Taipei	0923	0945	1052	1152	1200	1225	1220	1355
Keelung				1223			1245	

	Tzu Chiang (1004)	Chu Kuang (4)	Chu Hsin (54)	Chu Kuang (6)	Chu Hsin (74)	Express (106)	Chu Hsin (56)
Kaohsiung	0900	0910	0935	1000		1030	1100
Tainan	0931	0945	1010	1035		1108	1135
Chiayi	1011	1029		1119		1159	1222
Changhua		1129	1158	1218		1307	
Taichung	1112	1145	1215	1236	1300		1336
Miaoli	1156		1313	1333	1359		1439
Hsinchu	1220	1305	1344		1429	1442	1505
Taipei	1315	1410	1455	1501	1538	1555	1610
Keelung			1527				

	Chu Kuang (8)	Chu Hsin (58)	Express (108)	Tzu Chiang (1006)	Chu Kuang (10)	Chu Hsin (60)	Express (110)	Chu Kuang (12)
Pintung			1142					
Kaohsiung	1135	1200	1220	1300	1322	1350	1420	1440
Tainan	1210	1238	1258	1332	1357	1429	1456	1515
Chiayi	1256	1322	1346	1409	1444	1513	1544	1559
Changhua	1355	1424	1450		1542		1650	1701
Taichung	1411	1446		1512	1600	1632	1706	
Miaoli		1543	1653		1653		1806	
Hsinchu	1534		1635	1619	1723	1751	1837	1831
Taipei	1635	1709	1746	1713	1825	1900	1945	1940
Keelung								

		Chu Hsin (62)	Chu Kuang (14)	Express (112)	Tzu Chiang (1008)	Chu Hsin (76)	Express (114)	Chu Kuang (16)
Pintung	屏東						1624	
Kaohsiung	高雄	1500	1535	1600	1630		1700	1740
Tainan	台南	1535	1610	1639	1701		1741	1816
Chiayi	嘉義	1622	1654	1726	1739		1829	1801
Changhua	彰化	1720	1754	1837	1827		1938	2000
Taichung	台中	1740	1810		1842	1900		2017
Miaoli	苗栗		1910			1951		2114
Hsinchu	新竹	1901		2014	1953	2022	2118	2141
Taipei	台北	2010	2035	2125	2049	2133	2225	2250
Keelung	基隆							2319

		Chu Hsin (64)	Tzu Chiang (1010)	Express (116)	Chu Hsin (66)	Chu Kuang (18)	Express (118)
Pintung	屏東						2223
Kaohsiung	高雄	1825	1920	2200	2230	2245	2300
Tainan	台南	1900	1951	2253	2323	2336	2354
Chiayi	嘉義	1947	2028	2356	0028	0042	0058
Changhua	彰化	2049	2117	0126	0159	0207	0225
Taichung	台中	2106		0148		0229	
Miaoli	苗栗	2159		0306		0345	
Hsinchu	新竹		2228	0345	0406	0424	0435
Taipei	台北	2335	2328	0528	0540	0554	0607
Keelung	基隆			0601			

Fares	Tzu Chiang	Chu Kuang	Fu Shing
Taipei-Taichung	NT$232	NT$205	NT$169
Taipei-Tainan	NT$451	NT$399	NT$329
Taipei-Kaohsuing	NT$516	NT$455	NT$376

There are also express fares which are lower than the above.

3 EAST COAST – DOWN

		Express (2001)	Chu Kuang (81)	Chu Kuang (31)	Express (3003)	Chu Kuang (33)	Chu Hsin (91)	Express (131)	Chu Kuang (35)
Taipei	台北	0700	0740	0820	0940	1010	1230	1310	1350
Ilan	宜蘭		0948	1028	1127	1218	1439	1525	1611
Hualien	花蓮	0956	1156	1232	1313	1422	1509	1555	1818

		Express (133)	Chu Kuang (37)	Express (135)	Chu Kuang (39)
Taipei	台北	1510	1740	1930	2350
Ilan	宜蘭	1720	1957	2147	0225
Hualien	花蓮	1928	2203	2350	0453

	Express (21)	Kuang Hua (1)	Kuang Hua (3)	Express (23)	Kuang Hua (5)	Kuang Hua (7)	Kuang Hua (9)	Kuang Hua (11)
Hualien 花蓮	0547	0810	1026	1140	1305	1448	1705	1905
Taitung 台東	0959	1021	1415	1600	1649	1840	2057	2254

4 EAST COAST – UP

	Express (132)	Chu Hsin (32)	Express (134)	Chu Kuang (34)	Chu Hsin (82)	Chu Kuang (92)	Express (3004)	Chu Kuang (36)
Hualien 花蓮	0655	0800	0855	1015	1330		1510	1600
Ilan 宜蘭	0854	1004	1106	1234	1527	1540	1656	1804
Taipei 台北	1116	1237	1324	1454	1739	1823	1848	2017

	Express (136)	Chu Hsin (38)	Express (2002)	Chu Kuang (40)
Hualien 花蓮		1805	1930	2355
Ilan 宜蘭	1705	1956		0227
Taipei 台北	1947	2159	2329	0445

	Kuang Hua (2)	Express (22)	Kuang Hua (4)	Express (24)	Express (24)	Kuang Hua (8)		
Taitung 台東	0600	0747	0915	1146	1307	1515	1710	1905
Hualien 花蓮	0947	1149	1301	1531	1721	1901	2058	2252

Taipei-Hualien	Chu Kuang	NT$238
	Chu Hsin	NT$196

There are also express fares which are lower than the above.

5 ALISHAN FOREST RAILWAY (NARROW GAUGE)

Chiayi-Alishan

Train	Chiayi	Alishan	Alishan	Chiayi	
Chung Hsin (301)	0740	1130	Chung Hsin (302)	0750	1125
Kuang Fu (1)	0800	1210	Kuang Fu (2)	0820	1205
Local Train (51)	0850	1400	Local Train (51)	1010	1515
Chung Hsin (305)	1330	1715	Chung Hsin (306)	1305	1637
Kuang Fu (5)	1400	1805	Kuang Fu (6)	1335	1730

Fares	Kuang Fu	NT$373 one-way
	Chung Hsin	NT$346 one-way
	local train	NT$171 one-way

Taiwan — Around the Country

TAIPEI 台北

Taipei isn't exactly the world's most beautiful city nor its most interesting. Indeed, with the exception of certain features like the Chiang Kai-shek Memorial Hall, Lungshan Temple, Chunghua Bazaar, the Botanical Gardens and the area around the National Palace Museum, it's probably one of the plainest and ugliest capital cities in the area. It's certainly a very large and busy city which bustles with the activity of business, commerce and government. The transport system is well organised and people on the whole are very friendly but, unless you have money to burn on expensive night clubs and restaurants, it's definitely over-rated as a tourist attraction. The things that are worth seeing and the places that are worth visiting are largely to be found elsewhere on the island.

Orientation

Most travellers enter and leave Taiwan through Chiang Kai-shek International Airport 中正國際機場. The airport is 34 km from Taipei near Taoyuan. Public shuttle buses run between CKS airport and Taipei railway station 台北火車站 and between CKS airport and Taipei domestic airport (Sungshan airport) 台北空港. Both take about 50 minutes in normal traffic but if you are travelling during rush-hour allow at least another 15-20 minutes. The snarl-ups which happen at these times have to be seen to be believed! There are two types of buses between CKS airport and the railway station – the non-stop variety and the two-stop variety. It doesn't really matter which type you take if you intend staying at a budget hotel. The buses cost NT$73 and operate in either direction between 6.35 am and 10.30 pm daily every 10-15 minutes. It's unlikely you'll have to use the bus between CKS airport and Taipei domestic airport but if you do it runs on the same schedule and costs NT$32.

There is another shuttle bus service – the Gray Line – which connects CKS airport with the *President Hotel, Grand Hotel, New Asia Hotel* and the *Lai Lai Shangri-La Hotel* but it costs NT$200 one-way and operates only once per hour between 8.05 am and 5.45 pm on the journey to the airport and between 10 am and 6.50 pm on the journey from the airport.

A taxi from central Taipei to CKS airport will cost around NT$700 during the day although the meter will only show NT$350. The charge at night is higher. The reason for this is that taxi drivers often have to wait a long time for a return fare at CKS airport.

Three of the most popular budget hotels as well as the *YMCA* and the *YWCA* are located conveniently close to the Taipei railway station but there are others spread out over the city so it's a good idea to get to grips with the public bus system as soon as possible since this is excellent. On the other hand this is no mean feat and finding the right bus stop outside the railway station is another matter entirely! It's also worth remembering that anything vaguely resembling a queue will disintegrate the moment the bus arrives. After that it's the law of the jungle. This only seems to happen at the station – elsewhere it's pretty civilised. Make sure you buy a card of bus tokens before you attempt to board a bus as the conductresses get flustered if you delay matters. A card with 10 tokens costs NT$60 and can be bought at the small kiosks you'll find near most bus stops (they also sell cigarettes and newspapers). Just hand them NT$60 and say, 'bus tokens'. Most rides cost one token. If you can't handle jumping in at the deep end of the public transport system immediately on arrival, taxis cost NT$23 for the first km and NT$5 for each additional half km. You'll rarely meet a taxi driver who doesn't turn on the meter immediately and tipping isn't necessary. Few of the drivers speak any English so have the name of your destination written down in Chinese before you get in.

Both the tourist offices – the Taiwan Visitors' Association and the Tourism Bureau – are a fair way from the centre of town but you'll be able to pick up most of what you need from CKS airport on arrival. The railway station, bus stations, GPO, Immigration Office, Provincial Police Administration Office (for mountain permits), the head office of the Taiwan Bank (for changing money) and Chunghua Bazaar are all within easy walking distance of each other in the centre of the city.

Information

Tourist Information There are two tourist offices in Taipei but the Taiwan Visitors' Association, 5th floor, 111 Mingchuan E Rd (tel 594-3261/5) isn't worth visiting since they don't have any more information of use to you that you won't already have picked up at CKS airport. The Tourism Bureau, 9th floor, 280 Chunghsiao E Rd, Section 4 (tel 721-8541/751-8445), on the other hand, is worth a visit as they have a lot of information you cannot obtain elsewhere as well as all the usual stuff (*This Month in Taiwan*, maps of the island, street plans, leaflets about the major tourist attractions of the island, etc). Their office is a little difficult to find since there's nothing in English or Chinese on the outside of the building where it's situated but it's the second brown and cream coloured high-rise block back from Kwangfu N Rd opposite Sun Yat Sen Memorial Hall. The lifts are in the centre of the building and you'll see the Tourism Bureau name plate on the left-hand side of the lifts along with many others. Make sure you ask for a current list of rail, bus, boat and flight timetables and prices as well as an explanation of the Taipei public bus routes. The women who deals with enquiries here speaks excellent English and is very friendly. The office is open Monday through Friday from 9 am to 4 pm and on Saturdays from 9 am to 12 noon. Buses which go there include Nos 27, 31, 73, 204, 212, 240, 259 and 504.

Banks Unless you're changing money at one of the large hotels you must go to the Bank of Taiwan to change travellers' cheques. It's on the corner opposite the Presidential Building. On the other hand, you can change bank notes into Taiwanese dollars for a rate better than what the bank offers at the gold shops in the city centre.

Bank of Taiwan
: 120 Chungkin South Rd, Section 1 (tel 371 7171)

American Express
: 137 Nanking East Rd, Section 2 (tel 563 3182)

Bank of America
: 205 Tun Hwa North Rd (tel 731 4111)

Chase Manhatten Bank
: 72 Nanking East Rd, Section 2 (tel 521 3262)

Citibank
: 742 Min Sheng East Rd (tel 731 5931)

Grindlay's Bank
: 2nd floor, 123 Nanking East Rd, Section 2 (tel 541 9251)

Lloyds Bank International
: 66 Nanking East Rd, Section 2 (tel 394 5105/10)

Bookstores The two best English-language bookstores are Caves Books, 107 Chunshan N Rd, Section 2 (tel 541 4754/9410) and Imperial Book, Sound & Gift Co, 615 Lin Shen N Rd, opposite the President Hotel. Both are open seven days a week.

Museums

Of all the things to see in Taipei, the number one attraction is the **National Palace Museum** in the suburb of Wai Shuang Hsi. This museum houses the world's richest collection of Chinese art and you should plan on spending at least a whole day there. The displays are changed

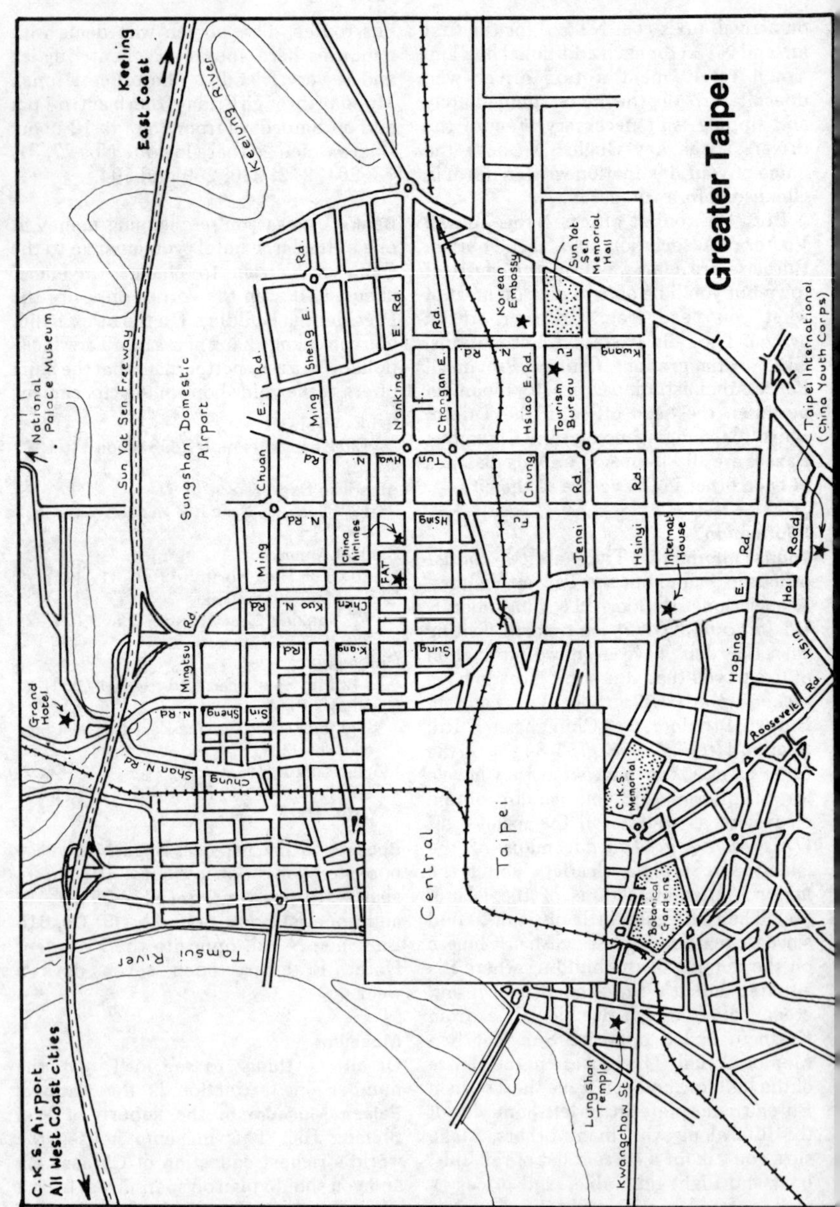
Greater Taipei
Keeling
East Coast
Keelung River
National Palace Museum
Sun Yat Sen Freeway
Sungshan Domestic Airport
Grand Hotel
C.K.S. Airport
All West Coast cities
Tamsui River
Central Taipei
Mingtsu Rd.
Min Chuan E. Rd.
Min Sheng E. Rd.
Nanking E. Rd.
Changan E. Rd.
Chung Hsiao E. Rd.
Jenai Rd.
Hsinyi Rd.
Hoping E. Rd.
Roosevelt Rd.
Hsin Hai Road
Chung Shan N. Rd.
Sin Sheng N. Rd.
Sung Kiang Rd.
Chien Kuo N. Rd.
Tun Hwa N. Rd.
Fu Hsing N. Rd.
Kwang Fu N. Rd.
China Airlines
FAT
Korean Embassy
Sun Yat Sen Memorial Hall
Tourism Bureau
Internat'l House
Taipei International (China Youth Corps)
C.K.S. Memorial
Botanical Gardens
Lungshan Temple
Kwangchow St

continually since at any one time there's only space to exhibit a small fraction of the total. The remainder is stored in air-conditioned caves behind the museum. Apart from the exhibitions themselves there are regular programmes on internal TV describing the development of Chinese pottery and painting (ear-phones are available for English speakers) and lectures on Tuesdays and Fridays at 10 am. The latter last two hours and cost NT$60 – get there early if you want a seat. There is a good restaurant and snack bar off to one side of the museum which sells reasonably priced meals. The museum shop has some excellent literature for sale as well as large prints of Chinese paintings which are outstanding value at only NT$42 per copy (if you want to mail them back home they also sell cardboard tubes). The museum is open daily from 9 am to 5 pm but try to avoid going there on Sunday as it gets very crowded. Entry costs NT$20. To get there from central Taipei take bus No 210, 213, 255 or 304 to the end of the line. No 213 can be caught either from outside the White House Hotel or the Hilton Hotel. No 304 can be found on Chunghua Rd (Section 1) or on Chungshan N Rd (Sections 2 and 3). If you take the 213 you'll pass the **National Revolutionary Martyrs' Shrine** en route. This monument, built in the style of the imperial pavilions at Peking, is open to visitors every afternoon.

The other museum which is worth a visit is the **National Museum of History**, 49 Nanhai Rd, open daily from 9 am to 5 pm. Entry costs NT$55. The museum houses over 10,000 items of Chinese art dating from 2000 BC to the present including a large number of bronze and jade pieces. Just at the back of this museum are the **Botanical Gardens**, an excellent place to relax in out of the noise and fumes of the traffic-jammed streets all around.

The recently completed **Fine Arts Museum**, 181 Chung Shan N Rd, Section 3, has been recommended by many travellers. It's the largest museum of its type in Asia and compares favourably with the Museum of Modern Art in New York. It houses displays of oil paintings, graphic art, Chinese landscape paintings, sculpture and other art works. It's open daily except Mondays.

If you have an interest in butterflies it might be worth trying to get to see the **Butterfly Museum**, 71 Chinan Rd, Section 1. The museum is open by appointment only between 9 am and 5 pm (ring 321 6256 and ask for Prof Chen Wei-shou but have a Chinese speaker with you as the professor doesn't speak English).

Memorials

The most impressive of these is the recently completed **Chiang Kai-shek Memorial Hall & Gardens**, Hsinyi Rd, Section 1, which is open daily from 9 am to 5 pm. Entry is free. The main building is a stunningly beautiful structure of white marble with an enormous blue-tiled traditional roof. You won't find anything quite like this place anywhere else on the island so it's well worth a visit. There's a classic re-interpretation of modern Chinese history in the photographic exhibition on the ground floor which is basically a eulogy about Chiang Kai-shek's glorious contribution to the Republic of China. It seems to end, however, around the time of the communist victory on the mainland in 1948. Buses which pass the memorial hall include Nos 20, 48, 67, 204, 235, 249, 253 and 263.

The other memorial hall is the **Dr Sun Yat-sen Memorial Hall**, Jenai Rd, Section 4, open daily from 9 am to 5 pm. It's one of the largest buildings in Taiwan and was constructed at a cost of US$4 million. Performances of Chinese opera are sometimes put on here on Saturday and Sunday afternoons – check with the tourist office for the times or in *This Week in Taiwan*. The shows are popular with local students so it's a good idea to make a reservation beforehand (ring 702 2411 and ask for extension 36). The performances are free of charge. Buses which go past the hall include Nos 19, 27, 31, 32, 33, 43, 70, 207, 212, 240 and 254.

Temples

The oldest and most famous of these is the **Lungshan Temple**, Kwang Chow St, right in the heart of the old city. The place was bombed out during World War II but has been faithfully restored since then. The most distinctive features of this temple are its incredibly ornate roofs though the stone sculptures, wood carvings and brass work are equally impressive. It's an interesting temple to stroll around at any time of day (open daily from 7 am to 10 pm) but special services are usually held in the evenings around 8 pm and there's chanting everyday at 6.30 am and 5 pm. Lungshan is basically a Buddhist temple though a lot of Taoist influence is evident and you will see images of deities such as Ma Tzu, Goddess of the Sea, the Goddess of Mercy and the red-faced Kuan Kung as well as those of the Buddha. If you're staying in the city centre it's a fairly easy walk but if you're coming from outside this area then bus Nos 1, 7, 11, 18, 49, 62, 201, 215, 229, 231, 233, 234, 242, 245, 265 and 310 can be taken.

The other temple well worth visiting is the **Confucian Temple** on Talung St off Chiu Chuan St. Built in traditional style with huge wooden gates, the temple is in complete contrast to Lungshan. Here the essence is one of simplicity and tranquility. In common with other Confucian temples there are no images here. If you're fortunate enough to be in Taiwan on Confucius' birthday (September 28th) it's worth getting a ticket from one of the tourist offices to see the dawn memorial festival which takes place here on that date. Some travellers have written in to say they find the **Tao Temple** next to the above temple more interesting and there's a kind of fantasy garden attached to it.

Other

If you're into bargain hunting then take off for a morning or afternoon stroll down Chunghua Rd, Section 1, or some of the streets adjacent to it where there are literally thousands of small shops and workshops selling everything from bamboo blinds to coral carvings, Chinese lanterns to jade and water colours to brass Buddhas. You can pick up some really pleasant curios and souvenirs relatively cheaply.

Two streets west of Lungshan Temple is Taipei's infamous **Snake Alley** where you can see one of the most gory sights in the world. In the evenings a great show is made of live snakes being slit open and the drained blood sold as a drink to men on their way to the nearby brothels (it's supposed to enhance performance). Live terrapins receive a similar fate by having their heads chopped off and their bodies rinsed out to make a potion which is supposed to be good for the eyesight.

Another exotic area of Taipei to explore is Dihua St in the old section of the city where wholesalers sell an unbelievably exotic and wide range of items. There are also some very attractive old houses to see here.

One thing you should take the opportunity to see whilst you're here is a performance of Chinese opera. It's sometimes put on at weekends at the Sun Yat-sen Memorial Hall. Otherwise it's usually possible to see it at the Chinese Armed Forces Culture and Activity Centre, 64 Chunghua Rd, Section 1. At certain times of the year there's a performance every night from 7 pm to 10.30 pm. Entry costs NT$20 with a student card or NT$40 without. This traditional style of opera is incredibly popular with the Taiwanese and seems to take up at least half of the programme time on television.

Every Sunday morning starting around 8 am you can watch hundreds of old and young Chinese doing *tai chi* in the park right in front of the Provincial Museum. It's quite a sight and many of the people bring their caged singing birds along with them.

If you're interested in Chinese ceramics

it's worth a visit to the **Classical Art Factory** where you can watch the artists painting the vases. To get there take bus No 217 from the Hilton Hotel and get off at Da Du Lu 11.

The **Taiwan Handicraft Promotion Center** where prices are government controlled has been suggested as a good place to buy these items. It's open every day of the week from 9 am to 5.30 pm. The address is 1 Hsu Chow Rd close to the Chiang Kai-shek Memorial Hall.

Places to Stay – top end

There's a vast choice of five– and four-star hotels in Taipei and new ones are opening up all the time. Most of them are in Taipei itself but some, like the *Holiday Inn* at Taoyuan, are outside the city itself. In a publication of this size it's obviously not possible to list them all so a selection has been made. They include the following (international standard hotels are marked with*):

*Ambassador Hotel**
63 Chung Shan North Rd, Section 2 (tel 551-1111), 500 rooms, singles NT$2980 doubles NT$3480-4400

Brother Hotel
255 Nanking East Rd, Section 3, (tel 712-3456) 304 rooms, singles NT$1900-2200, doubles NT$2500

*Century Plaza Hotel**
132 Omei St (tel 311-3131), 250 rooms, singles NT$1600-1800 doubles NT$2000-2200

Cosmos Hotel
43 Chung Hsiao West Rd, Section 1 (tel 361-7856), 300 rooms, singles NT$1300, doubles NT$1500-1600

Emperor Hotel
118 Nanking E Rd, Section 1 (tel 581-1111), 120 rooms, singles NT$1450, doubles NT$1550

Hotel Flowers
19 Hankow St, Section 1, (tel 312-3811), 200 rooms, singles NT$960-1100, doubles NT$1100-1300

*Gloria Hotel**
369 Linshen North Rd, (tel 581-8111), 245 rooms, singles NT$2150-2600, doubles NT$2400-3500

*Golden China Hotel**
306 Sung Chiang Rd (tel 521-5151), 240 rooms, singles NT$1650, doubles NT$1800-2000

*The Grand Hotel**
1 Chung Shan North Rd, Section 4 (tel 596-5565), 660 rooms, singles NT$1140-1240, doubles NT$1440-3300

*Hilton Internatioal Taipei**
38 Chung Hsiao West Rd, Section 1 (tel 311-5151), 527 rooms, singles NT$2500, doubles NT$2900-3700

*Holiday Inn International Airport**
269 Dah Shing Rd, Taoyuan, 391 rooms, singles NT$1450, doubles NT$1650

Holiday Hotel
31 Chung-Hsiao East Rd, Section 1 (tel 391-2381), 140 rooms, singles NT$1300-1400, doubles NT$1500

*Imperial Hotel**
600 Lin Shen North Rd (tel 596-5111), 338 rooms, singles NT$2500, doubles NT$2900

Kilin Hotel
103 Kangting Rd (tel 314-9222), 325 rooms, singles NT$1200, doubles NT$1400-1600

*Lai Lai Sheraton Hotel**
12 Chung Hsiao East Rd, Section 1 (tel 321-5511), 705 rooms, singles NT$3640-4000, doubles NT$3870-4690

Leofoo Inn
168 Chang Chun Rd (tel 581-3111), 238 rooms, singles NT$1700, doubles NT$1900-2100

*Majestic Hotel**
2 Min Chuan East Rd (tel 581-7111), 400 rooms, singles NT$1700-1800, doubles NT$2000-2100

*Mandarin Hotel**
166 Tun Hwa North Rd (tel 712-1201) 351 rooms, singles NT$2100, doubles NT$2400-2700

Hotel New Asia
139 Chung Shan North Rd, Section 2 (tel 511-7181), 102 rooms, singles NT$1200, doubles NT$1400

Olympic Hotel
145 Chung Shan North Rd, Section 2 (tel 511-5253), 190 rooms, singles NT$1100-1200, doubles NT$1200-1500

Hotel Orient
85 Hankow St, Section 1 (tel 331-7211), 98 rooms, singles NT$760-1100, doubles NT$1200

Pacific Hotel
111 Kun Ming St (tel 311-3335), 102

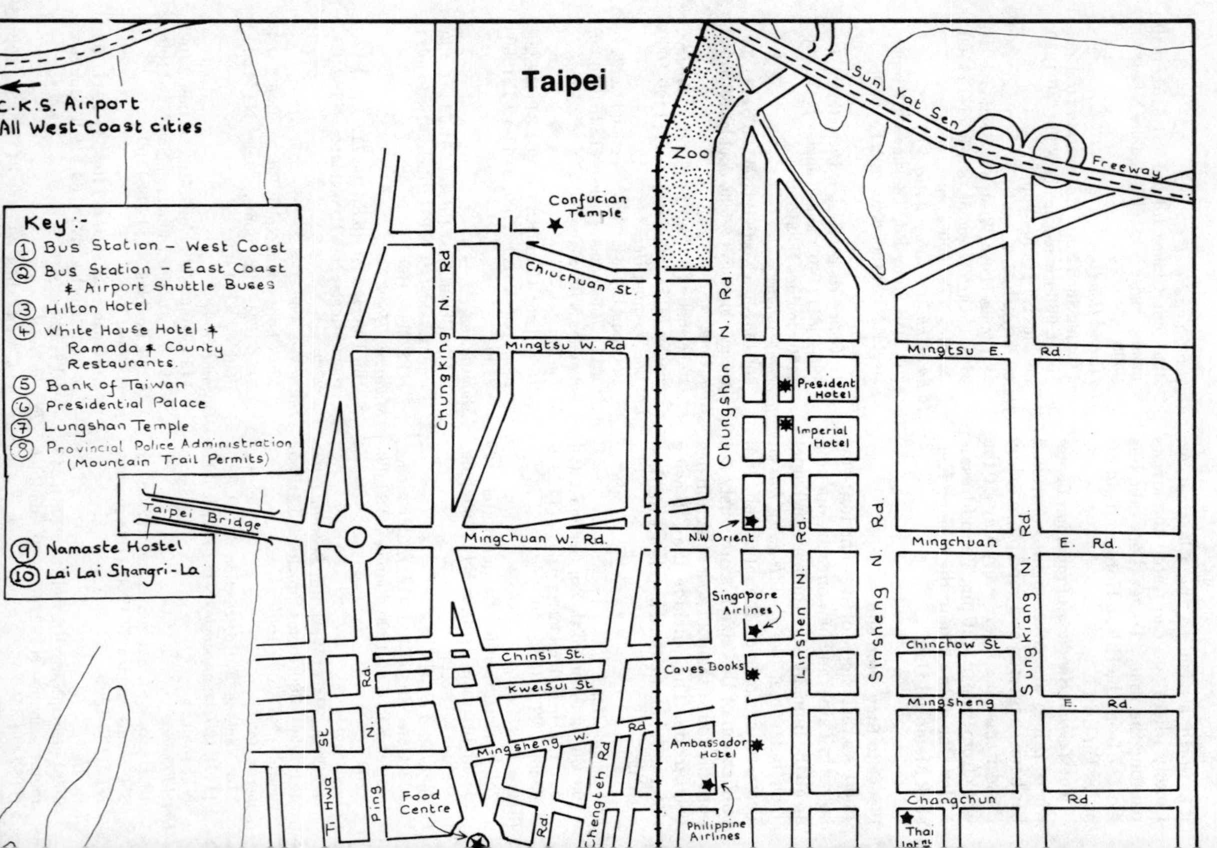
Taipei
C.K.S. Airport
All West Coast cities
Key:-
① Bus Station – West Coast
② Bus Station – East Coast & Airport Shuttle Buses
③ Hilton Hotel
④ White House Hotel & Ramada & County Restaurants.
⑤ Bank of Taiwan
⑥ Presidential Palace
⑦ Lungshan Temple
⑧ Provincial Police Administration (Mountain Trail Permits)
⑨ Namaste Hostel
⑩ Lai Lai Shangri-La
Sun Yat Sen
Freeway
Zoo
Confucian Temple
Chiuchuan St.
Chungking N. Rd
Mingtsu W. Rd
Mingtsu E. Rd.
Chungshan N. Rd
President Hotel
Imperial Hotel
N.W Orient
Taipei Bridge
Mingchuan W. Rd.
Mingchuan E. Rd.
Linshen N. Rd
Sinsheng N. Rd.
Sungkiang N. Rd.
Singapore Airlines
Chinchow St
Chinsi St.
Kweisui St
Caves Books
Mingsheng E. Rd.
Mingsheng W. Rd
Ambassador Hotel
Philippine Airlines
Changchun Rd.
Thai
T. Hwa St
Ping N. Rd.
Food Centre
Chengteh Rd

Keelung
Hualien
Kuanghua Bridge
International House
Sinsheng S. Rd.
Jenai Rd.
Hsinyi Rd.
Hoping E. Rd.
Chunghsiao E. Rd.
Taipei Hostel
Changan E. Rd.
Fuhsing Bridge
Tsinan Rd.
Linshen S. Rd.
Hsinyi Rd.
Chiang Kai Shek Memorial Hall
Roosevelt Rd.
Chungshan S. Rd.
Wulai Bus Stop
Kungyuan Rd.
Nanchang Rd.
Railway Station
Chunghsiao W. Rd.
G.P.O.
Hwaining St.
Chung King S. Rd.
Kwei Yang St.
Poai Rd.
Aikuo W. Rd.
Nanhai Rd.
National Museum of History
Botanical Gardens
Hoping W. Rd.
Yenping S. Rd.
Chunghua Bazaar
Kaifeng St.
Hankow St.
Wuchang St.
Omei St.
Kunming St.
Sining S. Rd.
Chengtu Rd.
Nei Chiang St.
Kangting Rd.
Kwei Lin Rd.
Kwangchow St.
Chunghsing Br.
Tamsui R.
Taichung
Tainan
Kaohsiung
1
2
3
4
5
6
7
8
9
10

rooms, singles NT$750-950, doubles NT$850-1150

Plaza Hotel
68 Sung Chiang Rd (tel 551-5251), 132 rooms, singles NT$1250, doubles NT$1400-1600

*President Hotel**
9 Teh Hwei St (tel 595-1251), 423 rooms, singles NT$2100-2400, doubles NT$2800-3400

*The Ritz Hotel**
155 Min Chuan East Rd (tel 597-1234), 221 rooms, singles NT$3200, doubles NT$3700-4300

*The San Polo Hotel**
172 Chung Hsiao East Rd (tel 772-2121), 407 rooms, singles NT$2200, doubles NT$2600

*Santos Hotel**
439 Cheng Teh Rd (tel 596-3111), 304 rooms, singles NT$2100, doubles NT$2100

*Taipei Miramar Hotel**
420 Min Chuan East Rd (tel 531-3456), 600 rooms, singles NT$2300, doubles NT$2500

*United Hotel**
200 Kuang Fu South Rd (tel 773-1515), 248 rooms, singles NT$2000.

Places to Stay – bottom end

In the centre of the city there is the very popular *Taipei Hostel*, 6th floor, No 11, Lane 5, Lin Shen North Rd (tel 02-295 2950/1) close to the Lai Lai Shangri-La Hotel. Dormitory beds here cost NT$70 a night with shared bathroom facilities, a washer and a spin-dryer and a useful notice-board. To get there from the airport take the Limousine Bus (NT$65) to the Lai Lai Shangri-La. Go up Lin Shen North Rd taking the first lane on the right-hand side. The buses are fairly chaotic, but from the railway station it's only a 10-minute walk. The Chinese address is 林森北路5巷11號6樓 .

Another popular place is the *Namaste Hostel*, 4th floor, 2 Shiu Chung St (tel 02-3813278/3317698). It's in the block at the back of the Hilton Hotel near the junction of Shiu Chung St and Kung Yuan Rd and there's a sign in English over the downstairs entrance. Beds here cost NT$90 per night. Rooms have fans and there is a restaurant (light meals), bar, recreation facilities and travel information. The Namaste is part of an island-wide chain of hostels and has 60 beds. The Chinese address is 台北市公園路16號4F .

Another place which offers dormitory-style accommodation and which has become popular recently is the *Formosa Hostel* (tel 02-531 9827). It offers beds for NT$90 in rooms which sleep between three and eight people. It has a pleasant atmosphere, a kitchen and a communal room with comfortable chairs. It's a little tricky to find but is in the same block as Philippine Airlines. As you come up Chungshan N Rd from the city centre take the second lane on the left-hand side after you have crossed Nanking E Rd. There's a very small sign at the entrance to the lane and an equally small one on the building where the hostel is. The hostel is on the third floor.

If you don't want dormitory accommodation then one of the cheapest places to stay and also one of the most popular is the *White House Hotel* 白宮大旅社 at 14-16 Hankow St (tel 311 7802/1602) diagonally opposite the Hotel Flowers which you can just about see from the railway station. There's a sign in English so you can't miss it. The cheapest rooms with fan and wash basin on the top floor cost NT$180/200 for singles/doubles though they may pretend that all these are full. The communal washing facilities are somewhat primitive but hot water is available. There are more expensive air-con rooms with own bathroom on the lower floors for NT$310 a double.

Further away from the centre is *International House* 台北國際學舍 18 Hsin Yi Rd, Section 3 (tel 707 3151/3) which has dormitory rooms for NT$100 and a range of more expensive rooms going up to NT$320 with air-con and own bathroom. The place is very well maintained, the bathrooms are spotless (though you're not allowed to wash clothes – laundry service available) and the staff speak English but only problem is that the dormitories and cheaper rooms are often full with long-term boarders. There's a TV lounge and library and a coffee shop which serves cafeteria-style meals between 7 am and 10 am, 11 am and 1.30 pm and 5.30 pm to 8 pm. The food is good and very cheap. If you miss the coffee shop, which often closes before it should, there's a Chinese restaurant next door which serves very good food at between NT$50-60 per dish. International House locks its doors at 12 midnight. To get there from the railway station take bus Nos 22, 38, 66, 70, 71, 209, 274 or 275.

Even further away from the centre is the *Taipei International*, 30 Hsin Hai Rd, Section 3 (tel 708 3932). This enormous building with restaurant, lounges and accommodation for 763 people is the headquarters of the China Youth Corps. The facilities here are superb as you might expect from a government-funded organisation and many foreigners stay here especially those looking for long-term cheap accommodation. The dormitories cost NT$100 per night or you can have private rooms for NT$250 a single and NT$300-600 a double. To get there from the railway station take bus No 237 or 209. Other buses which go there include Nos 3 and 76. This place is also the booking centre for the many other Youth Activity Centres scattered over the island – see the list under 'Accommodation' in the introductory section. The China Youth Corps also has another huge hostel with similar prices at 16 Chungshan North Rd, Section 4 (tel 596 2151) not far from the Grand Hotel. To get there take bus Nos 260 or 310 from the railway station.

Other possibilities are the *Taipei Youth Hostel*, 133 Tunhua N Rd (tel 721 5495) near to the Tourism Bureau which has dormitory-style accommodation for NT$70 per night (bus No 59 will get you there from near North Gate/GPO) and another youth hostel at 11-8 Fu Chou St.

Places to Eat

There's no shortage of cheap Chinese eateries in the streets around the railway station – Chung Hsiao Rd, Kai Feng St, Hankow St, Wuchang St, etc – but if you want an excellent choice of different Chinese dishes all in one location then try the *Food Centre* in the traffic island at the western end of Nanking W Rd on the top side of the railway station. This place is full of small stalls selling a wide variety of snacks and dishes. Just point to what you want. You can eat well here for around NT$60.

Two good restaurants on Hankow St both very close to the White House Hotel are the *Ramada* and the *County*. Both of them offer breakfasts (fruit juice, two eggs and ham, toast, butter, jam, coffee or tea) for NT$55 and set lunches for NT$90. They both do a la carte meals in the evenings but food at this time is considerably more expensive (soup, bread rolls, a fish dish followed by a meat dish and coffee start around NT$160).

In the evenings many travellers and ex-pat workers go to one or other of the European, American or Australian run 'pubs' which sell meals, draught and bottled beers and provide pub games (dart boards, pool tables, etc). Most of them are open daily from 11 am to 12 midnight. If you've been to Hong Kong they're very similar to the places there. With the exception of *The Ploughman's Cottage*, 305 Nanking E Rd, Section 3 (near the *Brother Hotel*) and *Zum Fass*, 55, Lane 119, Lin Shen N Rd,(near junction with Nanking E Rd and Sin Sheng N Rd), they are all located either on or very close to Shuang Cheng St near the *Imperial Hotel*, Lin Shen N Rd. This group of pubs includes the *Waltzing Matilda Inn*, *The Ploughman's Pub*, *The Horseshoe*, *Fiona's Farmhouse*, *The Hunter's Inn* and *The Victoria*. They're all quite similar in decor (usually mock farmhouse), atmosphere and price range and a lot depends on who you meet there. *The Ploughman's Pub* has the edge on prices for meals (a large helping of fish and chips, bread rolls and butter cost NT$180) but has no 'happy hour' whereas the *Waltzing Matilda* has a happy hour from 5 to 7 pm. *Zum Fass* isn't really a pub at all as it's too small and orientated towards groups of diners. The food is excellent but, apart from sausages and schnitzel, expensive. To get to any of the pubs in the vicinity of the *Imperial Hotel* take any of the buses going to Chungshan N Rd, Section 3 (Nos 17, 21, 29, 40, 47, 203, 208, 210, 213, 216,217, 218, 220, 224, 260, 301, 304, 308, and 310). If you're staying at the Taipei Hostel then you're within walking distance. Some of the pubs (eg the *Waltzing Matilda*) offer relatively cheap (NT$100-120) set meals at lunchtimes.

Getting There

There are two terminals for long-distance buses located on either side of the railway station. The left-hand side is for buses going down the west coast and the one on the right-hand side is for buses going down the east coast. The timetables are all in Chinese but the ticket offices usually have the destination in English as well as Chinese.

The West Coast

To Kaohsiung 高雄 There are 70 luxury, air-con buses daily round the clock which cost NT$363 and 75 air-con expresses from 6 am to 12 midnight which cost NT$309.

To Tainan 台南 There are 35 luxury, air-con buses daily from 7 am to 12 midnight which cost NT$325 and 26 air-con expresses daily from 7.25 am to 11.45 pm which cost NT$277.

To Chiayi 嘉義 There are 65 luxury, air-con buses daily from 7.20 am to 9.40 pm which cost NT$223.

To Taichung 台中 There are 35 luxury, air-con buses daily from 6.50 am to 10.40 pm which cost NT$172 and 73 air-con expresses daily from 6.15 am to 10.55 pm which cost NT$144.

The East Coast

To Ilan 宜蘭 There are eight buses daily to Ilan, the first bus at 11.30 am and the last at 7.20 pm.

To Lotung 羅東 There are 58 buses daily from 6.45 am to 8.45 pm. These buses pass through Ilan and so can be used to get to that place as well.

To Suao 蘇澳 There are eight buses daily to Suao, the first at 7 am and the last at 7.50 pm. Once past Fuling, the road down the east coast skirts along the edge of the mountain range which drops precipitously into the ocean. It continues to do this all the way down to Hualien so you're in for a spectacular ride if you choose the bus instead of the train. Taipei to Hualien can be covered easily in one day by bus if you set off early.

Getting Around

As mentioned earlier, the public bus system in Taipei is excellent but it's too complicated to get to know very well in the few days that you'll spend here. Bus numbers are included for the places you're likely to want to visit and for the accommodation but if you expect to be using the system extensively then go to the Tourism Bureau as early as possible and ask for a copy of the public bus numbering system. Another place which does a useful one-page precis of this is International House.

AROUND TAIPEI

Chinshan Beach 金山

On the north coast surrounded by wooded hills and close to the port of Keelung, Chinshan is perhaps the best beach close to Taipei. It's a huge bay and very popular with young people during the summer months. The China Youth Corps has a large hostel here located at the Huangkang village. There are direct buses from Taipei to Chinshan from the bus station on the eastern side of the railway station. Very close to Chinshan on the promontory which separates the bay from Keelung is the popular sight-seeing area of Yeh Liu 野柳 where there are many bizarre coral formations shaped as a result of erosion.

Wulai 烏來

An hour's bus ride due south of Taipei, Wulai is described in the tourist literature as 'the nearest aboriginal village to Taipei'. It might well have been that at one time but 'Taiwans answer to Disneyland' would be far more appropriate these days. All the same it's worth a visit not only because it's so outrageously kitsch but because it's located in a beautiful river gorge surrounded by forested mountains. Once you get off the bus, run the gauntlet of the tourist souvenir trash shops and head for the electric toy train on the other side of the river which links Wulai with the waterfall and the cable car to Yun Hsien 'Dreamland'. The trains run very frequently from 8 am to 6 pm and cost NT$16 one-way. If you prefer, you can walk the two km along a paved road. Where the train drops you can look at the waterfall, have a swim in the river (beautifully clean water!), pose with mini-skirted 'aboriginal' young women – for a price – and then take the cable car to 'Dreamland'. The cable cars run every 5-10 minutes and cost NT$75 return. Up there at the top you have a choice of boating ponds, skating rink, zoo, big dipper, space invaders, ghost train, kids' playground, an expensive hotel and restaurant and a whole lot more tourist trash shops all set amongst tree ferns and forest and boulder-strewn mountain streams. It's certainly a lot cooler than down at Wulai and the Taiwanese love it! There's always hundreds of poeple up there.

To get to Wulai from Taipei go to the bus stop on the Taipei Park side of Kungyuan Rd opposite the hospital. Buses run five to six times an hour in either direction from 6 am to 9.40 pm. The fare is NT$21 and the journey takes about one hour (longer if you get caught in the rush hour). Forget all about queues on this bus.

HUALIEN 花蓮

Hualien is the largest town on the east coast of Taiwan. It's a pleasant, easy-going place though otherwise unremarkable except as an overnight stop on the way to Taroko Gorge unless you happen to be interested in a colourful but very artificial display of Ami aboriginal dances and folk songs put on specially for the tourists. It's a good place to pick up marble and onyx souvenirs though the prices of these in many shops which line Hualien's main street are by no means cheap. Both of these minerals are quarried in and around Taroko Gorge and there are several small factories and workshops out on the road to the airport.

Ami dances & folk songs

The Ami are one of the aboriginal tribes of Taiwan and inhabit the area around Hualien and Taroko Gorge. As you might expect in a country geared to the creation of economic wealth, they have been almost completely assimilated into the mainstream and few facets of their culture remains. The dance performances which they put on are purely for the benefit of tourists but perhaps worth seeing if you have time to spare whilst in Hualien. You can see these performances at the Ami Cultural Village 阿美文化村 about 15 minutes from the centre of Hualien daily at 2.30 pm and 7.30 pm. To get there either take a taxi or enquire at one of the travel agents on the main street in the centre of Hualien.

Places to Stay – top end

Hualien has three international standard hotels with swimming pool, air-con and other such luxuries. The large 346-room *Marshal Hotel* (tel 038-326123) at 36 Kung Yuan Rd is comparatively new and costs NT$1200 for singles, NT$1200-1400 for doubles. The 170-room *Astar Hotel* (tel 038-326111) is situated on a bluff looking out over the Pacific at 6-1 Min Chuen Rd. Singles here cost NT$650-1000 and doubles NT$1200-1400. The 237-room *CITC Hualien Hotel*, 2 Yong Shing Rd (tel 038-221171), costs NT$1600 a single and NT$1800 a double. At 50 San Min St the *Toyo Hotel* (tel 038-

326151) has 70 rooms costing NT$800 for singles and NT$1000 for doubles. There are a couple of places at Tien Hsiang in the Taroko Gorge. The *Tien Hsiang Lodge* (tel Tien Hsiang 20) has 16 rooms at NT$800 for singles, NT$900 for doubles. The *Wenshan Guest House* (tel Tien Hsiang 25) has 12 rooms at NT$500-550 for singles, NT$600-800 for doubles.

Places to Stay – bottom end

The best deal for budget accommodation in Hualien is the *Teacher's Hostel* 601 Chung Cheng St (tel 038-325280), which costs NT$110 per person per night. It's a clean place with hot water available from 4 pm to 10.30 pm. Tell them you're a student. The doors close at 10 pm. A cheaper place but one which is nowhere near the same value is the *Youth Hostel*, 84 Chungshan Rd, which costs NT$150 a single and NT$300 a double. The private rooms are partially air-con – in other words it works at night when you least need it. It's a pretty scruffy place with indifferent management. The plumbing is in an advanced state of disrepair and the showers tend to be fully occupied every morning with laundry activities. The Youth Hostel has a sign up in English whereas the Teachers' Hostel doesn't.

Other than the above two places, you're up for something considerably more expensive in one of the hotels. One of the cheapest is the *Hotel Yuan San*, 177 Chungshan Rd, which costs NT$250 a single and NT$380 a double. Rooms have their own bathroom, fan, crisp, clean sheets and are well-maintained. A towel and toothbrush are also provided! Note if the room has a TV in it you pay NT$30 extra – if you don't want one tell them though you might have some difficulty getting this across as they don't speak a word of English. Two other hotels include the *Hotel Golden Dragon* 金龍大旅社, very close to the old railway station (tel 23126/7) which costs NT$400 a single and NT$500 a double, and also the 大新大旅社, 101 Chungshan Rd (tel 322125/6) which costs NT$350 a single and NT$450 a double. Another hotel which has been recommended is the *Elevator Hotel*, up the main street from the bus station and then first street right past the Youth Hostel. They normally charge NT$300 for a room with air-conditioning, TV, own bathroom (with towels, soap and toothbrushes) but are open to negotiation down to NT$200.

Places to Eat

The main street of Hualien (Chungshan Rd) is very well supplied with good, cheap, ready-prepared food cafes. There's little to choose between them but they all have a good variety of dishes available. Just point to what you fancy. You can eat well at these places for NT$40-50.

Getting There

Trains The old railway station is now closed and all trains leave from the new station about two km from the centre of town. Public bus No 3 connects the bus station with the new railway station. The service operates in either direction every 10-15 minutes and the fare is NT$6 (buy bus tickets at the old station from the bus ticket office and at the new station from the kiosk next to the bus stop – they don't take money on the bus).

Buses The bus station is located on Chungshan Rd next to the old railway station. It's from here that you take buses going through Taroko Gorge to Tienshan 天祥 and further along the East-West Cross Island Highway to Lishan 梨山 and Taichung 台中. These public buses are all very well and certainly cheap but they have one big disadvantage which is that they don't stop anywhere in the Taroko Gorge to let you get down and admire the breathtaking views or take photographs. As there's nowhere else in this part of Asia which is anywhere near as spectacular as Taroko Gorge it's a great pity to pass through it so quickly. One way to avoid this is to take the bus as far as the start of

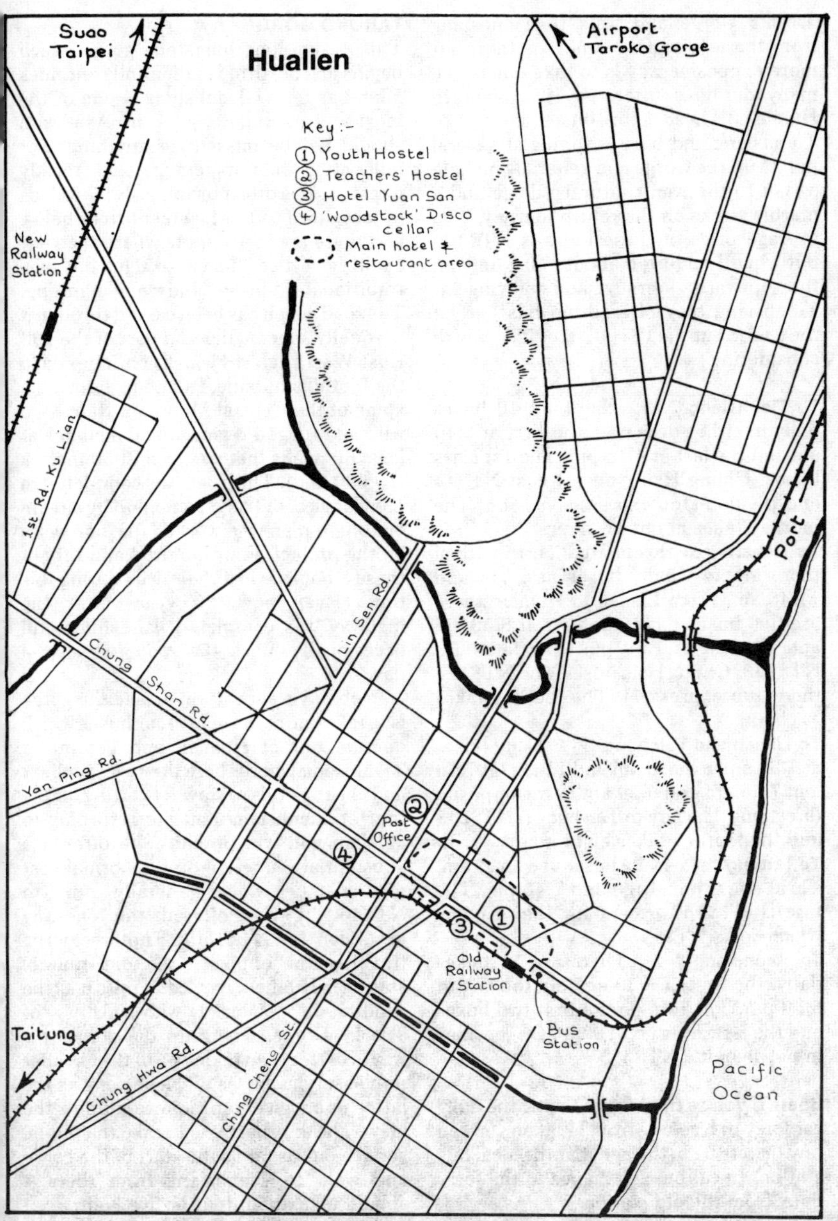
Hualien
Suao
Taipei
Airport
Taroko Gorge
Key :-
① Youth Hostel
② Teachers' Hostel
③ Hotel Yuan San
④ 'Woodstock' Disco cellar
Main hotel & restaurant area
New Railway Station
1st Rd. Ku Lian
Lin Sen Rd.
Chung Shan Rd.
Yan Ping Rd.
Post Office
Old Railway Station
Bus Station
Port
Taitung
Chung Hwa Rd.
Chung Cheng St.
Pacific Ocean

Taroko Gorge and walk to Tienhsiang from there (about 19 km). Another, but more expensive way is to take one of the many tour buses offered by rival agents in Hualien. These tour buses go up to Tienhsiang and back stopping at several points up the Gorge and generally include a visit to the Ami Cultural Village and a marble works on the return journey. The average price of these tours is NT$400 but when I enquired about going only on the outward journey and staying at Tienhsiang they offered me this part of the tour at NT$150 so it's worth considering.

To Tienhsiang 天祥 There are 10 buses daily in either direction, the first at 6.40 am and the last at 4.15 pm. The 1st class buses (Chung Hsing buses) cost NT$44 and the non-stop expresses NT$36. The journey takes about 1½ hours.

To Lishan 梨山 From Hualien to Lishan there are two daily buses at 7 am and 11.45 am. From Lishan to Hualien there are five buses daily, the first at 8.50 am and the last at 1.30 pm. The fares are NT$133 (Chung Hsin buses) and NT$111 (non-stop expresses). The journey takes 4½ hours.

To Lishan and Taichung 台中 Daily buses at 7.30 am, 8 am, 9 am and 11 am (at 7.15 am, 7.55 am and 9.20 am in the opposite direction). The fare to Taichung is NT$248 and the journey takes eight hours.

To Taitung 台東 Daily buses at 8 am, 9 am, 11.30 am, 2 pm, 4 pm and 7.40 pm. The fare is NT$167 except for the last bus which costs NT$148.

To Kaohsiung 高雄 There are 11 buses daily, the first at 6.30 am and the last at 6.30 pm. The fare on the first two buses and the last three is NT$298. On the ones in between it's NT$315.

Boats If you're thinking of taking the daily car ferry to Keelung from Hualien you can buy tickets from the agent at the local bus station. Local bus No 2 goes to the ferry quay from the old station.

TAROKO GORGE 大魯閣

This 19-km-long limestone gorge which begins just north of Hualien and continues inland as far as Tienhsiang is one of the most spectactular sights in Asia and should not be missed for anything. For mile after mile its craggy and thickly forested sides drop precipitously thousands of feet down to the turbulent river below and there are many spots where the view could have been taken straight out of a traditional Chinese landscape painting. The road which has been carved through it is equally spectacular and part of the 193 East-West Highway which continues on to the foothills outside Taichung across the spine of the Central Mountain Range – a wild and rugged region which includes at least 60 peaks that rise over 3050 metres (10,000 feet). This road was completed in 1960 at a cost of US$11 million by a team of 10,000 men who worked for four years on the project. Four hundred and fifty of these labourers lost their lives during this time. Even now, 20 years after the highway was completed, landslides still occasionally block the road for several days.

Probably the best way to see the gorge is to take one of the many tour buses which operate out of Hualien and get off at Tienhsiang where there are two excellent and cheap hotels to stay. By getting off the tour at Tienhsiang and not returning to Hualien you will probably be offered a substantial reduction on the normal cost of the tour which generally runs to NT$400 (I was offered the one-way excursion for NT$150). Enquire at the travel agent opposite the old railway station in Hualien – you can't miss it as the window is plastered with posters of Taroko Gorge. Going up the gorge this way is better than taking on of the cheaper public service buses to Tienhsiang as the latter don't give you time to admire the view. The alternative is to take the public service bus as far as the start of the gorge and walk to Tienhsiang from there – should take about four or five hours.

op: Sea of clouds at dawn, Alishan
.eft: Sacred tree (thousands of years old) on rail journey to Alishan
ight: View from Alishan

Top: Chiang Kai-Shek Memorial Hall, Taipei
Left: Warning sign on Taroko Gorge road
Right: Taroko Gorge

TIENHSIANG 天祥

Tienhsiang is a superb place to stay and relax for a few days. There are plenty of hiking possibilities in the area and much to see for those with an interest in geology, butterfly, bird and plant life. One place you should make the effort to go and see are the hot sulphur springs down at the bottom of the gorge at Wunshan, two or three km up the road from Tienhsiang. They're not signposted but you turn off to the right at the entrance to the third tunnel from Tienhsiang and follow the steps down the side of the gorge, across a small suspension bridge and down another flight of steps to the river. The springs are almost too hot to get into! Also at Tienhsiang is a pagoda and temple which are reached by crossing a long suspension bridge and while they're of no historical interest the views from the top of the pagoda are excellent.

Places to Stay

Most travellers stay at the *Catholic Hostel* which has been popular for years. It used to be a beautiful spot with Swiss chalet-type buildings and landscaped gardens but a lot of reconstruction went on during 1983 and 1984 and they were the first casualties. During that time the services suffered and it wasn't such good value but things will hopefully be back on a better footing by now. A bed in the dormitory (which the management isn't too keen to make you aware of) costs NT$80. There are also small double tatami rooms for NT$150 and single/double rooms for NT$200/300. It's sometimes a hassle to get clean sheets but if you insist they will be provided. Hot water is provided in the winter months. There's no provision for meals here but they do have cold drinks.

The other place to stay here is the *China Youth Corps Activity Centre* just a little further up the road from the *Catholic Hostel*. It's a gleaming white modern concrete structure which blends into the surroundings like an oil refinery on a beach. There's accommodation here for 344 people but the dormitories are often full with China Youth Corps groups out on hiking holidays. It costs NT$120 in the dormitories, NT$360-1200 a double or NT$600 for a four-bed room. Like all these places it has dining facilities and lounges.

Places to Eat

There are three cafes at the back of the bus station which have a good variety of ready-prepared food, soft drinks and beer. NT$75 will buy you a good meal. If you fancy a splurge one evening then try the *Tienhsiang Lodge* at the bottom side of the parking lot next to the river. A set meal here will cost you NT$120.

If you're planning on walking down the gorge there are several soft drinks and basic snack places strung out along its length where space allows.

Getting There

If you're heading towards either Lishan or Hualien it's advisable to book a ticket as early as possible (the woman who manages the ticket office speaks some English) as buses tend to arrive full. Unless you've booked a seat expect to wait around for some while.

To Hualien There are thirteen buses daily, the first at 6.50 am and the last at 5 pm (some of these buses start from Tienhsiang but most come through from Taichung or Lishan). The fare is NT$33 and the journey takes 1-1½ hours.

To Lishan There are buses at 8.10 am, 8.50 am, 9.20 am, 10.20 am, 11.20 am, 12.20pm and 1.20 pm. The first and last buses go only as far as Lishan whereas the rest continue on to Taichung. The fare to Lishan is NT$71 and the journey takes about 2½ to 3 hours. From Lishan to Taichung takes a further 3-3½ hours.

The journey to Lishan from Tienhsiang though not as dramatic as that through the Taroko Gorge nevertheless has its own beauty. The road winds and twists its way

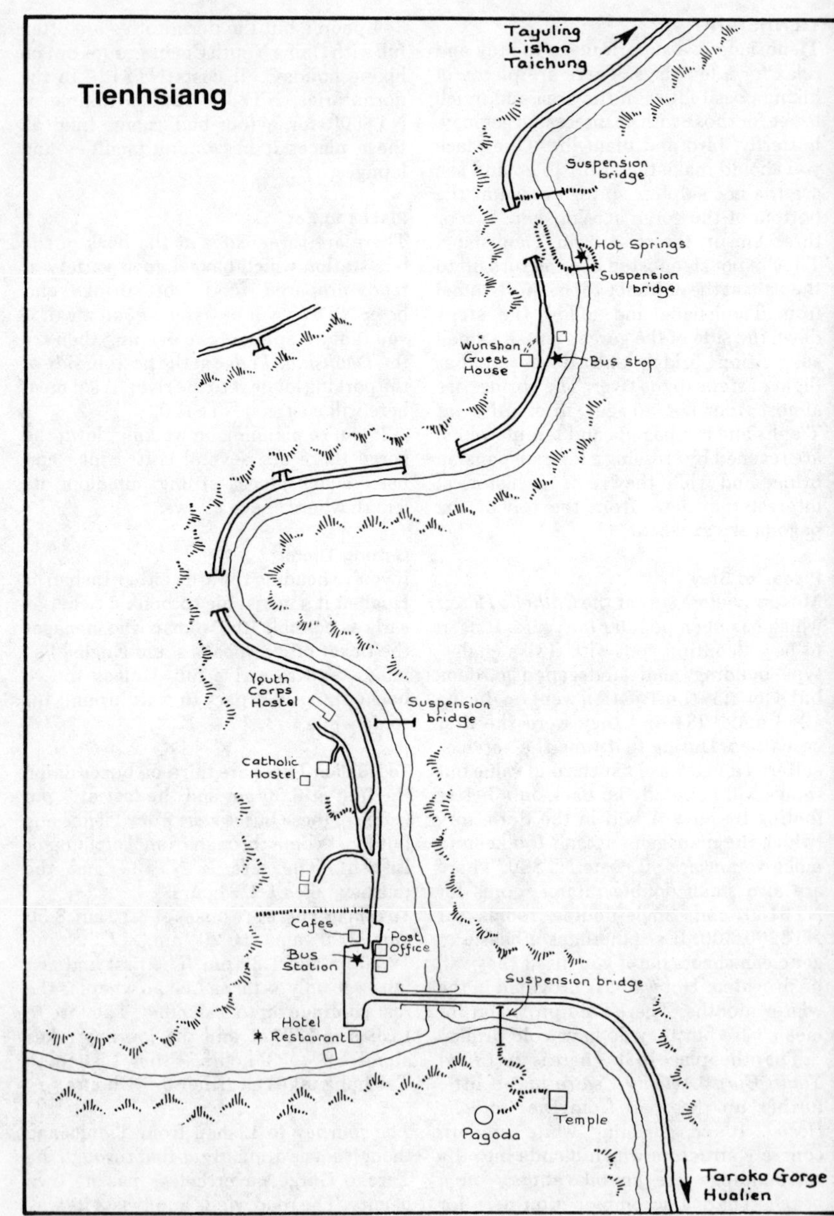
Tienhsiang
Tayuling
Lishan
Taichung
Suspension bridge
Hot Springs
Suspension bridge
Wunshan Guest House
Bus stop
Youth Corps Hostel
Suspension bridge
Catholic Hostel
Cafes
Post Office
Bus Station
Hotel Restaurant
Suspension bridge
Pagoda
Temple
Taroko Gorge
Hualien

up the pine-forested mountain slopes with views of terraced farms here and there until it reaches its highest point at Tayuling (2565 metres or 8415 feet). From here off to the south you can see Mt Hohuan which at 3580 metres (11,207 feet) is the second highest mountain in Taiwan. At this point there is a hostel belonging to the China Youth Corps (NT$60 per person in tatami rooms sleeping two to three people, no showers or hot water but a beautiful setting and very peaceful) and a branch road which leads to Wushe and Lushan via a 3275 metres (10,743 feet) high pass at Wuling. There's no public transport down this branch line but with a Mountain Pass you can go hiking down it. On the other side of the Tayuling Pass the road gradually descends through apple, pear and plum orchards which have been established since the East-West Highway was built. These orchards have been planted on very precipitous slopes cleared of the original pine forest – some of it unwisely judging from the amount of erosion which is taking place in parts. Many of the branches of the fruit trees are supported by elaborate bamboo props to prevent them breaking off when laden with fruit. The road eventually leads to the resort town of Lishan at 1926 metres (6318 feet).

LISHAN 梨山

Lishan is still in the process of changing from a small town into a tourist resort though the word 'resort' is perhaps a dubious word to use since once you've appreciated the views and fresh air and visited the small museum there's nothing else to do here. You can go hiking but even here there are many restrictions to movement since most of the area is given over to orchards, many of which are fenced around. It's also a very expensive place for accommodation. Probably the best part of Lishan is the journey up there.

The small 'Aboriginal Museum' on the crest of the hill above town is well worth a visit. It's open from 9 am to 4.30 pm daily and is free. Aboriginal artifacts are housed on the 1st floor and on the ground floor there are a series of topographical models and photographs of the central highlands, the building of the East-West Highway and the hydro-electric schemes in the valley below Lishan. There's also a small section given over to the natural history of the area.

Places to Stay

There's only one cheap place to stay at Lishan. Like many others it has only a Chinese name but it's on the roadside and easy to find. From the bus station walk up the hill past the turn-off on the right-hand side and it's the third building on the left next door to the *Li Yuan Restaurant*. Here they have tatami rooms for NT$80 per night. The rooms are in the basement and there are no windows so it's a bit grim but OK for an evening. Clean bedding is provided and it's unlikely you'll have to share with anyone. There are more expensive rooms available upstairs.

All the other hotels here – however modest they might look – are very expensive and you should not expect anything for less than NT$450 single. On the other hand, if I ever visited Lishan again I'd put the expense at the back of my mind and stay at the incredible *Lishan Guest House* (tel 045-989501) which is built in traditional Chinese temple style. With the exception of the Grand Hotel in Taipei you won't find anything like this anywhere else in Taiwan – especially at the price. You should phone ahead for a booking if possible as it's very popular. Rooms here cost NT$550 a single and NT$600-650 a double for single occupancy and NT$700-750 a double for two people. There are also more expensive suites available. All rooms have their own attached bath. Meals are available here at NT$40-70 with breakfast, NT$90 with lunch and NT$90 with dinner which is excellent value. Facilities at the hotel include a recreation room, swimming pool, coffee shop, giftshop and landscaped gardens. The staff are very friendly.

Places to Eat

Other than the restaurant at the *Lishan Guest House*, one of the best restaurants here is the *Li Yuan Restaurant*. It's not particularly cheap but they make excellent food and have an extensive menu with English translations of the dishes' names. (The menu makes for interesting reading with such esoterica as 'ox phallus in brown souce', 'fish head in sand pot', frank beef in five pot' and 'fried pig's intestinal'!). We settled for fried chicken and cashews and egg plant in hot garlic sauce which came to NT$200 including rice.

Lishan is, of course, the place to buy cheap fresh fruit. In season you can pick up apples, pears, plums and apricots. Buy them from the people who set up barrows at the side of the road.

Getting There

As at Tienhsiang, it's a good idea to book a day in advance as many of the buses turn up full.

To Hualien There are five buses daily at 8.50 am (two buses), 11.15 am, 12.30 pm and 5.10 pm. The fare is NT$100 and the journey takes about 4½ hours.

To Taichung There are thirteen buses daily, the first at 6.50 am and the last at 5.10 pm.

There are also several buses daily to Ilan and Suao if you're heading north from here and would like to go back a different way.

TAITUNG 台東

A small, compact port city, Taitung is the major centre of population down the east coast of Taiwan. Other than an interesting temple complex dedicated to Matzu, Goddess of the Sea, on the hill overlooking the city, its major interest to travellers is as a taking off point for Lanyu (Orchid Island) and Lutao (Green Island).

If you find yourself waiting around in Taitung and want something to do then it's worth making a trip to Chipen, a small place about 20 minutes by bus from Taitung to the south. There are a number of hot springs here, some by the river (free) and others by the hotel (entry NT$30). Some 15 minutes' walk away from the hotel into the valley is a Buddhist monastery with two beautiful Buddha images, one from Burma and the other from Thailand. Buses to Chipen leave every half hour from the local bus station behind the fish market in Taitung.

Places to Stay

Cheap hotels are not that easy to find here though there are plenty of them which look like they might be cheap. On enquiring, however, you'll find that most of them want NT$200-250 a single which is somewhat expensive for the facilities which most of them offer. The newer hotels around the railway station ask for NT$400-500 though they're sometimes open to negotiation. One place where you can find a cheap bed is the *Yang Jou Hotel* 洋洲大飯店 near to the fire station and the Lanyu shipping office (tel 322477, 322230) which has tatami rooms for NT$70 per bed or NT$100-150 a single. The single rooms are very basic with a double bed and a fan. Bathrooms are communal. They also have better air-con rooms with double bed, own bathroom and TV for NT$300. The manager's brother who may well meet you off the train from Hualien speaks very good English and is helpful even if you don't want to stay there.

The 金龍大旅社 which is the first hotel you come to after turning right immediately after leaving the railway station has basic double rooms for NT$200 with clean bed linen, fan and hand basin. None of the staff speak a word of English. Another in the price range is the 林雲英 which is located as shown on the street plan. Slightly up market is the *Hotel Jin An* 金安旅社, 96 Shin Sheng Rd (tel

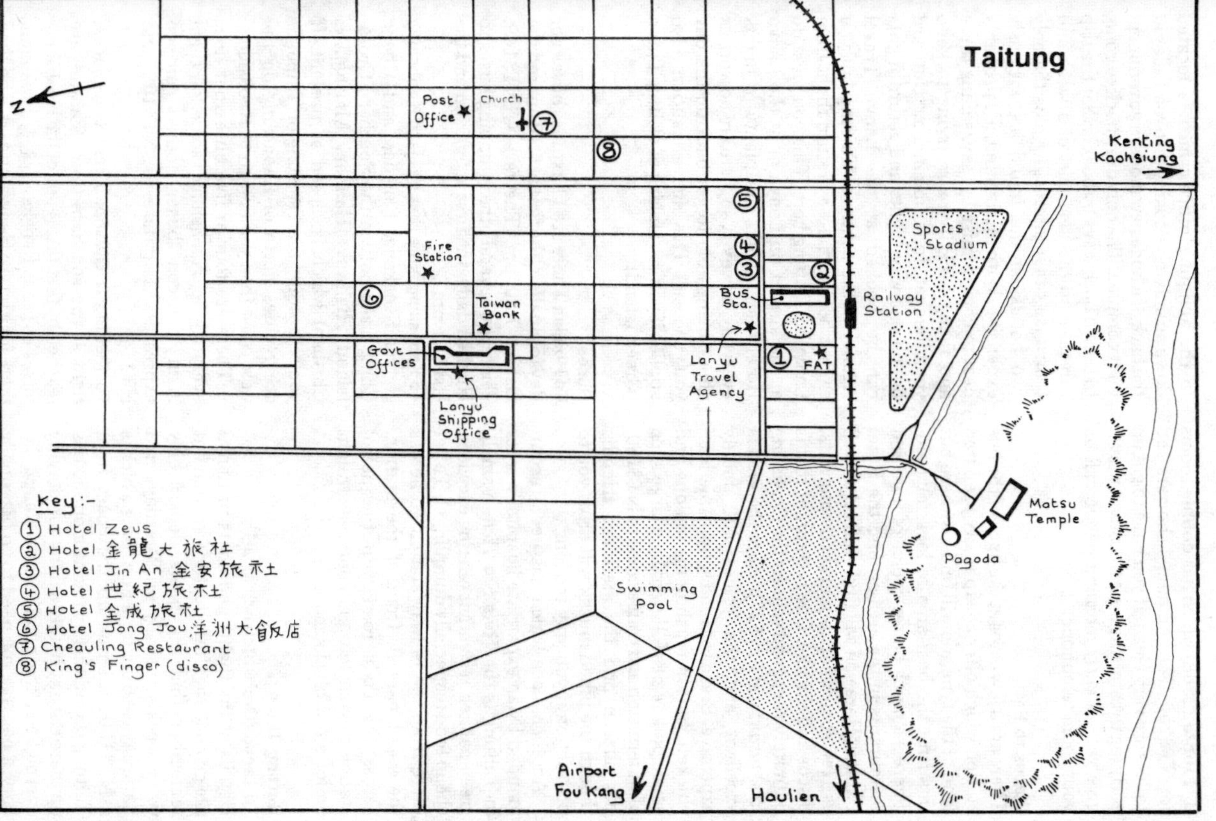
Taitung
N
Post Office
Church
Kenting
Kaohsiung
Sports Stadium
Fire Station
Bus Sta.
Railway Station
Taiwan Bank
Govt Offices
Lanyu Travel Agency
FAT
Lanyu Shipping Office
Matsu Temple
Pagoda
Swimming Pool
Airport
Fou Kang
Haulien
Key:-
① Hotel Zeus
② Hotel 金龍大旅社
③ Hotel Jin An 金安旅社
④ Hotel 世紀旅社
⑤ Hotel 金成旅社
⑥ Hotel Jong Jou 洋洲大飯店
⑦ Cheauling Restaurant
⑧ King's Finger (disco)

331168/322368) which has double rooms for NT$250. The communal showers and toilets are very clean. If you have to get up early (eg to catch the boat to Lanyu) they'll give you an early morning phone call on your room telephone.

Places to Eat

There are a few cafes at the back of the bus station which offer cheap ready prepared food of the type you will find elswhere but this isn't the best area to look for food. There's a much better choice of food and restaurants in the area around the Hotel Capital. Here you will find seafood as well as a few somewhat up-market restaurants, discos and the like. One restaurant that is definitely very good value is the *Cheauling Restaurant* (tel 327527). Here the food is excellent and the prices not unduly expensive. Bread rolls and soup, 'American' chicken, button mushrooms, onions and sauce plus vegies followed by a large slice of watermelon and coffee come to NT$180. It's air-con and the staff are friendly though the piped muzak will drive you to distraction if you stay too long.

Another place which has been recommended by an expatriate hospital worker in Taitung is the *Tung Sin Tien*, a small, green-painted restaurant offering excellent, cheap food (especially dumplings). To get there from the railway station go across the small park in front of the station, across the main road with the petrol station to your left and continue straight on for a few blocks more.

Getting There

To Lanyu (Orchid Island) 蘭嶼
Details of the flights and boats to Lanyu are given in the 'Introductory' section but remember that the boats depart only twice weekly, usually on Tuesdays and Saturdays at 6 am from Fou Kang which is a NT$160 taxi ride up the coast from Taitung (avoid this by taking a public bus up there the day before sailing and staying overnight at the hotel in Fou Kang). To book a passage you need to go personally to the shipping office which is located down an unlikely-looking dirt-road alley at the back of a huge new modern government built complex. The only drawback to going to Lanyu both ways by boat is that the trip can take up the best part of a week and Lanyu isn't that interesting plus the only two hotels on the island are viciously expensive. With this in mind, it's probably best to compromise by, say, sailing there and flying back if you're trying to keep your budget to a minimum. Outward bound one-way flights and return flights can be booked at the Lanyu Travel Agency in the centre of Taitung but you cannot book a one-way return flight from Lanyu to Taitung here. This you must do at the airport on Lanyu or at the Lanyu Hotel there. There are plenty of flights everyday, however, so there are no worries about being able to get back on the day you choose. The above caution also applies if you're thinking of visiting Lutao (Green Island).

Buses

To Hualien There are 11 express buses per day to Hualien, the first at 6.40 am and the last at 7.20 pm. The fare is NT$148. There are several other stopping buses to Hualien daily, the first at 5.05 am and the last at 1 pm.

To Kaohsiung Note that buses to Kaohsiung go via Fengkang, Fangliao and Cheng Ching Lake not via the Southern Cross-Island Highway (Haituan, Meishan & Chishan) which is closed at present. If you're heading for Taichung or Taipei or other cities north of Kaohsiung on the west coast then you first go to Kaohsiung.

There are four or five buses per hour everyday to Kaohsiung, some of them luxury air-con buses, others air-con expresses. The fare is NT$168 and NT$148.

To Kenting & Oluanpi These two places, right at the southern tip of Taiwan, are reached by first taking any of the Kaohsiung buses as far as Fengkang 楓港, changing there for a bus to Hengchun 恒春 and then changing again for another bus to Kenting 墾丁. If you're lucky you may find there's a bus going direct to Hengchun from Taitung – there are a few of them. Taitung to Hengchun costs NT$98 and takes 3½-4 hours. Hengchun to Kenting costs NT$11 and takes about half an hour. There isn't much point in asking 'Information' at Taitung bus station anything unless you speak Chinese. They just giggle when English is spoken. There are some beautiful views to take in on the journey from Taitung to Kenting.

LANYU (ORCHID ISLAND) 蘭嶼

The tourist literature about Lanyu and the photographs which are selected to accompany it beguile many a tourist into believing that this island is a living museum of a unique aboriginal culture where age old traditions, coming of age ceremonies and the like survive intact into the late 20th century and where they are, to some extent, protected. Unfortunately, this isn't the case and you're going to be sorely disappointed if that's what you're expecting to find. The curiously decorated boats which once symbolised the transition from boyhood to manhood by their makers – photographs of which grace all the tourist literature about the island – are still there but they look somewhat unused if not moribund. Members of the Yami tribe (the aboriginals of this island) are now almost indistinguishable from their counterparts on the main island and live in ugly concrete boxes (courtesy of the government), watch TV and drink beer. In other words don't come here expecting the sort of fascinating tribal society that you can find elswhere in Asia in such places as Thailand, Borneo or the Philippines.

Lanyu is still worth visiting on the other hand for that relaxing, small-island ambience where nothing is hurried and you can wander around all day hardly meeting a soul (except the occasional field worker who will hassle you for a cigarette!) The 'beaches' that are talked about in the literature are largely a fantasy consisting of a very coarse grey-black volcanic pebble which will wear the skin off your feet within minutes and some pretty powerful waves that you'll find it very difficult to swim in. The only two hotels on the island – the Yayu and the Lanyu – are outrageously expensive and the food which they offer only average. If none of this bothers you, then go to Lanyu. It does have a certain mysterious beauty and it can certainly be very relaxing. One more thing – don't expect to frolic among the orchids. They're very difficult to find!

Places to Stay

The cheapest of the two hotels on Lanyu is the *Hotel Yayu* (tel 089-323864/320033) located in Yayu village between the airport and the Taitung ferry jetty. I personally preferred this place to the Lanyu Hotel as it was less pretentious (the staff at the Lanyu try to affect that out-of-date aloofness you might associate with an international-class hotel). The Yayu is tatty at the edges, the fans don't work during the day and cut off in the middle of the night, the toilets don't flush and the food begs for a little inspiration but the staff make up for it in friendliness and spontaneity. All the rooms have their own bathroom and cost NT$400-600 single and NT$600-900 double. There are also rooms for three people at NT$1400 and rooms for four people at NT$1600. Meals cost NT$40 for breakfast and NT$100 for lunch and dinner. There's also a bar which opens in the evening. The hotel also offers bus trips around the island every day which take three hours and cost NT$250 – probably worth it unless you prefer walking.

The *Lanyu Hotel* (tel 089-326111/2/3) is somewhat better appointed and the meals are of a better standard but it's also more expensive. Rooms cost NT$400-700 a single and NT$700-1200 a double. There are also rooms for three people at NT$1100-1500 and rooms for four people at NT$1300-1700. Meals cost NT$50 for

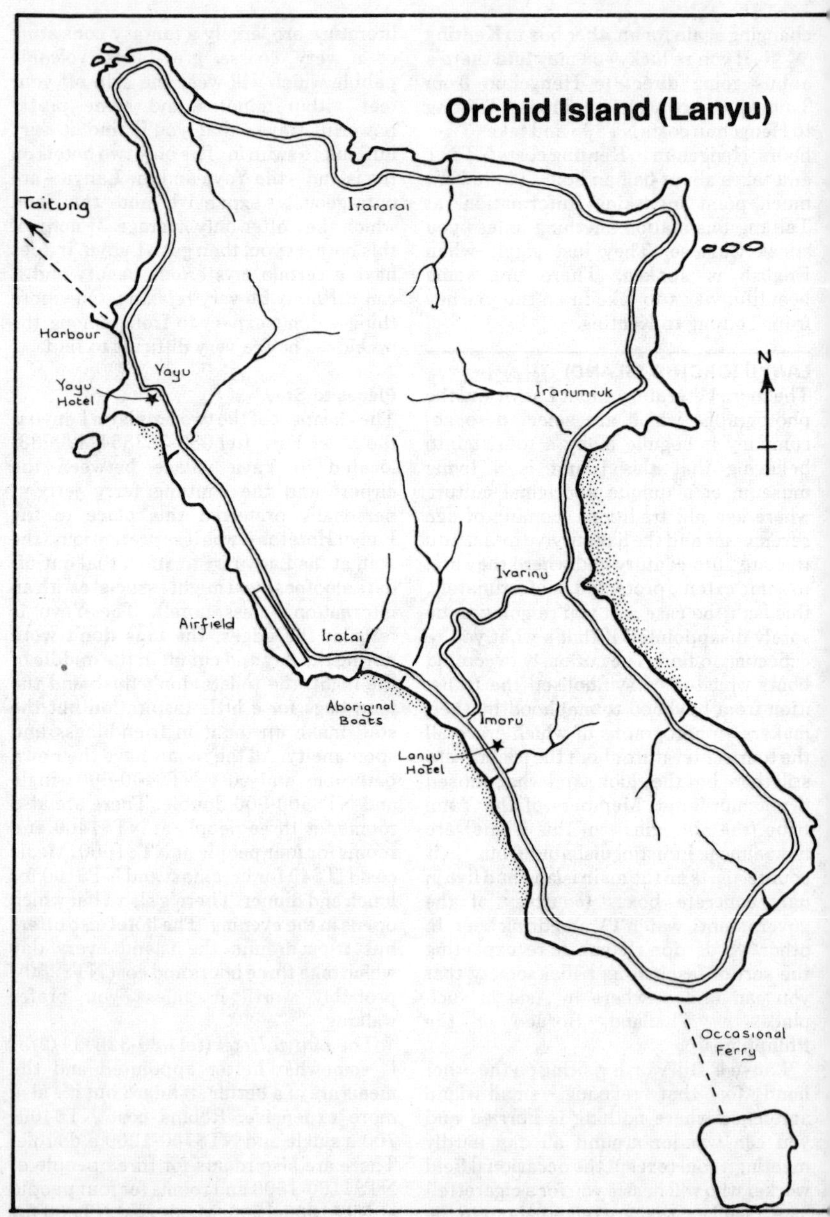
Orchid Island (Lanyu)
Taitung
Harbour
Yayu
Yayu Hotel
Irarai
Iranumruk
N
Ivarinu
Airfield
Iratai
Aboriginal Boats
Imoru
Lanyu Hotel
Occasional Ferry

breakfast, NT$120 for lunch and NT$180 for dinner. Like the Yayu they offer bus trips around the island every day for NT$250. They also have their own bar and coffee shop.

Both these hotels have their own mini buses which meet incoming flights and offer free transport to the hotels. If you're coming by boat, however, don't expect anything to be waiting. Everyone who got off the boat I was on either had to hire a taxi or walk.

If you can't afford the charges at the two above hotels and you think it's worth hiking around with your baggage for a couple of hours then it might be worth trying the Catholic Church at Irati village between the airport and the Lanyu Hotel. They might be able to put you up on the floor in a school but no-one here speaks English.

If you don't particularly want to eat at the hotels there are one or two cafes at Imoru village (where the Lanyu Hotel is situated) and at Yayu village (where the Yayu Hotel is located) but the food is nothing to write home about and the prices are much the same as those at the hotels.

Getting There

Flights Flight tickets back to the main island can be bought from the lobby of the Lanyu Hotel – see the flight schedule in the Introductory section. You need to be at the airport at least half an hour before the flight is due as there is a baggage and passport check to pass through (goodness knows where anyone would be able to hijack these tiny planes to!). Both the hotels offer free transport to the airport.

Getting Around

There are one or two irregular public buses which connect the main villages on the island but it's unlikely you'll ever find out where they go to or what times they run at. The best transport you've got on this island are your own two feet and the hotel mini-buses.

KENTING 墾丁

Kenting has the warmest sea and best beaches in Taiwan. It's also a mecca for those who never tire of that mysterious fascination for the extremities of islands and continents since it's within a few minutes' bus ride of Oluanpi at the southern tip of Taiwan. And if soft, yellow, coral sand, warm sea and island extremities are sufficient to bring you here then there's also an extensive tropical botanical garden laid out among the hills which overlook Kenting. On the other hand, if you prefer a little bit of space in which to enjoy all these things then get here during the week because at weekends the place fills up with dozens of busloads of China Youth Corps, Taiwanese tourists and expatriate American workers. It's not quite so idyllic at those times.

The Beach

Of course – but note that if you go onto the beach through the grounds of *Kenting House Beach Restaurant* in the mornings or early afternoons there's a checkpoint beyond the restaurant where officials will refuse to let you through unless you've bought a NT$20 ticket at the "Front Desk' (which is where you enter the grounds). Avoid this bullshit by turning right at the restaurant just beyond the 'Front Desk', going over the bridge and through the beach cottages – or go down the road past the *Teachers' Hostel* (though this is a longer way round). There's no check coming back through the grounds from the beach. You can ignore all the signs saying 'No photography, no sketching, no note-taking, etc' since everyone is doing it.

Kenting Botanical Gardens

(Kenting Park) 墾丁公園

Four km from Kenting town on the hills overlooking the tip of the peninsula are the extensive grounds of the botanical gardens. To get there you take a public bus from the traditional Chinese gateway just opposite the Kenting Hotel. These buses take you past *Kenting House* (the huge hotel on the slope just below the park) to the park entrance. There are 12 buses daily in either direction and the fare is NT$5. The journey takes about 10 minutes. Coming back from the park, the last bus leaves at 6.05 pm. Entrance to the park costs NT$20. As botantical gardens go, they're not the most interesting in the world but it is worth going up there for the views – there's an observation tower and a sea-viewing platform. In addition there are two limestone caves with stalactites, a small gorge and a refreshment centre. Walking round the park will take you several hours and, on a clear day, you can see Lanyu.

Oluanpi 鵝鑾鼻

This place is the Land's End of Taiwan and as such attracts tourists by the bus load at weekends. There's virtually nothing there except a lighthouse and a view of the Bashi Channel which separates Taiwan from the Phillipines. Buses run from Hengchun to Oluanpi 11 times daily, the first at 6 am and the last at 6.30 pm. If you'd prefer to walk, it's about 8½ km from Kenting.

Places to Stay

The only top end hotel in Kenting is the 89-room *Kenting House* (tel 088-861301/4) high up above the town itself and close to the entrance to the park. The rooms here cost NT$700 a single and NT$900-1100 a double. There is a choice of Chinese and western restaurants, a swimming pool and coffee shop.

One of the cheapest and most popular places with travellers are the few private rooms which are available for rent on the first floor above the house next to the motorcycle shop which in turn is next door to Kenting Hotel (there's usually a sign outside when they have a vacancy). It costs NT$100 a room. Clean sheets are provided and the bathrooms are clean. A friendly Chinese family runs it. If there's no room here then probably the next best place is the *Teachers' Hostel* (tel 088-892304). The hostel is a large, modern building set in its own gardens right next to the sea and run by friendly staff. Meals are available too. At weekends in the summer months it's likely to be full. Accommodation here costs NT$65 in a tatami room or NT$160 a single or NT$320 a double. It's excellent value if you can get in. Down the same lane as the *Teachers' Hostel* is the *Catholic Hostel* which also has large dormitory rooms for NT$70 a bed but it's nowhere near the same standard as the *Teachers' Hostel*. It's also likely to be full with middle-aged conventioners or the like but it's worth trying if you're looking for cheap accommodation.

After the above the next best is the *Kenting Hotel*, 271 Kenting Rd (tel 088-892901/2) not to be confused with *Kenting House* which is much more expensive. This hotel is the large white concrete building just opposite the traditional Chinese gateway to Kenting Park. Tatami rooms here cost NT$100 a bed but as a westerner you're more than likely to be left with the whole room to yourself (with a key) no matter how many people turn up. Sheets and a table fan are provided and the rooms are even partially air-con! The communal bathrooms have hot and cold water and are spotlessly clean except when the place is full of youth groups at the weekends (their memory seems to fail them when it comes to flushing toilets). Other than the tatami rooms there are doubles for NT$540 – there are no single rooms and you pay the full price if you singly occupy a double room. They have their own restaurant on the first floor.

Two other good value hotels are the *Hong Bin Hotel* 鴻賓旅社 which costs NT$100 a single and NT$200 a double (there are no tatami rooms) or there is the 北平大飯店 which is excellent value at NT$150 for a single without air-con, NT$200 for a single or NT$300 for a double with air-con. The rooms are very

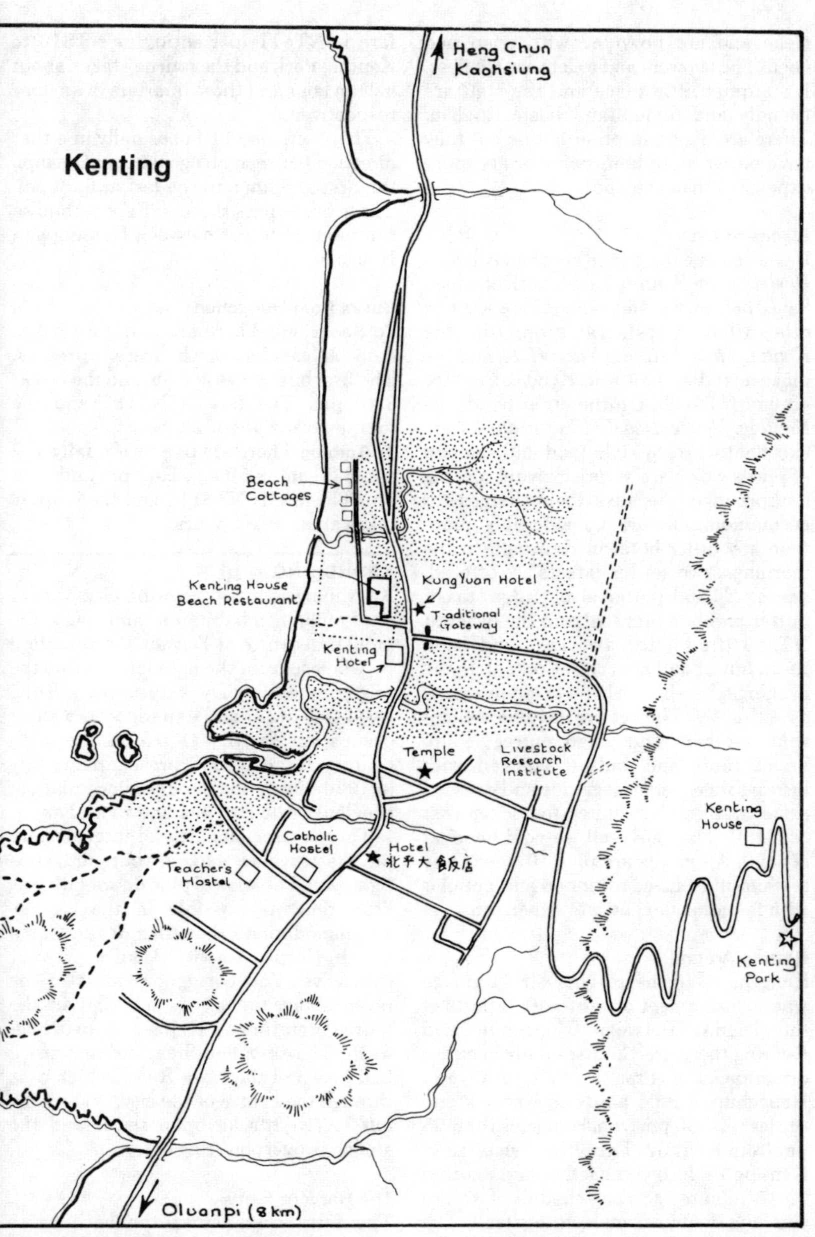
Kenting
Heng Chun
Kaohsiung
Beach Cottages
Kenting House Beach Restaurant
Kung Yuan Hotel
Traditional Gateway
Kenting Hotel
Temple
Livestock Research Institute
Kenting House
Catholic Hostel
Hotel 北平大飯店
Teacher's Hostel
Kenting Park
Oluanpi (8 km)

clean and are provided with crisp bed linen. The showers and toilets are spotless. It's a quiet little place and the staff are friendly and understand basic English. There are plenty of other hotels but they have either no tatami rooms or are more expensive than the above.

Places to Eat

If you're not eating at either the *Teachers' Hostel* or the *Kenting Hotel*, both of which have their own restaurants, there are two other Chinese restaurants opposite the *Kenting Hotel – Kuang Yuan Hotel* and the place next door to it where you can eat for around NT$100. On the other hand, the *Kenting House Beach Restaurant* offers excellent western-style food and seafood at prices which are surprisingly reasonable ('surprisingly' because their charges for accommodation are considerably more than any other hotel in Kenting). In the mornings, two set breakfasts are offered, one at NT$50 (oatmeal porridge, toast, butter and jam and tea) and the other at NT$80 (fruit juice, two eggs and ham, toast, butter and jam, coffee or tea). In the evenings there's an a la carte menu as well as set meals. The set meals are excellent value. A ham and salad entree, soup, bread rools and butter, chicken with brown sauce, vegies, egg rice and dressed salad, watermelon and coffee or tea cost NT$180. They also sell ice-cold beers at NT$60. All prices are plus 10% tax. The restaurant is air-conditioned and popular with fastidious expatriate Americans.

Getting Around

Hengchun is the nearest main bus terminal where you can get buses to other parts of the island. Between Hengchun and Kenting there are 13 buses daily in either direction, the first at 6.30 am from Hengchun or 8.05 am from Kenting and the last at 5.30 pm from Hengchun or 6.05 pm from Kenting. The above buses go to Kenting Park so you need to add another 10-15 minutes to the schedule if you're catching the bus from Kenting itself. The fare is NT$11 to Kenting or NT$16 to Kenting Park and the journey takes about half an hour and three quarters of an hour respectively.

There are also 11 buses daily in either direction between Hengchun and Oluanpi, the first at 6 am and the last at 6.30 pm. These buses pass through Kenting and so can be used to get between Kenting and Hengchun.

Buses from Hengchun

To Kaohsiung There are about 50 buses daily, at least half of which are expresses. The first bus leaves at 6 am and the last at 8.40 pm. The fare is NT$87 and the journey takes about 2¾ hours.

To Taitung There are five buses daily at 7 am, 8.20 am, 9.50 am, 2.40 pm and 4.05 pm. The fare is NT$111 and the journey takes about 3½-4 hours.

KAOHSIUNG 高雄

Kaoshiung is a fast growing city of over one million inhabitants and also the industrial centre of Taiwan. It was settled by Chinese from the mainland during the reign of the Ming Dynasty emperor Yung Lo (1403-1424) and experienced a short occupation by the Dutch in the 17th century. It received its present name only in 1920 during the Japanese occupation; previously the city was known as Taku.

There's precious little of interest here for the traveller and, if your budget is tight, you'd be wise to plan on spending as little time as possible in the city as accommodation other than at the China Youth Corps Activity Centre is very expensive. You can ignore most of the raves about the city you'll find in the tourist literature as it's just a heap of hogwash. The so-called 'beaches' are just a bad joke and the Love River, which runs through the centre of the city, is anything but lovely. It's an open sewer and the stench is overpowering.

The Harbour Ferry

The ferry ride across the harbour to

Chichin Island is just about the only thing worth doing in the city itself. It's here that you'll see the sort of Chinese fishing junks that are generally associated with Hong Kong. To get to the ferry take No 1 bus from the urban bus stand in front of the railway station to the fish dock (buy a couple of bus tokens first – NT$4 each). The ferries run from early morning till late at night every 10 minutes or so and cost NT$2 each way. The trip across the harbour takes 5-10 minutes.

Foukuangshan Buddhist Monastery 佛光山

This recently established Buddhist monastery which is still not complete is about an hour's journey outside Kaohsiung. It's principal attraction is the enormous golden coloured Buddha (32 metres high) which is visible for miles around. The monastery has a dormitory for pilgrims and guests where you can stay overnight for a small donation and very cheap vegetarian meals are available. To get there take a bus from the suburban bus stand on the right-hand side and at the back of the highway bus terminal to Fengshan 楓港. This costs NT$8 and takes about 20 minutes. Tell the conductress and the people in the adjacent seats that you're heading for Foukuangshan and they'll tell you where to get off. It's very unlikely they won't point you to the exact bus you want but if they don't you want the light green buses. This second bus will take you to within a few minutes walk of Foukuangshan for NT$6.

Santimen Aboriginal Village 三地門

If you don't mind commercialised displays of aboriginal 'culture' then Santimen is a good place to go to if only to get out of the city for a few hours. The principal attractions here are the stone slab houses which are built in the foothills and the large suspension bridge across the river. There are several buses daily from the highway bus terminal which cost NT$35 and take about 1½ hours. If you like you can also go via Pingtung 屏東 – take the same bus as you would for Foukuangshan. The fare to Pintung is NT$20 and the journey takes about 45 minutes.

Places to Stay – top end

Ambassador Hotel Kaohsiung
202 Min Sheng 2nd Rd, Kaohsiung (tel 07 211 5211), 457 rooms, singles NT$1800-1900, doubles NT$2000-3000

King Wang Hotel
329 Chi-Hsian 2nd Rd (tel 07-281 4141), 150 rooms, singles NT$1400, doubles NT$ 1600

Grand Hotel Kaohsiung
Cheng Ching Lake, Kaohsiung (tel 07 383 5911), 108 rooms, no singles, doubles NT$1500-1700

Hotel Kingdom
42 Wu-Fu 4th Rd, Kaohsiung (tel 07 551 8211), 312 rooms, singles NT$1700-1800, doubles NT$1900-2200

Hotel Major
7 Ta-Jen Rd, Yen-chen District, Kaohsiung (tel 07 521 2266), 220 rooms, singles NT$1350-1500, doubles NT$1700

Southland Hotel
139 Chung Cheng 4th Rd, Kaohsiung (tel 07 221 6033)

Summit Hotel
426 Jeouru 1st Rd, Kaohsiung (tel 07 384-5526), 211 rooms, singles NT$1200, doubles NT$1400

Harbour Hotel
245 Pi-Chung St, Kaohsiung (tel 07 561-2371), 42 rooms, singles NT$600, doubles NT$800

Places to Stay – Bottom End

The cheapest accommodation you will find in Kaohsiung is the *China Youth Corps Hostel*, 189 Chung Cheng 4th Rd (tel 07-2211060). It's a huge place full of friendly people who will go out of their way to help you. The dorms cost only NT$30 a bed, but ring first as it's often full.

Anywhere other than the *Youth Hostel* and you're up for NT$250-300 for a single room. And you'll be lucky at that. One of the few places where there's a chance of a cheaper room is the *Hotel Hua Pin* 華賓大旅社 221 Nan Hua Rd (tel 228809/

228800). This hotel has three rooms on the very top floor (actually on the roof) for NT$180 with fan, TV and crisp, clean sheets but (apparently) no access to a bathroom. The rooms on the lower floors cost NT$280 a single with air-con and own bathroom. I was told by several Chinese budget accommodation seekers independently that this place had the cheapest rooms in Kaohsiung. After running around many other hotels in the vicinity I reluctantly had to agree with them. If the *Hua Pin* is full then take any of the hotels nearby as they're all similarly priced at around NT$300-350 a single (plenty of them).

Places to Eat
There are several ready-prepared food cafes on Chienkuo Rd opposite the railway station and the highway bus terminal where you can eat well for between NT$56-60 but the best one is next door to the Duke Hotel, 233 Lin Sen 1st Rd very close to the YMCA. They have some of the best food of this type I've tasted in Taiwan. Excellent place. If you'd like something other than this type of food then try the seafood restaurant next door to the *Hotel Hua Pin*. The foods they have are all displayed on ice – just take your pick and have it cooked for you. The price varies from between NT$40-70 depending on what you have (fish, prawns, octupus, shrimps, etc).

If you want somewhere to go in the evenings then try one or other of the coffee shops which line Chungshan 1st Rd. They're popular with well-heeled young people in the evenings and are not cheap.

Getting There
Buses There are three bus stations in Kaohsiung, all of them in front of the railway station at the junction of Chungshan Rd and Chienkuo Rd; the one on the left is the urban bus stand (for buses around Kaohsiung City), the one directly facing you in the centre is the long-

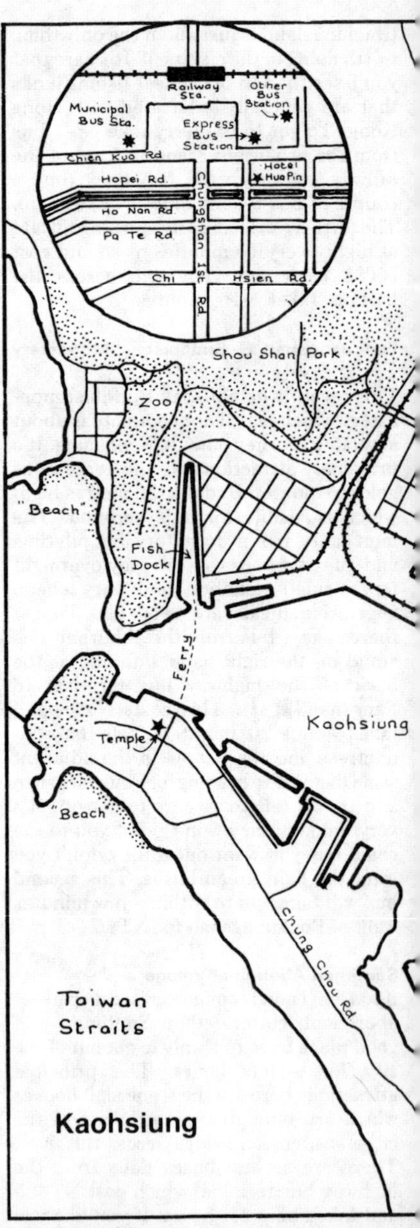

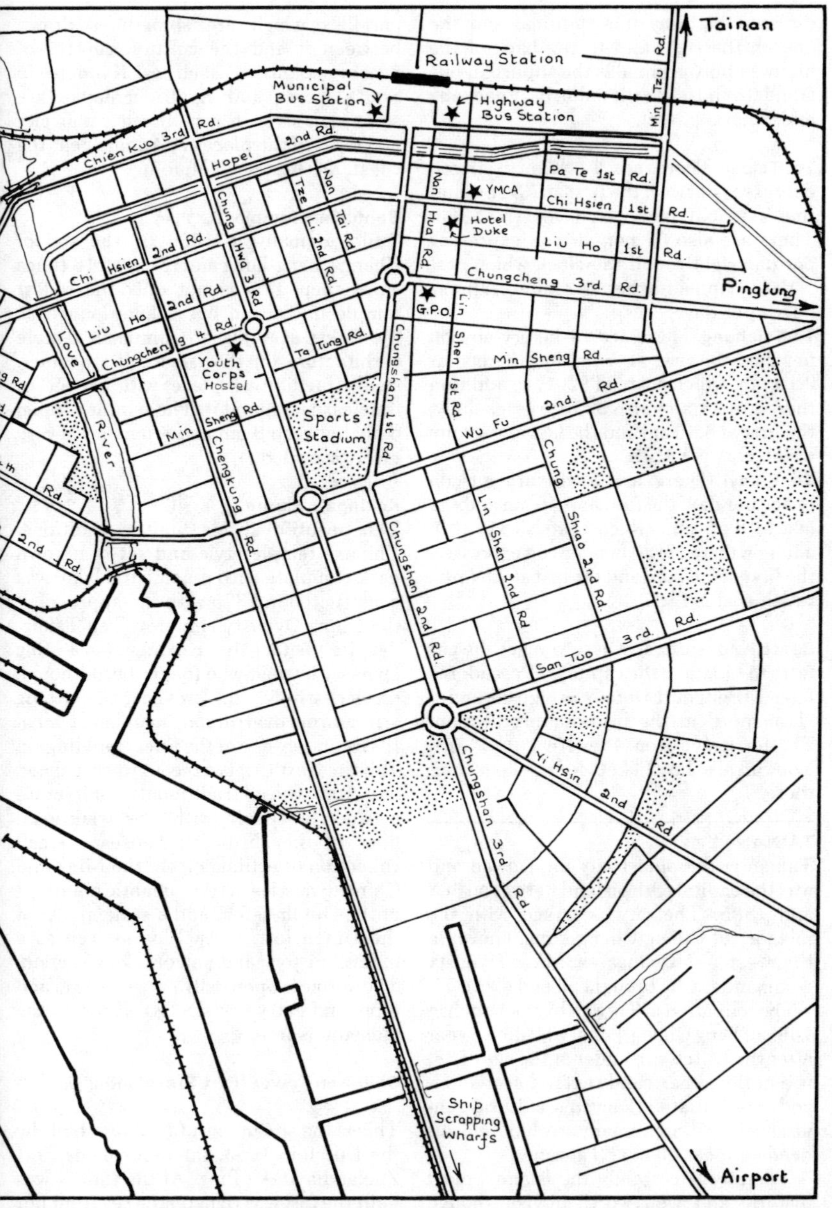

Tainan
Railway Station
Municipal Bus Station
Highway Bus Station
Min Tzu Rd.
Chien Kuo 3rd Rd.
Hopei 2nd Rd.
Pa Te 1st Rd.
YMCA
Chi Hsien 1st Rd.
Hotel Duke
Liu Ho 1st Rd.
Chungcheng 3rd. Rd.
Pingtung
G.P.O.
Chi Hsien 2nd Rd.
Liu Ho 2nd Rd.
Chungcheng 4 Rd
Youth Corps Hostel
Chung Hwa 3 Rd
Tze Li 2nd Rd.
Nan Tai Rd
Nan Hua Rd
Ta Tung Rd.
Lin Shen 1st Rd
Min Sheng Rd.
Chungshan 1st Rd
Love River
Min Sheng Rd.
Sports Stadium
Wu Fu 2nd. Rd.
Chengkung Rd.
Chung Shao 2nd Rd.
Lin Shen 2nd Rd
Chungshan 2nd Rd.
San Tuo 3rd. Rd.
Yi Hsin 2nd Rd
Chungshan 3rd Rd
Ship Scrapping Wharfs
Airport

distance highway bus terminal and the one on the right and to the back of the highway bus terminal is the suburban bus stand (for buses to the suburbs, Fengkang and Pingtung, etc).

To Taipei There are 14 luxury air-con expresses per day, the first at 7.30 am and the last at 3 pm, which cost NT$363. There are also 56 non-air-con expresses per day right round the clock which cost NT$310 and a further 93 limited express buses per day.
To Taichung There are 14 luxury air-con per day, the first at 7 am and the last at 9.10 pm, which cost NT$201. In addition there are 28 non-air-con expresses daily, the first at 6.40 am and the last at 8.40 pm which cost NT$172.
To Chiayi There are 37 luxury air-con buses per day, the first at 6.40 am and the last at 8.55 pm, which cost NT$102. In addition there are 20 non-air-con expresses, the first at 6.57 am and the last at 7.57 pm, which cost NT$87.

Boats Kaohsiung is where you get the car ferry to Makung, the capital of Pescadores Island (Penghu). Details are given under 'Transport' in the introductory section. The ferries go from Pier No 1 (號碼頭). You can also buy tickets for the boat from there.

TAINAN 台南

Tainan is the oldest city on Taiwan and was the capital of the island between 1663 and 1885. The city is linked with the memory of Cheng Cheng-kung, known in the west as Koxinga, a Ming Dynasty commander who brought an end to the 37-year occupation of Taiwan by the Dutch in 1661. Cheng Cheng-kung, who died a year after the Dutch surrender at the age of 38, is a national hero and revered as a demigod. He initiated Taiwan's cultural renaissance and monuments to him and his deeds appear all over Taiwan.

The city is certainly the island's most historic and well worth a visit though parallels which are sometimes drawn between it and the cultural centres of nearby countries such as Kyongju in South Korea and Kyoto in Japan are somewhat over-drawn. It's a small city and most of the places at Anping near the coast, are best seen on foot.

Confucian Temple 孔子廟

Built originally in 1666 by the son of Cheng Cheng-kung and restored 16 times since then, this is not only the oldest temple in Taiwan but acknowledged as the finest example of Confucian temple architecture on the island. It's a quiet, shady meditative place with an air of timelessness about it. The temple is open daily between 9 am and 6 pm and is very rarely crowded.

Koxinga's Shrine 延平郡王祠 成功廟

This beautiful shrine, built in traditional Chinese temple style and set in its own park complete with ornamental lake, was constructed in 1875 with the approval of the Ching Dynasty emperor, Teh Tsung, despite the fact that Koxinga was a Ming Dynasty loyalist who fought hard, though unsuccessfully, to prevent the Ching armies from overrunning mainland China. It's definitely one of the finest buildings in Taiwan. Next to it is a recently constructed museum whose traditional architecture clashes hideously with the traditional lines of the shrine. It houses a small collection of artifacts from the Ming and Ching dynasties, a few romantic paintings of the Dutch defeat and a scale model of the Dutch fort at An Ping as well as a natural history and paleontology section. The shrine is open daily between 9 am and 6 pm and entry costs NT$4. Entry to the museum is free.

Chih Kan Tower (Fort Providentia) 赤崁樓

This is the site of one of two forts built by the Dutch in 1653, the other being Fort Zeelandia at An Ping. At the time it was built the fort was right on the sea front but silting over the centuries since then has put the shore line several km to the west. The fort itself was destroyed in an earthquake in 1862 and only tiny sections of it remain. The two raised halls which stand there now were built in 1875 and house a small museum containing historical relics and a photographic rave about Taiwan's economic miracle.

Kai Yuan Buddhist Temple 開元寺

One of the oldest Buddhist temples in Taiwan, Kai Yuan is a treasure house of Chinese iconography and temple decoration. It's actually not one but several temples connected by gates and passageways and its three pagodas are often used to illustrate tourist literature on Tainan. The temple is located on the northern outskirts of town. To get there take bus No 6 or 17 from the railway station to the end of the line (about 10 minutes' journey).

An Ping Fort (Fort Zeelandia) 安平古堡

An Ping is located several kilometres west of Taiwan and, like the city itself, was once on the sea front. The Dutch built Fort Zeelandia here in 1624 with bricks imported, incredibly, from Holland and though the fort was largely destroyed in a cyclone in the late-19th century substantial parts of it are still visible. Most of the buildings which stand there now were built in the mid-70s as a kind of tourist attraction over the ruins of the former fort. There's an observation tower from which excellent views of the surrounding countryside and coastline can be had and a small museum containing scale models of the original Dutch fort. Entry to the museum and observation tower is NT$8. An Ping has a very quiet, relaxing atmosphere and the area around the fort is well landscaped with old trees and gardens. It's well worth making the effort to go there. From Tainan take bus No 15 from either Hsi Men St or Chung Cheng Rd which takes you right to the fort. The fare is NT$6 and the journey takes about 15 minutes.

There's another fort – or the remains of it – about two km from An Ping at Chin Cheng Li. This is the Everlasting Fort or Yi Tzai Chin Cheng designed and built by French engineers commissioned by the Chinese authorities in 1874. Much of it has disappeared but the gates and some cannon remain.

Other

Tainan is full of temples of one sort or another and you'll come across quite a few as you wander around the town. Two of the most notable are the Tien Hou Kung on Yungfu Rd which is dedicated to Matsu, Goddess of the Sea, and the Wufei Miao or Five Imperial Concubines' Temple on Wu Fei St which was built in 1746 to commemorate the suicide of five concubines of Ling Chin, a Ming Dynasty loyalist who also commited suicide rather than submit to the conquering Ching armies.

Places to Stay – top end

There are three tourist hotels in Tainan. The most luxurious is the *Tainan Hotel*, 1 Cheng Kung Rd (tel 06-228 9101) which has 152 rooms at NT$1000 a single and NT$1200 a double. Cheaper are the *Oriental Hotel*, 143 Min-tsu Rd (tel 06-222 1131) which has 94 rooms at NT$600-800 a single and NT$900 a double, and the *Chengkung Hotel*, 11 Pei Men Rd (tel 06-222 8151) which has 47 rooms at NT$550-600 a single and NT$700 a double.

Places to Stay – bottom end

The best place to stay in Tainan is the *Tainan Theological College Hostel* 青年路, 274 Ching Nien Rd. Although it's a good 10 minutes' walk from the station it's well worth the effort as it's a beautiful place to stay. The hostel is an old, roomy, wooden house with mosquito netting all around the verandahs and run by very friendly people who also speak good English. It costs NT$100 per bed with clean sheets in the dormitories but very few people seem to stay there. The grounds are locked from 10 pm to 6 am though you could probably

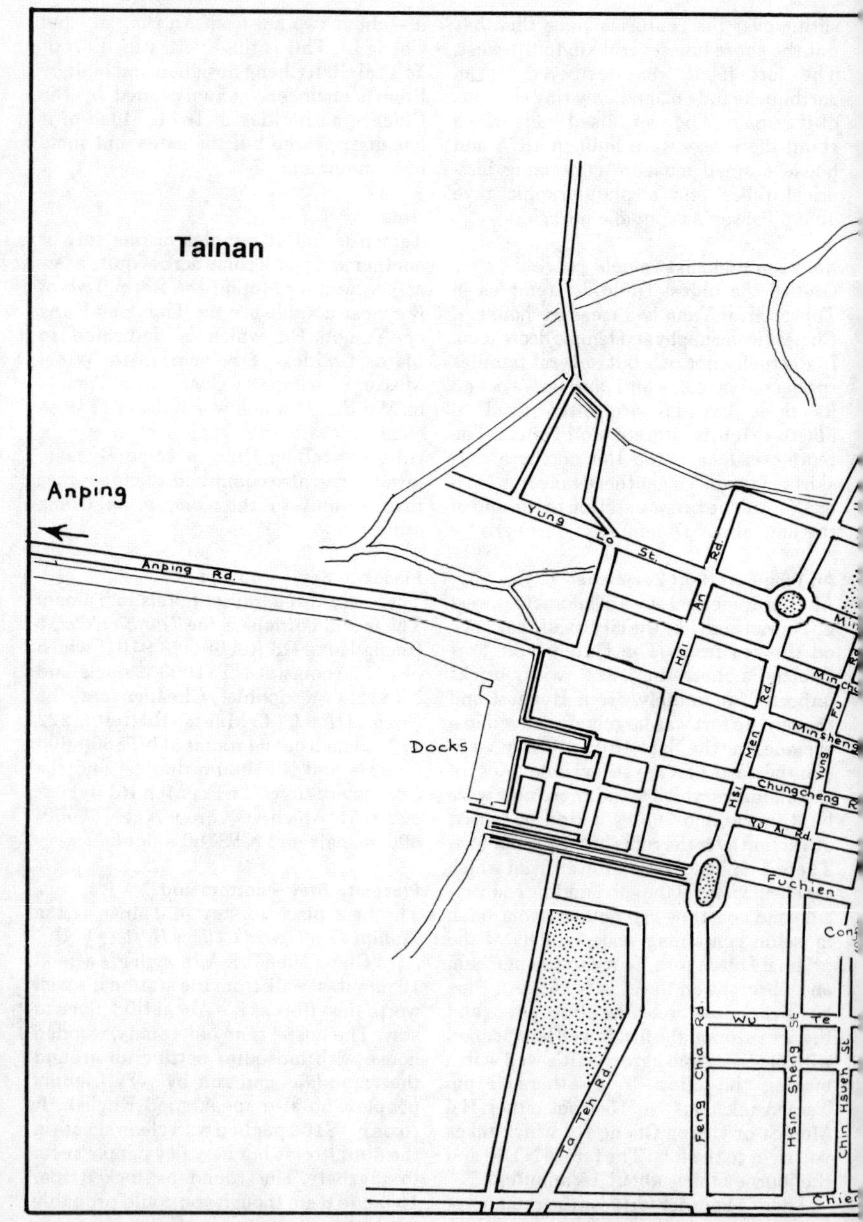
Tainan
Anping
Anping Rd.
Yung Lo St.
Hai An Rd.
Min Chu
Minsheng
Hsi Men Rd.
Yung Fu
Chungcheng
Yu Ai Rd.
Fuchien
Docks
Ta Teh Rd.
Feng Chia Rd.
Wu Te
Hsin Sheng St
Chin Hsueh St

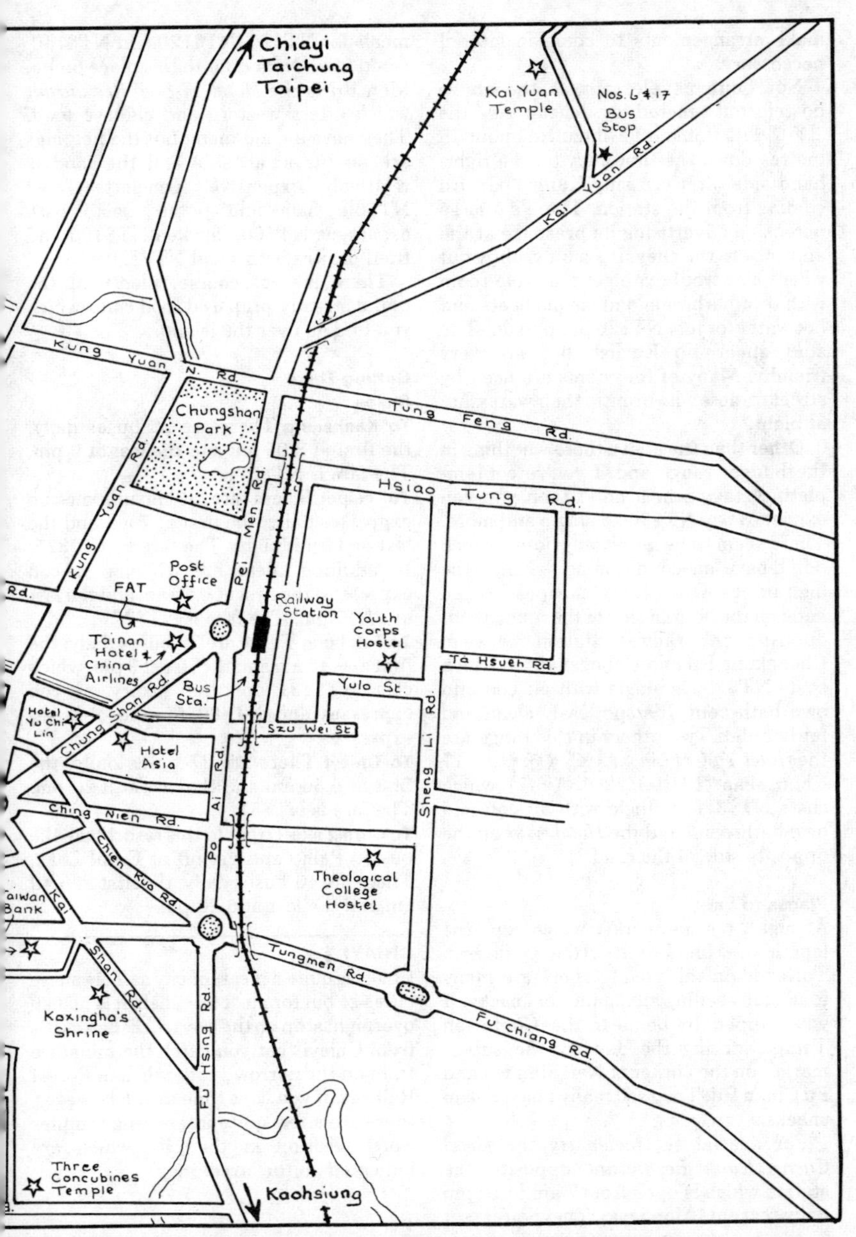
Chiayi
Taichung
Taipei
Kai Yuan Temple
Nos. 6 & 17
Bus Stop
Kai Yuan Rd.
Kung Yuan N. Rd.
Chungshan Park
Tung Feng Rd.
Hsiao Tung Rd.
Kung Yuan Rd.
Pei Men Rd.
Post Office
FAT
Rd.
Railway Station
Youth Corps Hostel
Tainan Hotel & China Airlines
Ta Hsueh Rd.
Bus Sta.
Yulo St.
Chung Shan Rd.
Hotel Yu Chi Lin
Szu Wei St
Hotel Asia
Sheng Li Rd.
Po Ai Rd.
Ching Nien Rd.
Chien Kuo Rd.
Theological College Hostel
Taiwan Bank
Kai Shan Rd.
Tungmen Rd.
Fu Chiang Rd.
Koxingha's Shrine
Fu Hsing Rd.
Three Concubines Temple
Kaohsiung

make arrangements to come in later if neccessary.

Not quite as pleasant as the above hostel but incredibly cheap is the 新園大旅社 just off Mintzu Rd about 75 metres down the first alley on the right-hand side after crossing Kung Yuan Rd coming from the station. There's a large neon sign advertising its presence at the entrance to the alley. It's a bit grubby but where else would you get a double room with own bathroom and clean sheets and hot water for just NT$20 per person? The staff speak no English but are very friendly. Many of the rooms are used by street traders who bring in their wares late at night.

Other than the above there's nothing in the budget range and if you're contemplating staying in a hotel then you can expect to pay NT$300 a single and more. There seem to be hardly any hotels which don't have air-conditioning – hence the high prices. One of the 'cheapest' is the hotel on the bottom side of the roundabout opposite the railway station between Chengkung Rd and Chungshan Rd which costs NT$250 a single with air-con and own bathroom. It's spotlessly clean and fairly quiet. Two others in this range are the *Hotel Yu Chi Lin* 玉麒麟大旅社, 117 Chungshan Rd (tel 220185/6/7) which costs NT$370 a single with air-con and own bathroom, and the *Hotel Asia* on the opposite side of the road.

Places to Eat

At night, try the market which runs the length of Min Tsu Rd (the Chih Kan Tower is on this road). There are many food stalls selling all manner of snacks. If you happen to be near the Confucian Temple during the day try the supermarket on the corner of Nan Men Rd and Fu Chien Rd. They sell really tasty, cheap snacks.

For special set meals try the *Hotel Cheng Kung Restaurant* opposite the station which is open from 7 am to 10 pm daily except Mondays. They offer set meals for NT$70, NT$120 and NT$150. Good food. Next door to this place on Pei Men Rd is the *Hotel Yi Low Restaurant* which offers western and chinese food. They have a good menu but the helpings are on the small side and the food is relatively expensive. Omelettes cost NT$60, ham and potato salad with asparagus NT$60, chicken NT$100 and fried prawns with salad NT$120.

There are, of course, plenty of the popular ready-prepared food cafes which you find all over the island.

Getting There

Buses

To Kaohsiung There are 22 buses daily, the first at 8.05 am and the last at 9 pm. The fare is NT$37.

To Taipei There are 33 luxury air-con expresses daily, the first at 7 am and the last at 12 midnight. The fare is NT$325. In addition there are 37 non air-con expresses, the first at 6.20 am and the last at 11.45 pm. The fare is NT$277.

To Taichung There are 56 buses daily, the first at 6.45 am and the last at 9 pm, which cost NT$131 for the luxury air-con expresses and NT$99 for the ordinary expresses.

To Chiayi There are 27 buses daily, the first at 6.50 am and the last at 9.20 pm. The fare is NT$51.

To Coral Lake To get to this resort take the bus to Paiho and get off at Coral Lake. There are 13 buses daily, the first at 6.40 am and the last at 6.20 pm.

CHIAYI 嘉義

Chiayi is quite a pleasant city as Taiwanese cities go but for most travellers it is just an overnight stop on the way to Alishan as it's from Chiayi that you catch the minature train on the narrow guage Alishan Forest Railway. If you have time to kill, however, there are a few quite interesting temples worth visiting in the city which are indicated on the street map.

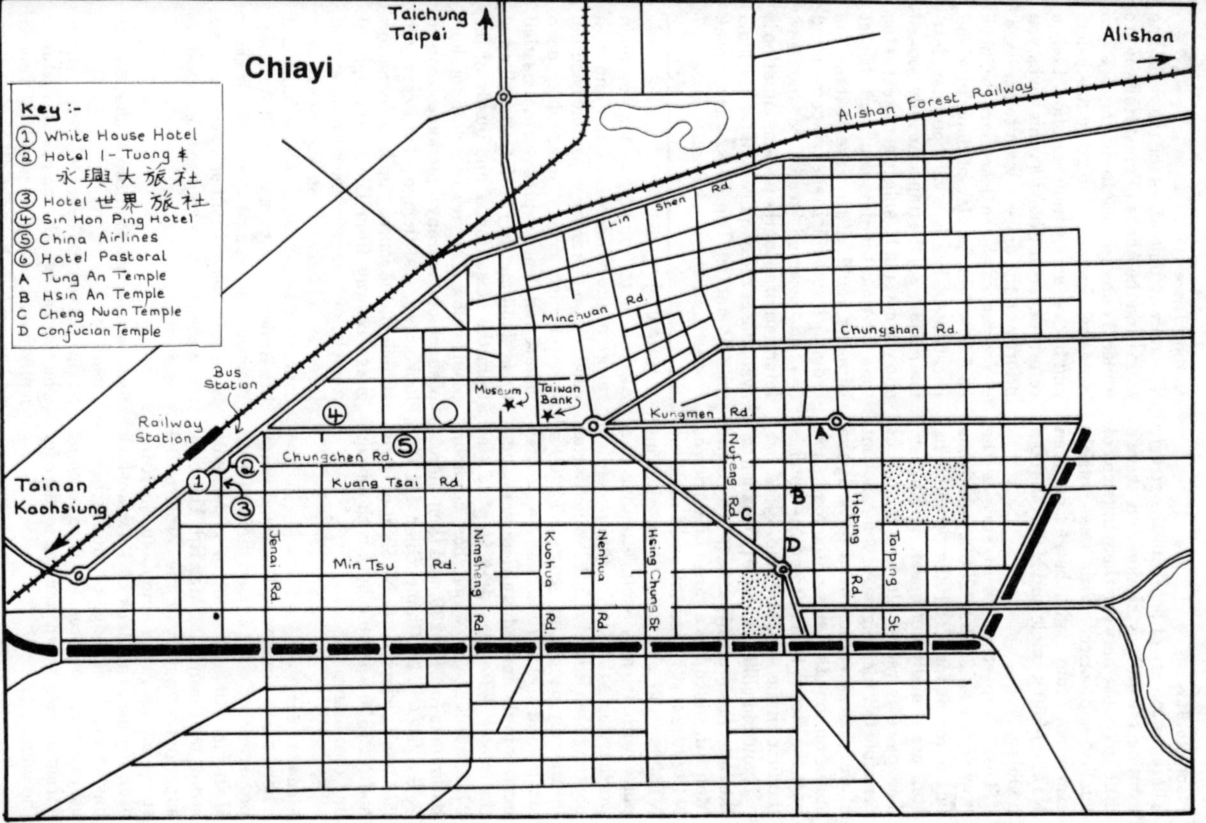
Chiayi
Taichung
Taipei
Alishan
Alishan Forest Railway
Key :-
1 White House Hotel
2 Hotel I-Tuong
永興大旅社
3 Hotel 世界旅社
4 Sin Hon Ping Hotel
5 China Airlines
6 Hotel Pastoral
A Tung An Temple
B Hsin An Temple
C Cheng Nuan Temple
D Confucian Temple
Lin Shen Rd.
Minchuan Rd.
Chungshan Rd.
Bus Station
Railway Station
Museum
Taiwan Bank
Kungmen Rd.
Chungchen Rd.
Kuang Tsai Rd.
Tainan
Kaohsiung
Jenai Rd.
Min Tsu Rd.
Nimsheng Rd.
Kuohua Rd.
Nenhua Rd.
Hsing Chung St
Nufeng Rd.
Hoping Rd.
Taiping St

Places to Stay

There are plenty of hotels in the streets fronting the railway station and there's little to choose between them in terms of quality and price. With one notable exception, they all charge between NT$200-250 a single and NT$300-400 a double.

The cheapest place to stay is the 世界旅社 (tel 223492/223692) which has tatami rooms for NT$100 a person. The staff are friendly but speak no English. The place is rather old and dusty but certainly OK for a night. As you come out of the railway station head towards the statue on the other side of the road. Just past the statue turn left and the hotel is the first on the left-hand side.

If you don't like the above place then try the *Hotel Pastoral* 田園大旅社 434 Kung Men Rd, which has a range of singles at NT$220, 240, 270 and 350 and doubles at NT$300, 330 and 380. It's a pleasant place with friendly staff. Another one worth trying is the *Sin Hon Ping Hotel* also on Kung Men Rd (tel 222317) which is run by friendly people and costs NT$200 a single and NT$270 a double. Other hostels in the immediate vicinity include the *Hotel I-Tuong* 一同大飯店 , (tel 2722250/272251), which has common bathrooms for NT$230, and then there's 永興大旅社 710 Chung Chen Rd (tel 278246/7) which costs NT$280 a single and NT$350 a double both with air-con and own bathroom.

Places to Eat

There are a number of the usual ready prepared food cafes around the station on Hsin Hai Rd and a lot of restaurants strung out down Kung Men Rd. There's a supermarket/bakery on the corner of the street at the first roundabout on Kung Men Rd past the Bank of Taiwan which has an excellent range of sandwiches at very reasonable prices. If you're catching a train it's well worth stocking up here for the journey.

Getting There

The railway timetables for the main-line trains and the Alishan Forest Railway are under 'Trains' in the introductory section. Note that if you want to go up to Alishan and back again by train you should buy a return ticket in Chiayi as this gives you priority on the day you want to get back.

You can only buy a ticket back to Chiayi at Alishan on the day of departure and because Alishan is a very popular destination many of the trains are fully booked and you may not be able to get a seat at the time (or even the day) you want. If that happens you'll either have to take the ordinary train (which takes all-comers and has no reserved seats) or the bus. Information about the booking situation is available at the enquiry counter at Chiayi railway station. The clerks there speak English and are very helpful.

ALISHAN 阿里山

Alishan is the most popular mountain resort in the whole of Taiwan and with good reason. It's an incomparably beautiful area of high craggy mountains, deep valleys and dense cypress forests nestled up at 2333 metres (7465 feet) well away from the noise, fumes and bustle of the plains below. The views are nothing short of spectactular in any direction you care to look. And, as though that were not sufficient, the journey up here by narrow guage railway from Chiayi through 50 tunnels, over more than 80 bridges and three switchbacks is an experience that cannot be equalled outside of India and the Andean countries of South America. Whatever else you do, don't miss Alishan. Note that there is no bank at Alishan so make sure you take enough ready cash up there with you.

Sunrise over Mt Morrison & the 'Sea of Clouds'

Seeing the sun rise over Mt Morrison from Chu Shan above Alishan has the status of a pilgrimage among the people of Taiwan and watching their antics is almost as enjoyable as the spectable itself! Spike Milligan would love it. Everybody but everybody gets up religiously at about 3 am (the hotels are all geared to waking people up for this!), drag themselves up to the bus stand and buy a ticket for the mini-buses which take people to Chu Shan. It's as near to panic stations as anyone can manage at that ungodly hour and strictly first come, first served, so get there early or you'll be queueing for at least an hour. There are hundreds of people involved in this mad rush. Tickets on the mini-buses cost NT$32 one-way (or twice that return – but it's more pleasant to walk back). Once at Chu Shan about half of these people tuck into an expensive breakfast at Sunrise House while the rest hang about shivering outside on the observation terraces. If you're on a budget make sure you bought coffee, Ovaltine, tea, pancakes or eggs back at the bus stand – stalls are always set up there and the food is cheap.

Breakfast over, people wait with baited breath as the dawn comes up, cameras at the ready, and the muted tones of earlier conservations gradually rise to fever pitch. Then, as the sun rises over the distant forested peaks and the cloud-blanketed valleys below, the assembled throng surges madly to the edge of the parapet, there to attain collective and simultaneous orgasm amid gasps of awe and wonder. Telephoto lenses collide with upraised arms and skulls for a piece of the action while amateur photographers with every attachment imaginable dripping from their machines reel off film after film and contort their stubby bodies into postures rivalling those of the Kama Sutra. It's pure Fellini and not to be missed for anything!

All this, of course, if it's a clear dawn and mist doesn't shrowd the mountain tops and Chu Shan itself. If this happens gloom envelopes the crowd and it ebbs away dejectedly towards the mini-buses and back to Alishan. If this does happen when you're there don't follow them but wait another half hour or so as the mist often clears shortly after sun-up and you'll get what you came to see anyway – the sea of clouds in the valleys below with the forested peaks rising up out of it. It's one of the most beautiful sights you will ever see.

There's no need to go up to Chu Shan by mini-bus if you prefer to walk. It takes about an hour to do this via the road and the short-cut pathways through the forest. The latter are paved with stone all the way so you can't get lost though a torch would be useful – it's pretty dark under the trees even when there's a full moon.

Walking Trails around Alishan

There are any number of walking trails through the forest around Alishan, most of them signposted though these are sometimes missing at crucial junctions (not that it matters a jot). Most of these paths are indicated on the map. It doesn't matter which way you go but don't miss the museum, giant tree, the Three Generations Tree and the Two Sisters Pond (the latter sometimes dries up if there's been no rain for a while). The museum which is free and well worth a visit has excellent collections of the butterflies and snakes found in the area, a topographical model of the area, soil and wood samples. To go around all these places will take a leisurely morning or afternoon. There are a number of places to stop for a tea, soft drink or snack along the way.

The Plum Wine Trail

If you're thinking of going on this one you can do it in joggers if it's not been raining recently. Otherwise you really need a pair of stout boots. It's about a four-hour round trip though, of course, this depends on how long you spend drinking plum wine at the farm. It's excellent wine though you shouldn't expect it to resemble too closely the commercial variety that you get out of a bottle with a respectable label on it (it tends to be on the young side and cloudy and is likely to lead to a bad case of

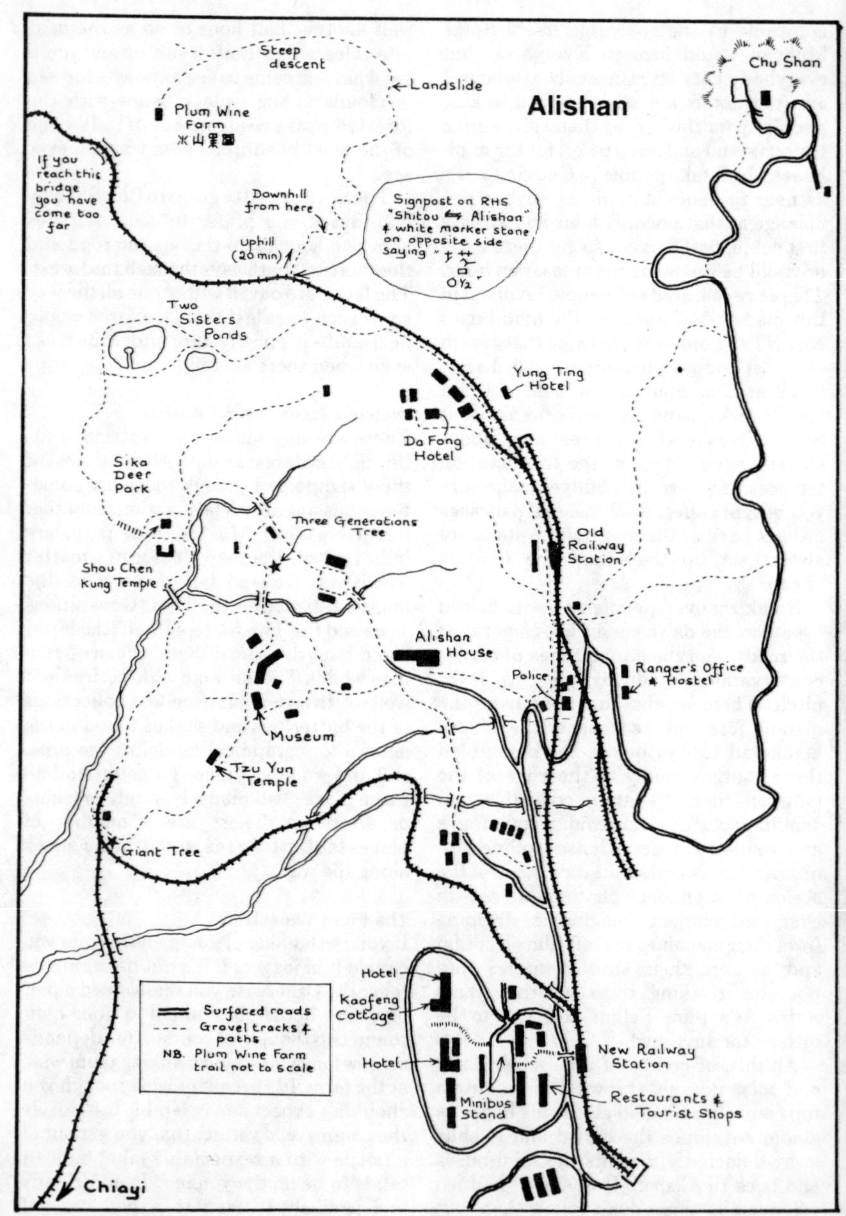
Alishan
Chu Shan
Steep descent
Landslide
Plum Wine Farm
水山果園
If you reach this bridge you have come too far
Downhill from here
Uphill (20 min)
Signpost on RHS "Shitou ⇆ Alishan" & white marker stone on opposite side saying
Two Sisters Ponds
Yung Ting Hotel
Da Fong Hotel
Sika Deer Park
Three Generations Tree
Old Railway Station
Shou Chen Kung Temple
Alishan House
Police
Ranger's Office & Hostel
Museum
Tzu Yun Temple
Giant Tree
Hotel
Kaofeng Cottage
Surfaced roads
Gravel tracks & paths
NB. Plum Wine Farm trail not to scale
Hotel
Minibus Stand
New Railway Station
Restaurants & Tourist Shops
Chiayi

flatulence the next morning!). Take a long stick with you on this trail in case you come across a snake – Taiwan has plenty of them and many are venomous. If you can't make the trek then you can sample the wine at Kaofeng Cottage.

Places to Stay

Kaofeng Cottage 高峯大山 (tel 052-278404/277546) has been the most popular place with travellers for many years. It's run by a very friendly bunch of English-speaking young women. They will probably meet you as you get off the train from Chiayi and ask you if you want a room – most of the other hotels also have runners who meet the trains – some of them with flags! It's a beautiful place and absolutely spotless. The tatami rooms – each with their own bathroom – are some of the best you will come across and cost NT$300. There's also a cheaper dormitory for NT$120 per person. Depending on when you go up to Alishan, however, you may find that the dormitory and the tatami rooms are full. If that happens you will have to take a private single room without bathroom for NT$400 or share a suite with own bathroom for up to NT$1000. Plenty of clean linen and duvets are provided. They have a (usually deserted) bar which sells small snacks, coffee, Ovaltine and plum wine. If you need something later in the afternoon and the girls at reception look tired remember they got up at 2.30 am that morning to wake you up!

If the Kaofeng is full there are two other hotels, one on either side of the Kaofeng but they only have rooms for NT$700-800 and up. If you don't mind dormitory accommodation then the *China Youth Corps Hostel* has beds for NT$80. There are also two pretty basic hotels just beyond the old railway station which are cheaper than the above two – the *Da Fong Hotel* and the *Yung Ting Hotel* – but at 3 am they're a long way from the mini-bus stand (but closer to Chu Shan if you're planning on walking).

If you need somewhere comparatively luxurious to stay in Alishan there is the *Alishan House*, 2 West Alishan, Shan Lin Village, Wu Feng Hsiang Chiayi (tel 05-267 9811/4). The hotel has 54 rooms and charges NT$800 a single and NT$1000 a double.

Places to Eat

There are several fairly simple restaurants just below the railway station which usually display what they have in glass-sided refrigerators at the front of the shop. There's little to choose between them. Just point to what you'd like cooked up but note that none of the restaurant owners speak English (though you can often find someone eating there who can). The prices are reasonable though somewhat higher than similar places down on the plain.

If you'd like a western-style breakfast (ham and eggs, toast, coffee, etc) then go to *Alishan House* where you can get this for NT$80. They also offer lunch and dinner if you'd like a splurge.

Getting There

Trains The train schedule and fares on the narrow guage Alishan Forest Railway are included under 'Trains' in the introductory section. If you're a railway buff then it's worth having a stroll onto the railway sheds just beyond the new station at Alishan to see the beautiful old steam engines which used to pull the carriages up from Chiayi and which are still used for shunting and pulling logs down from Tungpu, a further two hours' journey into the mountains.

Buses Since a road was constructed several years ago (sealed all the way) it's now also possible to get up to Alishan by bus. The fare is NT$71 and the journey takes about 2-2½ hours so it's quicker and cheaper than the train. There are generally seven buses daily in either direction (the first from Alishan at 8.30 am). Perhaps the best thing to do is to take the train in one direction and the bus in the other since both journeys have their attractions.

TAICHUNG 台中

Taichung is a major cultural and educational centre and fast-growing market city. Like Taipei and Kaohsiung it attracts many expatriate workers, businessmen and students but for the budget traveller it's an expensive place with few points of interest.

Confucian Temple

Located on Shuangshin Rd about 15 minutes' walk from the centre of town and close to the recently completed Martyrs' Shrine, this beautiful temple has the same quiet, meditative atmosphere as other Confucian temples on the island though it's considerably larger than its counterpart in Tainan. It's open daily from 9 am to 5 pm. To get there take bus Nos 20, 24, 40, 41 or 42 or walk.

Pao Chueh Temple

This 60-year old Buddhist temple on Chien Hsing Rd is remarkable for having one of the largest statues on the island – the 31-metre (101 ft) high statue of Milefo (the Maitreya Bodhisattva). Services take place here at 5 am and 7 pm and chanting can sometimes go on for up to two hours if enough people are present.

Changhua 彰化

A short train or bus journey south of Taichung is the city of Changhua where there is another huge statue of the Buddha. Begun in 1961, the 22-metre (72 ft) high statue took five years to complete and consumed about 300 tonnes of concrete. You can climb up inside the Buddha and look out over the countryside through the eyes. The old cannons on the terrace are a reminder that the site was once the location of an old fort.

Sun Moon Lake 日月潭

Photographs of this very popular resort area in the foothills of the Central Mountain Range grace virtually every publication aimed at tourists. Before the area was dammed during the Japanese occupation to create the lake and provide hydro-electric power which was once sufficient for the whole island, these valleys were the home of the Ami aboriginals. There is still an 'aboriginal village' and museum of sorts but like others around the island which have been subjected to too much outside influence they're very disappointing. The lake and surrounding area is certainly very beautiful and there are a few temples worth visiting but it's very commercialised and during the summer months packed out with holiday makers from all over Taiwan. Nevertheless, at 726 metres (2500 ft), and so a lot cooler than down on the plains, it can be a good place to go and relax for a few days.

Buses to Sun Moon Lake depart from the bus terminal next to Taichung railway station. There are 'Golden Horse' buses at 8 am, 9.50 am, 10.30 am, 1.30 pm and 3.30 pm which cost NT$46 and take about two hours. There are also other buses at 7.20 am, 8.20 am, 9.20 am, 10.20 am, 1.20 pm and 1.40 pm but these take a little longer. On the return journey 'Golden Horse' buses depart Sun Moon Lake at 10.30 am, 12.30 pm, 4 pm and 6 pm.

Places to Stay

There are two luxury-class hotels in Taichung. The *National Hotel*, 257 Taichung Kang Rd, Section 1 (tel 04-229 6011), has 270 rooms and charges NT$1650 a single and NT$1850 a double. The *Park Hotel*, 17 Kung Yuan Rd (tel 04-220 5181), has 122 rooms and charges NT$1000-1400 a single and NT$1150-1700 a double. Somewhat cheaper are the *Taichung Hotel*, 152 Tzu Yu Rd, Section 1 (tel 04-224 2121), with 179 rooms at NT$900-1300 a single and NT$1400, and the *Lucky Hotel*, 68 Min Chuan Rd (tel 04-229 5191), which has 121 rooms at NT$1000-1100 a single and NT$1200 a double.

Budget accommodation is very difficult to find here but if you don't mind dormitory accommodation then try the *China Youth Corps Hostel*, 262-1 Lihsing Rd (tel 042-232702) next to the Martyrs' Shrine, where you can stay for NT$40 per night. Other than this there is a cheap place suggested by the *YMCA* (which itself has no accommodation) but it's a long way out of town past the Hotel National out on Taichung Kang Rd and very inconvenient. You can stay there for NT$70 a night but it's best to give them a ring first if you want to stay there – tel 512121. The only other place which can be classed as budget accommodation is the *Wan An Lu She Hotel* but even this isn't particularly cheap at NT$170 a single plus NT$20 tax and NT$30 for each additional person in a room. To get there walk down Chung Cheng Rd (opposite the railway station) until you get to San Min Rd where you turn right. Carry on past the Far Eastern Store and another set of traffic lights and you will come to a number of food stalls on both sides of an alley on your right-hand side. The hotel is located at the end of this alley in a small courtyard. It's not all that obvious. The standard of accommodation here is very basic and it might well be worth spending another US$1-2 for something considerably better.

Other than the above, you're up for a pretty costly overnight stay here. The *Grand Garden Hotel* 華園大旅社 at 65 Chung Cheng Rd (tel 225056/7) is amongst the cheapest but only just. It isn't anywhere near so grand as its name suggests so don't let that put you off. It's a very pleasant, spotlessly clean place with friendly management and very convenient for the transport terminals. They have a range of rooms here for between NT$320-540 a single or double with air-con and own bathroom.

You might also like to try the streets on either side of the railway tracks where there are number of fairly simple hotels but beware of assuming that because a place looks cheap it is cheap. This often isn't the case.

Places to Eat

There are all the usual ready-prepared food cafes all around the railway station where you can eat well for around NT$60-70 and more in the alley near the *Wan An Lu She Hotel* but two of the most popular cafes with students and other young people are situated in the same block as the *YMCA* on Shih Fu Rd as you walk away from Chungshan Park. If you want western-style food or a good Chinese meal try one or other of the restaurants in the Ku Kuang Lou block on the corner of Shih Fu Rd and Kungyuan Rd facing the park. Quite a few expatriates go for their breakfast in the basement coffee shop here. Another excellent place for western-style food is Taichung's only 'pub', the *Ship's Tavern*, 217 Taichung Kang Rd, Section 1 (tel 299042), near the Hotel National. This is an expatriate watering hole owned and run by an Australian. It has a very easy-going atmosphere (much better than those of the pubs in Taipei), sells draught and bottled beer, excellent food at reasonable prices (NT$120 and up), has a darts board and pool table and a 'happy hour' from 5 pm to 7 pm. It's a great place to spend the evening. To get there take a taxi from the centre – should cost about NT$40.

Getting There

There are three bus terminals in Taichung. The one located right next to the front side of the railway station has buses going to Sun Moon Lake, Puli and Wushe. On the other side of the railway tracks, reached by a footbridge, is the terminal for buses to Kaohsiung, Tainan and Chaiyi. The other terminal a few minutes' walk from the railway station at the start of Nanking Rd has buses going to Hualien, Lishan and Hsinchu. Buses to Sun Moon Lake are covered above.

Confucian Temple
Martyrs' Shrine
Youth Corps Hostel
Li Hsing Rd
Stadium
Paochueh Temple
Shuang Shih Rd
San Min Rd
Chung Hua Rd Sec. 2
Wu Chuan Rd
Chin Hua N. Road
Chien Hsing Rd
Ta Ya Rd
Taichung
"Ship's Tavern" (1km)

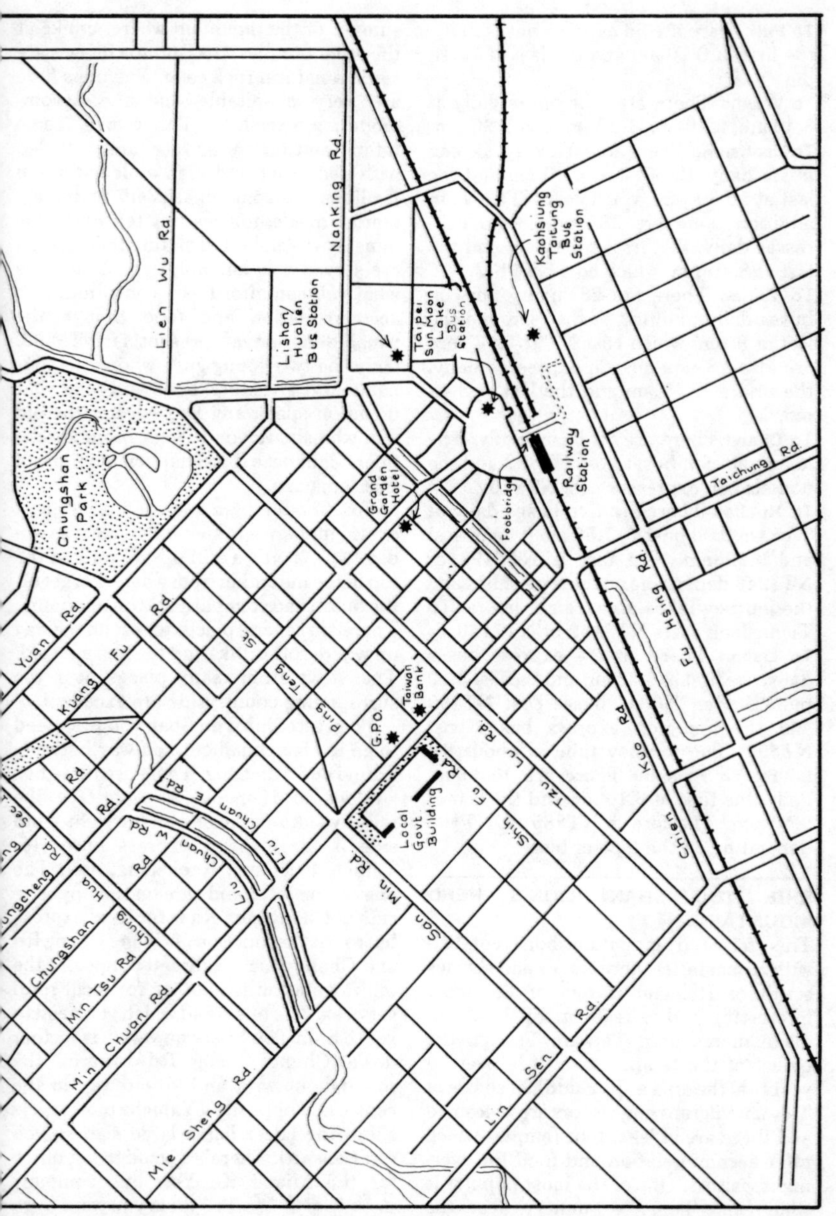

Nanking Rd
Lien Wu Rd
Lishan/ Hualien Bus Station
Taipei Sun Moon Lake Bus Station
Kaohsiung Taitung Bus Station
Railway Station
Footbridge
Taichung Rd
Grand Garden Hotel
Chungshan Park
Yuan Rd
Kuang Fu Rd
Ping Teng St
Taiwan Bank
G.P.O.
Local Govt Building
Fu Hsing Rd
Kuo Rd
Chien
Shih Tzu Rd
Li Chuan E Rd
Liu Chuan W Rd
Chung Hua Rd
Chungcheng Rd
Chungshan Rd
Min Tsu Rd
Min Chuan Rd
Mie Sheng Rd
San Min Rd
Lin Sen Rd

To Puli There are 36 express buses daily, the first at 6.10 am and the last at 10.10 pm.
To Wushe There are four buses daily at 8.40 am, 9.20 am, 1.20 pm and 2.20 pm.
To Kaohsiung There are 80 luxury, air-con buses daily, the first at 6.30 am and the last at 10.30 pm, which cost NT$201. In addition there are 28 non-air-con expresses daily, the first at 6.40 am and the last at 8.40 pm, which cost NT$172.
To Tainan There are 28 luxury, air-con buses daily, the first at 6.45 am and the last at 9 pm, which cost NT$131. There are also 28 non-air-con expresses daily, the first at 7.15 am and the last at 8.45 pm.
To Chaiyi There are 82 buses daily. The luxury air-con buses cost NT$82 and the non-air-con expresses cost NT$75.
To Hualien There are five buses daily at 7.15 am (two buses), 7.55 am (two buses) and 9.20 am. The fare is NT$195 or NT$248 depending on the type of bus and the journey takes about eight hours. To Tienhsiang costs NT$152 or NT$140.
To Lishan There are 14 express buses daily, the first at 6.35 am and the last 3.10 pm. 'Golden Horse' buses cost NT$99 and the non-stop express buses cost NT$95. The journey time is about 3½ hours. **To Hsinchu** There are 46 buses daily, the first at 6.10 am and the last at 9.50 pm. The fare is NT$85 or NT$65 depending on the type of bus.

SHIH TOU SHAN (LION'S HEAD MOUNTAIN) 獅頭山

This forested mountain honeycombed with monasteries, hermitages and shrines south of Hsinchu is one of the most interesting and refreshing trips you can make in northern Taiwan. Though the oldest of the temples is a little over 70 years old the area is the Buddhist centre of Taiwan. Pilgrims and visitors are welcomed and there are at least four temples which offer accommodation and food for overnight visitors. One of the most popular is Shui Lien Tung, a nunnery near the summit of the mountain where, unlike at the other temples, the Buddha images are set in a natural rock cave. The nuns here are very hospitable and the accommodation excellent. The rooms, some tatami and others private, are provided with clean linen and a fan while bathroom facilities are communal. Very tasty vegetarian meals, followed by tea which the nuns grow, smoke and mature themselves, are served at 6 am and 6 pm. You leave what you can afford as a contribution to accommodation and food though the usual donation at present is NT$200. Only the two young guys who write your name in the visitors' book and take your donation speak any English but the old nun who shows you to your room speaks fluent Japanese if you happen have any of that language.

You should plan on staying at least overnight here – better still make it a two-day trip – as it's a stiff up-hill walk to the top of the mountain from where you get off the bus. Keep your baggage to a minimum. There are several places to rest on the way up where soft drinks and the like are sold. The views from many places over the surrounding countryside are excellent.

To get to Shih Tou Shan you first need to go to Hsinchu about half way between Taipei and Taichung. There are three bus stations in Hsinchu. As you face the railway station, the one on the right-hand side is for highway express buses (to Taipei, Taichung, Kaohsiung, etc). The one on the left-hand side on the opposite side of Chung Hua Rd is for local express buses. At the junction of Chung Cheng Rd and Chung Hua Rd directly opposite the railway station is another for local rural services. The bus stand which you need to get to Shih Tou Shan, however, is further down Chung Cheng Rd towards the roundabout with an old gateway in the centre and opposite a Yamaha motorcycle shop (the latter has a large sign so you can't miss it). There's a small ticket office for the Miaoli Ke Yun bus company 苗栗汽車客運. Tell them you want to go

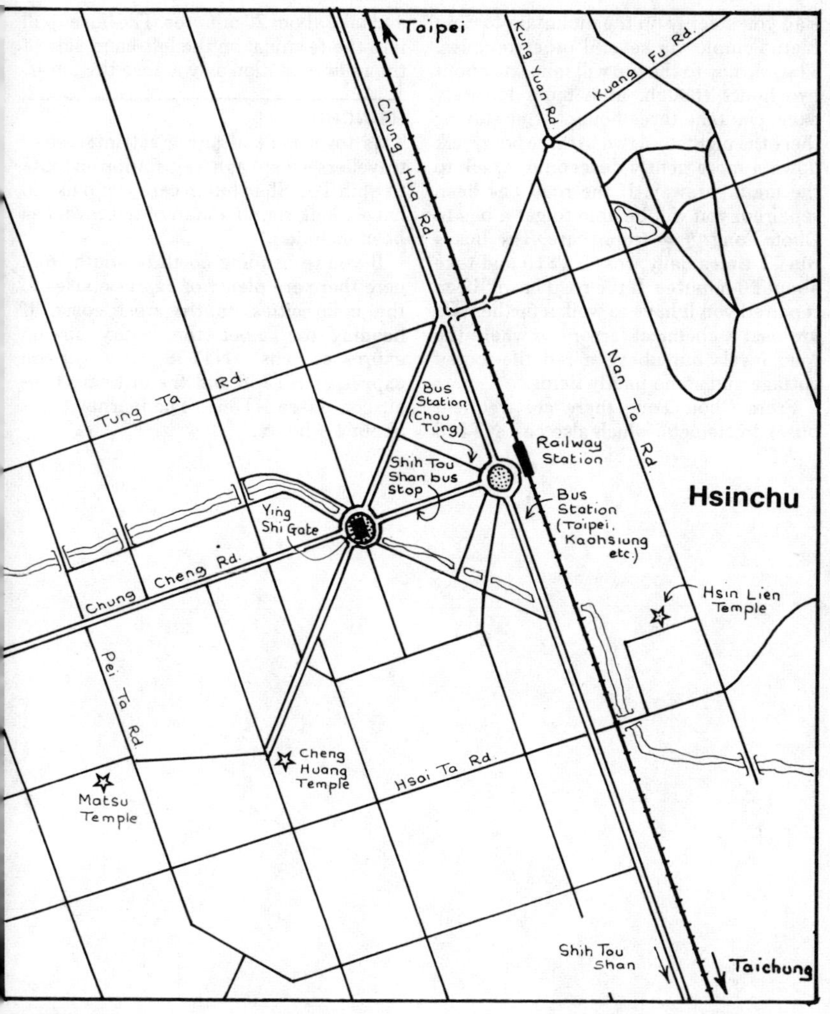

to Shih Tou Shan and they'll put you on one of their buses which go to Nanchaung 南庄. The fare is NT$31 and the journey as far as the mountain takes about 40 minutes. The drivers will tell you where to get off. There are 12 buses daily, the first at 7.20 am and the last at 6.20 pm.

The place where you get off the bus is really the back entrance to Shih Tou Shan so if you'd prefer to enter via the main gateway then simply reverse the directions given here for getting to the mountain. From where you are dropped flights of stone steps and sections of gravel track lead you steeply up the mountain to Shiu Lien Temple via several other temples. The journey to the top will take you about two hours though, at a more leisurely pace, can take three hours. After staying there the night it's a two to three hour walk down a more gently descending track to the main gateway. If the road has been repaired, you will be able to get a bus to Chou Tung 竹東 from there. The buses run 11 times daily, cost NT$15 and take about 20 minutes. If the road hasn't been repaired you'll have to walk a further two km past a chemical factory to where the road levels out above a red tile-roofed cottage and some paddy fields.

From Chou Tung there are frequent buses to Hsinchu which also cost NT$15 and take about 20 minutes. The buses pull into the terminal on the left-hand side of the railway station as you face the latter.

HSINCHU

This town isn't of any great interest to travellers except as a way-station en route to Shih Tou Shan but in case you'd like to have a look round a map of the town has been included.

If you're heading north or south from here there are plenty of express buses to the main cities on the west coast. If heading to Taipei, the luxury air-con expresses cost NT$88, the air-con expresses NT$68 and the ordinary non-air-con buses NT$61. The journey takes about 1½ hours.

Index

Lobby + 2nd + 3rd levels

Bathhouse · Hilton Hotel Basement
38 Chung Siao West Rd.
Section 1 311 51 51

Wall-hung - New Garden Park 17-21 Pagoda Pond
Area

Cruise - Red Chamber @ + of Chunghua
Bazaar +
Cheng-tu Rd. (upstairs)

Hon-Low Theatre.

Lonely Planet travel guides
Africa on a Shoestring
Australia – a travel survival kit
Alaska – a travel survival kit
Bali & Lombok – a travel survival kit
Burma – a travel survival kit
Bushwalking in Papua New Guinea
Canada – a travel survival kit
China – a travel survival kit
Hong Kong, Macau & Canton
India – a travel survival kit
Japan – a travel survival kit
Kashmir, Ladakh & Zanskar
Kathmandu & the Kingdom of Nepal
Korea & Taiwan – a travel survival kit
Malaysia, Singapore & Brunei – a travel survival kit
Mexico – a travel survival kit
New Zealand – a travel survival kit
North-East Asia on a Shoestring
Pakistan – a travel survival kit kit
Papua New Guinea – a travel survival kit
The Philippines – a travel survival kit
South America on a Shoestring
South-East Asia on a Shoestring
Sri Lanka – a travel survival kit
Thailand – a travel survival kit
Tramping in New Zealand
Travellers Tales
Trekking in the Nepal Himalaya
USA West
West Asia on a Shoestring

Lonely Planet phrasebooks
Indonesia Phrasebook
China Phrasebook
Nepal Phrasebook
Thailand Phrasebook

Lonely Planet travel guides are available around the world. If you can't find them, ask your bookshop to order them from one of the distributors listed below. For countries not listed or if you would like a free copy of our latest booklist write to Lonely Planet in Australia.

Australia
Lonely Planet Publications, PO Box 88, South Yarra, Victoria 3141.
Canada see USA
Denmark
Scanvik Books aps, Store Kongensgade 59 A, DK-1264 Copenhagen K.
Hong Kong
The Book Society, GPO Box 7804.
India & Nepal
UBS Distributors, 5 Ansari Rd, New Delhi.
Israel
Geographical Tours Ltd, 8 Tverya St, Tel Aviv 63144.
Japan
Intercontinental Marketing Corp, IPO Box 5056, Tokyo 100-31.
Malaysia
MPH Distributors, 13 Jalan 13/6, Petaling Jaya, Selangor.
Netherlands
Nilsson & Lamm bv, Postbus 195, Pampuslaan 212, 1380 AD Weesp.
New Zealand
Roulston Greene Publishing Associates Ltd, Box 33850, Takapuna, Auckland 9.
Pakistan
London Book House, 281/C Tariq Rd, PECHS Karachi 29, Pakistan
Papua New Guinea see Australia
Singapore
MPH Distributors, 3rd Storey, 601 Sims Drive #03-21, Singapore 1438
Spain
Altair, Riera Alta 8, Barcelona, 08001.
Sweden
Esselte Kartcentrum AB, Vasagatan 16, S-111 20 Stockholm.
Thailand
Chalermnit, 108 Sukhumvit 53, Bangkok, 10110.
UK
Roger Lascelles, 47 York Rd, Brentford, Middlesex, TW8 0QP.
USA
Lonely Planet Publications, PO Box 2001A, Berkeley, CA 94702.
West Germany
Buchvertrieb Gerda Schettler, Postfach 64, D3415 Hattorf a H.